BERNIE FEDERKO

BERNIE FEDERKO

My Blues Note

Bernie Federko
with Jeremy Rutherford

Library of Congress Cataloging-in-Publication Data

Names: Federko, Bernie, 1956- author. | Rutherford, Jeremy, 1975– author.
Title: Bernie Federko : my blues heaven / Bernie Federko, with Jeremy
    Rutherford.
Description: Chicago, Illinois : Triumph Books LLC, [2018] | Includes
    bibliographical references and index.
Identifiers: LCCN 2018023882 | ISBN 9781629373706 (alk. paper)
Subjects: LCSH: Federko, Bernie, 1956– | Hockey players—Canada—
Biography. | St. Louis Blues (Hockey team)—History. | Sportscasters—United
    States—Biography.
Classification: LCC GV848.5.F42 A3 2018 | DDC 796.962092 [B]—dc23
LC record available at https://lccn.loc.gov/2018023882

This book is available in quantity at special discounts for your group or organization. For further information, contact:

Triumph Books LLC
814 North Franklin Street
Chicago, Illinois 60610
(312) 337-0747
www.triumphbooks.com

Printed in U.S.A.
ISBN: 978-1-62937-370-6
Design by Amy Carter
Page production by Patricia Frey
All photos are courtesy of the author unless otherwise noted.

To My Three Sons—

I never thought I was worthy to write an autobiography, but now that it is all finished, worthy or not, I am so very elated that you all chose to convince me to do so. Being a dad has been, without a doubt, the greatest achievement of my life, and I am truly thankful for that. One day you will understand when you have children of your own. Jordy, Dusty, and Drew—don't wait too long; I look forward to reading this storybook with them. Only Mom and I can say that with no pressure and a big smile.

CONTENTS

INTRODUCTION

IF YOU'RE EVER in a car driving across the prairies of Saskatchewan on the Yellowhead Highway, you may come across a sign that reads "Welcome to Foam Lake, population 1,123, elevation 1,842 feet."

The highway borders Foam Lake on the south side, while the north side is bordered by the railway tracks. You didn't really go north of the tracks unless you were going to the cemetery, so we always hoped to avoid that. There are eight streets that run north and south and five that run east and west. In Saskatchewan, the size of the town depends on how many grain elevators flank the railway tracks, and in our case we had six or eight, which meant we were a big town. In my day, the only building south of the highway was the Foam Lake Union Hospital, where I was born. As for the name Foam Lake, there really is no lake. There might have been a lake at one time, but that must have been long before I came along.

As you can imagine, being in the prairies, Foam Lake was flat—*extremely* flat. There's an old saying: "From your front porch, you could watch your dog run away for three days." But it was home for me, and I didn't know anything else. In the book *If You're Not from the Prairie*, Canadian author David Bouchard captures this well:

"When travelers pass through across our great plain,
They all view our home, they all say the same:
'It's simple and flat!' They've not learned to see,
The particular beauty that's now part of me."

We lived on a street that I will never forget. That's because our address was 236 Forget Street, which of course is French and is pronounced "for-jay." Our house was tiny, with three bedrooms, one bathroom, a kitchen, and a living room all packed into maybe 800 square feet. That probably would have been big enough if I were an only child, but Nick and Natalie Federko had four boys: twins Ron and Don, myself, and Ken. The house may have been small for that big of a family, but it was perfect for us.

Winter seemed like it lasted 13 months a year, but that's okay when you love to play hockey. We were on the ice for hours on end, and 40 below zero was a warm day. We felt it in our bones, but we just didn't care. We were kids and it was fun. Bouchard also expounds on this in *If You're Not from the Prairie* as well:

"Do you know what to do to relieve so much pain
Of burning from deep down that drives you insane?
Your ears and your hands right into your toes—
A child who's been cold on the prairie will know!"

At the time, I thought growing up in small-town Saskatchewan was a disadvantage, but I didn't know any better. Many great hockey players, including the great Gordie Howe, had roots in the province. Now looking back, that humble upbringing made that little boy's heart and soul grow into something that I would've never envisioned—a Hall of Fame career in the National Hockey League.

Here's the story of my life, and if I'd read this book before I lived it, I never would've believed it.

In true hockey fashion, you're going to come across a lot of nicknames in the following pages. I never had one myself—I was always just Bernie—but I had friends who went by "Lutey," "Babs," and "Rammer," just to name a few. Don't worry though, I've provided a nickname glossary in the back of the book so that you can keep everybody straight.

Enjoy!

1

A PRAIRIE TALE

I DIDN'T WANT to be a figure skater. Mom wanted me in the class, and Mom, she was in control. She had to be. She had four boys.

I don't know how old I was, probably four or five, and I don't remember an awful lot. I know it was 10 to 12 weeks of lessons, and at the end they had what was called a "carnival." It was like a recital, where you went through a routine skating to the music. We had skits with costumes, and all the girls were dressed in white cartons of milk. I was dressed in brown like chocolate milk. Why? Because I was the only boy in the class.

It was extra ice time, I guess, and when I look back on it, it was probably a good thing for me. The kid that plays for the Carolina Hurricanes now, Jeff Skinner, he was a figure skater, and he's an unbelievable skater. But if you wanted to be a hockey player like I did, you didn't want to be a figure skater. Back then, you were the wrong gender if you were a figure skater.

I wanted to play on an organized hockey team, but that idea went up in smoke when the Foam Lake Skating Arena burned to the ground. The rink was directly across the street from our house, so I vividly remember the flames that night. My brothers, they remember hosing down the side of our house to keep it from getting too hot. Everybody in the entire neighborhood was afraid, Mom and Dad included, thinking we were all going to lose our houses. The rink was so close we would actually put on our equipment at the house and skate across the street. The roads were all gravel, and they didn't plow them, so it would get icy. It didn't matter if your skates were dull or not in those days. Who had a skate sharpener anyway?

I was a little kid, but I do remember how the fire crushed us all, because this was our organized hockey. This was the place in town where everybody hung out in the wintertime and now all of a sudden it was gone. In our neck of the woods, the closest rink was at least 15 miles away. Where were we going to play hockey now?

The debris from the Foam Lake Skating Arena was cleaned up and the ground was left vacant for several years before some housing was eventually built on the property. But before the homes went up, we played baseball in the lot. That was our summer activity. When you're from a small town, you learn that if you don't make up games to pass the time, your life will be extremely boring. There was only one channel on TV, so most of the time there was nothing to watch, especially during the day. Video games weren't invented yet, but even if they were, Mom would have kicked us out of the house anyway.

The alternative was always sports. We played kick the can, hide and seek, and we'd even invent games that only we could figure out. We left the house in the morning, came home for a quick lunch, and were back out doing something else until suppertime. And the funny thing? We never got bored. That was our life in Foam Lake.

The twins, who are three years older than me, were by far the best athletes in town, from the time they started school all the way through high school. Every time there was an award, whether it was the most valuable player on the basketball team or the volleyball team, or track and field, you name it, my brothers, one or the other, won them all. The other kids in the school would boo when my brothers won. It got to the point where my mom didn't even want to go to the award ceremonies because it was almost embarrassing. Since my dad was the secretary/treasurer of the school district and signed all the checks for the teachers, and my uncle was vice principal of the high school, and my other uncle was the algebra teacher, everybody thought we had everything rigged. But it really wasn't; they were just that good.

Because there were not a lot of boys my age around, I was forced to play with my older brothers, Ron and Don. Actually, they were forced to play with me. The twins were always hard on me, trying to make me cry all the time, because that's what older brothers do, right? But I think the fact that my brothers kept pushing me down was a good thing because it made me fight back. I thought that since Mom and Dad were forcing them to be with me and they didn't want me, I was going to make sure that I could prove myself. I wanted to show them that I was their equal. I think all of that motivated me, and I always felt that I had to compete at a higher level.

Whatever we played, I caught on quickly. I've always said that I've been really blessed that way. If you want to, let's say, play darts, even if I've never played darts, chances are in a very short while, I'm probably going to beat you. I think there are certain things that you're blessed with and certain things that you work for. They asked me that question at the Hall of Fame: What's your biggest attribute? I think mine was my sense and my awareness. I could see everything around me and adjust. It wasn't just peripheral vision, I could sense someone coming up from behind me. I could see where I should pass the puck before someone was there. I think playing a sport that's moving all the time, I was able to anticipate a lot of what was going to happen. I had good vision, and like I said, it wasn't just hockey. Heck, I could see a golf ball way underwater and tell you the make of the ball and what number it was.

Because the rink burned down, my dad would flood the back-yard so that we had a place to skate. My brother's friends would always come over after school to play pickup games, and when they drafted teams I was always the last pick. I'd score most of the goals and the next day we'd play again and I'd still be the last pick. I was always somewhat sensitive with that stuff, but at least I still got to play.

Growing up, I noticed that there were a ton of pictures of Ron and Don around the house, but there weren't a lot of me—and by that I mean there were none. Finding a baby picture of me was like trying to find a needle in a haystack. They were twins and they were the first born, so I guess the novelty just wore off when I was born. That was a standing joke in our family, and I remember bugging my mom about it all the time. I even used to ask her if I was adopted. Another thing I was always confused about was how she got "Bernard" for my first name. Somehow she came up with common names like "Ron" and "Don" and later "Ken" with my younger brother, and in the middle of this you get "Bernard?" How do you name your kid "Bernie?" See, I must have been adopted. She always laughed it off but never really explained why, other than to say she liked the name. Trust me, she must have liked the name, because she was the one who picked and she was in charge.

Mom was the brawn behind everything. She and dad were school teachers by trade, but when Dad got the opportunity to leave teaching and become secretary-treasurer of the Shamrock School District, he jumped at it. Mom quit teaching once Ron and Don were born and became a housewife, which is the most underrated title of all time. She made that house tick.

She was a great cook. When you walked in, you could smell the aroma of freshly baked bread or a wonderful apple pie. She had a knack for everything. She knew how to furnish the house. It was always decorated to a T. And without any daughters, she made sure that her four boys knew how to do everything. Every morning before we went to school we had to make our beds, and on Saturday morning we had to strip our beds and change the sheets. We vacuumed the couches and the carpet. Our house was tiny but it was always spotless. She taught us how to cook and how to peel potatoes. She taught us proper etiquette, how to set a table, where the knives and forks go. It still amazes me that lots of people don't even know that the fork is on the left. We've done the same thing with our kids, but it was because Mom taught us how to do that. We cooked, we did it all. If our parents were gone for the weekend, we could have survived anything.

Dad gave Mom a monthly allowance to take care of all the household needs, which included buying all of the groceries. I'll tell you, there was never a shortage of food in our house. We had a big freezer in our basement and it was restocked every fall with a side of beef and a side of pork, and a boatload of chickens. Dad went to work in the morning, came home for lunch, and when he came home at 5:00, we had dinner. And what she made for dinner, that's what we ate. Most of the time it was fantastic, but there were exceptions. The things you didn't like, though, you ate. I didn't like Brussels sprouts, but if I didn't eat them, I wasn't leaving the table. And if you didn't eat supper, then you couldn't have a snack later on. Because of that, all of us boys learned how to eat a lot of things we didn't like, which is a good thing. (But I still can't do Brussels sprouts.)

With that monthly allowance, Mom also had a lot of other things to take care of. She had to buy all of our clothes, so to make things work, she did a lot of things to save money, darning the holes in our socks and patching the knees in our pants. She even cut our hair and we hated that. We fought her, oh my goodness, so hard, because she wouldn't let us have hair over our ears. Her favorite word was that she was just going to "taper" it. What the hell is that? I don't know why she continued cutting our hair because we would get so mad that she would start crying. It got to the point where she would wait until Dad got home and was sitting in the living room. We would start yelling and all hell broke loose, and Dad would peek his head around the corner, stare at us, and we would start whimpering. I don't know why Dad was so intimidating, because he was only 5'6" and about 150 pounds. Heck, he was so passive and accommodating. He was always so politically correct that he even served a term as mayor of Foam Lake and didn't have any enemies; that tells you how good of a guy he was. But still, you didn't piss him off because on that rare occasion he lost his temper, he might take out a belt and whack you. It's funny that all these years later I can still remember those dreaded moments.

One Sunday morning coming home from Mass, I must have said something that Dad didn't like. We were coming up the back steps of the house and he grabbed the broom that was there to sweep the snow off the back porch and broke it on my ass. It was more funny than anything because he felt bad for having broke it on me. But honestly, it must have been a weak broom handle because it didn't hurt at all. I think it hurt him more than it hurt me. But I got the point. It was about respect. He taught us so much about that word.

Foam Lake was in the process of building a new rink, but that takes time in a small town. They finally finished the Foam Lake Recreation Centre when I was 10 years old. I hadn't played organized hockey for about four years, but I don't think it held me back. In fact, I think it might have helped me grow. The kids nowadays don't have enough ice time to hone their own skills because practices are so structured. But by working on them in the backyard rink for hours and hours, we got better and better. Still, we were excited when the new rink was finished.

It now wasn't across the street like the last one—it was about six blocks away—but the facility was state of the art and it was unbelievable. It was a double-building with a curling rink and skating rink. The curling rink had five or six sheets of ice, and the new skating rink even had spectator stands on both sides. We had real nice locker rooms and showers. The only bad thing was that it was not artificial ice, so in order to skate on it, the weather had to be cold enough. When that happened, they had to leave the back door open, so the air would come in and freeze it.

For the first time in four years, we were going to finally have organized hockey. With that, the competition in Foam Lake was heating up because a new family had just moved into town. Their last name was Hannotte and they had four boys, like us, and also like us, they were very competitive. Their one son, Allan, was the same age as me, and the big question was who was better, Allan Hannotte or me? It was like, "Oh man, this guy is better than you, Bernie." For the first time as a child, I understood what pressure was.

I always wanted to get better, so I took advantage of any ice time I could get. We had general skating most weekdays from 7:00 PM to 9:00 PM, and if the senior team wasn't practicing when general skating ended, it meant some extra stick and puck time. Peter Seidlyk was the caretaker of the rink. This rink didn't have a Zamboni, so everything had to be done by hand. Peter would have his son and me help him shovel the rink, and we could get some extra ice time after we finished. I had to be home by 10:00, but we would scrape the rink in 10 minutes and that would give us a half hour or 45 minutes to pass the puck around. That was a huge deal and thankfully my folks allowed me to do it as long as all my homework was done.

2

HABS FAN
AT HEART

IN 1967, THE Foam Lake Minor Hockey Association had a huge fundraiser and officially became known as the Foam Lake Jets. We had this great new rink, a new name, and best of all, new uniforms. They were blue, white, and red, and they were beautiful. We were so proud to be the Foam Lake Jets. I remember it was a big thing when we got our new sweaters. With no organized hockey for the last four years, we never, ever had team sweaters. We just wore whatever sweater someone bought for us. Most of the kids had Toronto Maple Leaf sweaters because they were Leaf fans. Not us. We were the only family in town that was fans of the Montreal Canadiens. Every Saturday night, we all sat down in front of the TV and watched *Hockey Night in Canada* on CBC, the only channel we had. Weekly, CBC alternated the broadcasts between Montreal and Toronto and we were always excited when the Canadiens were on. Jean Beliveau was the captain of the Canadiens and he was my favorite player. I adored him, so I wore No. 4 in his honor. In fact, that was the only number I ever wanted to wear. Now with our new sweaters I wanted so badly to be No. 4, and I was fortunate that, because I was a pretty good player, our coach let me pick first. That's how I got No. 4 that first year, and after that it was always saved for me.

There were many reasons why we were excited when the Foam Lake Jets sweaters came in, but the biggest reason was that we all matched. Having organized hockey back and being in a league now was absolutely the best feeling. I looked forward to every weekend because now we were playing real games. We had a half-dozen farm towns with rinks within a 30-mile radius, so we could travel and play against a lot of different competition. Now that we had a fancy new rink, we could even host some special events. Minor Hockey Day in Canada was always a big day and we now could be a part of it. We invited teams from out of the area to come and play us, and that always expanded our horizons because we didn't really know if we were good or not. I loved going up against the best, and now that was happening as we were playing teams from far across the province.

In 1969, I was 12 when I got asked to play in what was considered at that time to be the biggest Pee-Wee tournament in Saskatchewan. We had our Foam Lake team, but Kelvington, another town about 45 minutes away, wanted me to join their team. It was my first experience spending a couple of nights away from home and playing hockey. It was also the first time I ever went into the United States, because Weyburn was only about 30 miles from the U.S. border, so we went across to Crosby, North Dakota. That's when I met Barry Melrose for the first time.

Most know Barry as the voice of hockey on ESPN, but back then Barry was a defenseman for Kelvington and a really good one. He was competitive and he was always big for his age. When we played against each other, he was their star and I was ours, so we didn't like each other. But when we played on the same team, we really hit it off. He was our go-to defenseman and I was our go-to forward. We called him "Bubba," and I know what you're thinking, but no, Barry didn't have the mullet then. The Melroses were farmers. His dad was pretty quiet and Barry was not outspoken at all. I don't know what happened but I laugh when I see him now TV because he's got the gift of gab. He made his name with the Los Angeles Kings, coaching Wayne Gretzky, and then when he got on TV he started coming up with all these quirky sayings. All of a sudden people loved him, and now he's making a helluva living with his mullet on ESPN. But to me, Barry will always be "Bubba."

The tournament went great, and at 12 years old the seeds of playing the game were forever being planted. After that tournament, I went right back to playing with my Foam Lake team, and despite having a population of about 1,200, we had a pretty good team for the size of our town. That spring, our Pee Wee team invited a team from Saskatoon to play us on Minor Hockey Day in Canada. Saskatoon is the biggest city in Saskatchewan, with over 150,000 people, so that was a huge deal. We figured the kids were going to be way better than us, and since this was the first time we were playing a team from the big city, we were all nervous. We thought that we were going to get our butts kicked, but it was quite the opposite, as we beat them by about 15 goals. You think we were shocked? You should have seen their faces. That's when I knew we weren't just a small-town team.

A few weeks later, my thoughts became justified when our Foam Lake team combined once again with Kelvington and damn near won the Pee-Wee provincial championship in our division. We won three tight series travelling throughout the province. And then, to be in the final was so rewarding. We came so very close, losing the last series, but I will never forget the disappointment it brought. But everyone in town was so proud of us. Nobody in Foam Lake had ever won a provincial championship, so just being in the final was big news.

We even had a banquet a few weeks later and George Reed, the big running back at the time for the Saskatchewan Roughriders, was our guest speaker. I still have the trophy we received and George Reed's autograph is still on the bottom of it. I got to shake his hand, my first touch of fame. It was so memorable. We also got our team picture in the town newspaper, *The Foam Lake Review*. All this for finishing second. Imagine if we would have won.

From then on, hockey was different. That May I turned 13 and was finally a teenager. Almost every time we won a tournament, I won the MVP trophy and the Foam Lake paper would write about "Foam Lake's Bernie Federko blah, blah, blah…." It was something I was very proud of, but it didn't make me feel that I was any more special than anybody else. I was just having fun. I wasn't scoring all the goals. To me it was just as satisfying to have that other guy score a goal. I really got a charge out of having somebody feeling good about themselves. That is what teamwork is about. If we won, we won because of all of us.

And it was in the spring of 1971 that we really won what we had waited two years for. Another crack at winning the provincial championship. It was the Kelvington crew and our Foam Lake team going through another four series of hockey playoffs to be the best in the province. I will never forget that feeling. We played Nipawin in the final game. My dad was always very even-keeled, but I will always remember how excited he was that night. The game was in Nipawin and Dad had relatives that lived there and he was sitting there with them when we won. Finally, a championship for Foam Lake, and this time a picture in *The Foam Lake Review* with the trophy. How sweet it was.

My best friend on the team in Foam Lake was Ron Chaykowski. He was a really good player—big, strong, and tough. Ronnie was an only child, so he was kind of lucky in the fact that whenever he wanted something, he got it. I was somewhat envious of him having the best sticks and the best skates, but I always understood that my folks had three other siblings they had to shell out money for. It must have been really hard to be a parent back in those days because hockey has always been such an expensive sport. The sticks may be $200 apiece today, but at least they come with a warranty, and if you break one, they replace it. In those days, when you got a new stick, it might have only cost $5, but good luck if you broke it. There certainly wasn't a warranty on a wood stick, so when we got a new one, we would actually wrap fiberglass tape around the blade to make it a little bit stronger. That didn't always help, though. I remember the day my dad bought me a new stick, I was skating around the rink and, as I went around the back of the net, I accidently got the stick caught in the netting. I speared myself and broke the blade of the stick right off. I remember crying on the ice, and everybody was wondering if I was okay. I wasn't hurt. I was crying because I didn't know how I was going to talk Dad into buying me another one.

Being the third brother in line, I had all the hand-me-down equipment from Ron and Don. It's called middle-child syndrome, and it's even worse when you're preceded by twins because it's two things that have to wear out before you get something new. Those were the days when skates had a cardboard toecap and we taped the toe so that we wouldn't get them marked up. Unfortunately the tape didn't make the cap stronger. If you got a real hard shot in the toe, the cardboard busted and so did your toe. I always hoped my skates would break so that I could get a new pair, but no such luck.

When I was 15, Ronnie Chaykowski got new skates and I wanted a pair too. Thankfully my feet were as big as my older brothers' so it was finally time to stop with the leftovers. I begged my mom until she finally agreed, but not without a price. She made me a deal. My folks had always made us all take music lessons, and I had chosen the saxophone as my instrument of choice. Well, my mom was going to have one of her ladies' luncheons at the legion hall and her friend's daughter was going to play the piano at the luncheon. Mom convinced me that if I played two songs with her, she would take me to McLeod's to buy me a new pair of skates. Of course I sucked it up and embarrassed myself, but looking back, it was well worth it. We even got a standing ovation from the ladies.

In those days, the most popular skates were either CCM or Bauer. CCM had Tacks and Supertacks and Bauer had Black Panther, Super Pro, and Supreme. Ronnie Chaykowski of course had the best, the Bauer Supremes. I wasn't surprised that Mom gave me a budget, so unlike Ronnie, I had to settle for the second-best pair, the Super Pros. The great news was that they had the plastic toecaps, so my toes were finally safe. There was one drawback. In order to get a couple of seasons out of them, she bought them a couple of sizes too big. That was okay. I was so proud of those skates because they were better than what I had ever had. I also think Mom was proud of me too. I had earned them. It was worth it for everyone, except the people who had to sit there and listen to me play the saxophone.

As a 15-year-old, hockey was starting to become more of a passion in my life. Every tournament seemed to bring out the best in me and I was starting to open a lot of eyes in Saskatchewan. That spring I realized that I wasn't a kid anymore, and if I wanted to move ahead in hockey, I had to get bigger. I was almost six feet tall, but I was only 150 pounds and that was not going to cut it. One of the school teachers had a side business, so I took a part-time job, and that was the best thing that could have happened to me. I became part of his crew that did drywalling, mudding, and stippling ceilings. It was nice to make some money of my own. I bought a set of weights so that I could get stronger, and if I needed a new stick or better equipment, I no longer had to worry about playing the saxophone for deals.

So I was becoming more and more committed, but I was still young and liked to have fun. By this time, Ron and Don were graduating from high school and heading off to college at the University of Saskatchewan in Saskatoon. I will never forget their graduation, especially the after-graduation party at the lake, about 12 miles north of Foam Lake. Because we were a big Catholic family and because of our dad's status as mayor, we were looked at like the goody two shoes in town. Obviously, we weren't sup-posed to swear and drink. But trust me, we did both, just never at home because we would have gotten our asses kicked. I don't know how, but I somehow talked my folks into letting me go, and then talked my brothers into taking me with them. At age 15, I didn't really know what drinking was. Sure I had a beer a couple of times with Dad or my uncles, but I'd never gone overboard. Well, that certainly changed that night. I found out that one should never mix a few beers with a bottle of gin. I guess everybody who's done that could tell you the rest of the story. I was so drunk I puked my brains out, and to this day I still can't drink gin.

It wasn't pretty, but I give my brothers an awful lot of credit for not throwing me under the bus with my folks. But I guess I didn't learn my lesson because two months later, we went to a wedding in Saskatoon, and I was puking my brains out again. My mom said, "Who gave Bernie the booze?" Ron said to Mom, "What are you going bonkers for? It's not his first time." Unfortunately, I didn't get away with it this time and my folks grounded me for quite a while.

When Ron and Don went off to college that fall, it was really different because now I was the older brother, and instead of me being under Ron and Don's wing, I had Kenny under mine. It was the first time in my life that I wasn't sharing a room with Ken. I now had the room that was away from the other two bedrooms. Our house was tiny, so we're talking maybe 20 feet away, but I felt like a true teenager because I could sit in my room and listen to a transistor radio without disturbing Mom and Dad. We really only had one radio station that played music, but it was great to listen to the Top 40 hits. Kenny was a very good hockey player, so we started spending a lot of time together at the rink, but we were never on the same team. Because of my size, I was always able to play on Ron and Don's teams, but Kenny was smaller so he couldn't play on my teams. That kept Mom and Dad pretty busy, taking both of us to our games, but that was about to change because I was turning 16 soon.

On May 12, 1972, after six months of driver-education training, and a lot of practice with my dad, I passed my driver's test with flying colors on the first try. Dad had bought Ron and Don a newer car to take to university in Saskatoon, so I inherited their old car, which was fine by me. It wasn't exactly a dream car—a 1956 Viva Vauxhall—but to me it was perfect. It was a three-speed standard with a really sensitive clutch, but it had a cherry-red paint job. It was freedom to go where you want, when you want, but I guess it wasn't really that much independence when you live in a town that only has 10 streets.

It was great being 16. Tony, who was my school teacher and also my boss in my part-time drywalling job, started treating me more like an adult. After work on Saturdays in whatever town we were in, we went to the bar after finishing up the job and had a couple of beers before we went back to the shop to clean up. That was the advantage of having a drinking age of 18 in Canada—anybody can pass for 18, and I was no exception. Working for Tony was the best and I will always remember the fun times.

Meanwhile, my parents were getting phone calls from junior teams in Yorkton, Weyburn, Humboldt, Melville, and Estevan, almost all of the teams in the Saskatchewan Junior Hockey League. They all tried to talk my folks into letting me play junior hockey, but the answer was no. They didn't want me to leave home. They kept saying, "You're not going to leave home at 16 years old." Mom and Dad were all about education and getting good marks. They were so into education that if I didn't get straight A's they wouldn't let me play hockey. I got straight A's, but I wasn't leaving home.

A lot of the older guys in town knew that my parents wouldn't let me play junior hockey and tried convincing me to play senior hockey for the Foam Lake Flyers, who played in the Fishing Lake Hockey League (FLHL). That's right, they wanted a 16-year-old to play against guys as old as 40 years old. Most of them had played minor-pro and come home, like Wendel Clark's dad, Les, and his uncle Murray, or high-level junior back in their day. They would always say, "C'mon Bernie, you got to come out."

I said, "I'd love to play, but how?" They played in little towns 35–40 minutes away, and Mom and Dad weren't going to let me take the car that far, and plus we didn't get home until midnight or later and had school the next day. But I started practicing with them anyway, and on the opening night of league play, I just decided to play. My mom may have been turning a blind eye, but I know my dad didn't know I was playing. He happened to come to the rink to watch the senior team play our second game and he was surprised to see me. Somebody said, "Bernie is playing well," and that kind of let the cat out of the bag. I think he realized that night that I could play with the men, so it didn't take a lot to convince him to let me continue playing. It was a little scary at first playing against all these men but the first couple of games went well and I found out pretty quickly that I was every bit as good as these guys. They were all bigger and stronger than me, but I was faster and smarter. And all of our older guys, like Keith Harkness and Harold Sandberg, took care of me, so no one was going to run me. If that happened, all shit would have broken loose and no one would've messed with me again.

I was having so much fun, playing midget hockey with kids my age and then getting the chance to play senior hockey. I was the best young player in town, and now I knew that I could play against men. Maybe I should have been playing junior hockey against good players, but since Mom and Dad wouldn't allow it, this was the next best thing. To my amazement, I won the scoring title in the senior league that year as a 16-year-old, and even though it was just senior hockey, it gave me a lot of confidence going forward.

I went back to my midget team and continued to join forces with Kelvington in the provincial playoffs. This time we barely had enough players to put a team together, but we kept winning and our path took us to play Notre Dame College in Wilcox, the famous boys hockey school, for a two-game series. Since its inception, over 130 Notre Dame College students have been drafted into the NHL, including names such as Wendel Clark, Curtis Joseph, Vincent Lecavalier, Tyler Myers, Rod Brind'Amour, and Jordan Eberle, to name a few. It was obviously our toughest challenge, but amazingly we beat them. I took my game to a new level in that series and that was the first time in my life that I knew I had a bona fide chance of making hockey a career. From that point on, I could have easily made any Saskatchewan junior team, but my folks held their ground. They had no idea that I had a chance of playing professional hockey one day, but really, how could they?

Hockey, of course, was my favorite, but I continued to play every sport: football, basketball, track, baseball, and volleyball. Ron and Don had really gotten me into volleyball and that spring our team in Foam Lake won the Saskatchewan championship, which was pretty amazing. The reason that it was so amazing is that every school, regardless of how many students they had, played in the same class. We had 300 students and we were playing three other schools that all had enrollments over 3,000 students. Our P.E. teacher at the time was one of the top volleyball coaches in the province, and our structure was more advanced than a lot of the other schools. I was the setter and those were the days that I was light enough that I could really jump, so I was able to control a lot of the play. I actually even got an invitation to play for the Canadian national junior volleyball team later that fall, but I couldn't go to the tryouts. It was for a good reason, though, which I'll get into soon.

I also played football that year, and was the quarterback and punter. My folks never let Ron and Don play football, so it was beyond me why they let me play. I think Uncle Joe, my mom's brother, who reffed the football games, talked Mom into letting me play. I really enjoyed it, but I was glad when I got through the year without getting hit too hard or landing on one of Saskatchewan's famous stones. This is no joke: I remember the morning of every home football game, the P.E. classes would walk through the field and pick up all the loose rocks.

And speaking of jokes, I even pole vaulted, however, due to budget constraints, we were highly outmatched. We had metal poles and had no chance against the "modern" fiberglass poles other schools had. Let's just say I lost by several feet. It was almost embarrassing.

3

ON SHAKY GROUND

I LIKED BEING a well-rounded athlete, but going into my senior year at Foam Lake, I wanted so badly to play junior hockey. I understood my parents' thinking, but I really felt like I was missing out. Heck, I hadn't even been to a junior hockey game in person—but then came my big break. I received a letter in the mail from the Saskatoon Blades informing me that I had been placed on their protected list. I really didn't know what that meant or how I got on it, but it certainly sounded important. The letter also informed me that a Blades scout would contact me about coming to a rookie tryout camp in Saskatoon in early September. That scout was Father Mel Fenrich, who was the parish priest at the Roman Catholic Church in Foam Lake. Our family went to the Ukrainian Catholic Church in town, so we didn't really know Father Fenrich, but Dad had met him before. He came to the house one Saturday evening after his 5:00 mass and explained that he was friends with Blades head coach, Jack "Shaky" McLeod, whom he had known from their days at Notre Dame College in Wilcox. The scout's job was to put your name on a protected list, which Father Fenrich had done, and he was at our house to invite me to the Blades' camp.

This was not the Saskatchewan Junior Hockey League, it was the Western Canadian Hockey League, one of the three best junior development leagues in the world. It was shocking, but Father Fenrich was pretty convincing, and I couldn't believe Mom and

Dad were actually going to let me go to camp. The fact that Ron and Don were in college in Saskatoon, and would be able to keep an eye on me, was a huge factor in my folks' decision. Of course, it didn't mean I was going to make the team, but it was an amazing first step. I found out when the Blades' tryouts were and I couldn't believe the date. It was the same time as the camp for the Canadian national junior volleyball team. I loved volleyball a lot, but I guess when I put everything into perspective, it was an easy decision. My dream had always been to be a hockey player, so I couldn't turn down this opportunity. I had waited too long.

My brothers were impressed with the fact that I was headed to Blades rookie camp. I was excited, but this was the top tier and I didn't know where I was going to fit in. I was tall and scrawny, but I could handle the puck. At the camp, you would hear the bench coaches screaming, "Dump it in," and I'm thinking, *Why would I do that when I've got the puck?* Thankfully, Shaky McLeod and I had the same philosophy, and I think that helped me early in camp. He really liked my hockey sense.

The story goes that Shaky got his nickname after being diagnosed with polio when he was seven years old. When he got to junior hockey, he would shake so bad because of the effects of the polio, he couldn't get his laces through the eyelets on his skates. He would tell his teammates to head out to practice so he could tie them up alone, but one time his buddy came back in the locker room and said, "C'mon, Shaky, coach is waiting." So that's where "Shaky" came from. He played 106 games in the NHL with the New York Rangers and several more years with Vancouver, Saskatoon, and Calgary in the Western Hockey League. After his playing career ended in 1965, he spent four years coaching the Canadian national team before he started operating a flooring and sporting goods store in Swift Current. He got back into coaching with the Blades in 1970, inheriting a team that went 18–41–1 the year before. He turned them around quickly, going 46–11–11 in his third season and finishing runner-up in the WCHL final.

Shaky was beginning his fourth season when I got my tryout. There were a lot of people who figured I wouldn't make it, and going into the Blue and Gold exhibition game they were probably right. My brothers Ron and Don had heard that cuts were coming that night and Shaky didn't think I was ready for that level. But that night he was sitting in the bleachers, where he always watched the scrimmage games, and he saw me score a goal that might have saved me. I picked up the puck and carried it to the offensive blue line, where I got tripped and fell to my knees. As I fell, the defenseman moved toward me and I poked the puck through his skates. I got back on my skates, walked in, and scored. Maybe Shaky saw that goal and thought, *That was really good, I better give him another chance.*

The next day, there was an article in the *Saskatoon Star-Phoenix* that said that me and another guy named Marty Feschuk had been impressive in the camp. That was great, but they had my name wrong in the headline and in the article—it said "FEDORKO." Shaky called me "Fedorko" and when the reporter, John Cherneski, wrote the article, he probably didn't check the spelling. It's funny, 45 years later he still pronounces my name Fedorko. But that didn't matter to me because they kept me on the roster for the regular training camp, and Marty and I both ended up making the team.

I always say there was a bit of destiny in my career because what if Shaky had sneezed and missed that goal that I scored in the Blue and Gold game? Heck, I might've got cut in rookie camp.

The way I found out that I made the Blades was that the guys who got cut had to go see Shaky and no one ever asked me to go see him. No news was good news. One guy who did was my friend from Foam Lake, Ron Chaykowski. He was big and strong and had a decent rookie camp, but I guess he just wasn't quick enough. The Blades had a working relationship with the Saskatchewan Junior Hockey League team in Humboldt, so they tried to send Ronnie there, but that was Tier II and he didn't want to go. I think it was a big mistake on his part. Ronnie wound up going back to Foam Lake to play senior hockey and we could never figure out why he gave up. Maybe he was depressed, maybe he didn't have the drive, or maybe he was just hurt that I made it and he didn't. I never asked him. I don't know, but I know he really wanted to be a hockey player. To this day, I still think, *Why me and not him?*

This was a huge move for me. It was really a time now to grow up. I was going to be living away from home for the first time in my life. Saskatoon was only 150 miles away, but for a 17-year-old that was a long way away. The twins were both there attending college, and I always said that having them nearby is why my parents okayed the idea, but I couldn't stay with them. The team policy was that you boarded with a family. The Blades assistant general manager, Roy Will, was in charge of the process and he helped me get all squared away with that stuff. Roy and his wife, Mary Lou, knew that our family was Catholic, so they enrolled me into E.D.

Feehan Catholic High School, and found me a boarding home that was within walking distance from school.

My landlady was the mother of Bobby Schmautz, who at the time was playing with the Boston Bruins. She was a fiery lady who I'm going to guess was probably in her late fifties and believe me this was not your normal everyday household. Bob Hoffmeyer, who was one of my Blades teammates, became my roommate, but she also boarded three other people. One of them was a young kid named Allen, who was about 10 or 12 years old and had Down syndrome. Allen was a cute little kid, but he kept us on our toes. He always had something up his sleeve. He had a room on the main floor just like Bob and me, and every time I came home, Allen would always be hiding in our room trying to surprise me. He wasn't the only surprise I got while living there. Of course, my billet mom was responsible for providing us our three meals a day and let's just say that lunch for school was an adventure. Every day when I got to the cafeteria and opened the bag, your guess was as good as mine about what was in it. She would make the craziest combinations, like cheese and jam sandwiches. Cheese and jam! Really, it was like a cartoon. All my classmates just loved the suspense. We'd look to see what it was and then I'd throw it away. I was so lucky that the cafeteria food was pretty decent, and I could afford to buy it. Otherwise, I might have been in big trouble.

This was a whole new experience for me and I admit, I got a little homesick. I went from a town of a few square blocks to 10 square miles, so I had to learn my way around. I was also going to a new school and because none of my teammates were going to this school, I didn't know anybody. My class in Foam Lake would have been 90 students, but my class at E.D. Feehan was almost 800 students. I was playing for the Blades, so I was a somebody, and that made it easier making friends. But we played a 72-game schedule, so there wasn't a lot of free time to make new friends. It was like being in the pros all of a sudden, going from playing for fun to playing for a living. We practiced every day after school and I wasn't used to that. It was really hard for me to get into the swing of things because I was trying to keep my straight A's and, at the same time, prove that I could play hockey at this new level. But this experience was so amazing; it was important that I make the most of it.

I got to fly in an airplane for the first time in my life. In fact, we flew quite a few times during my years with the Blades. Our team was very lucky because it was very unusual for junior teams to travel by air. It was usually a hundred percent by bus. I'm sure that our owner, Jim Piggott, had a lot to do with it, but I think the main catch was that we had a very supportive and aggressive booster club. With the scheduling of some of our weekend road games, we would charter a Nor-Can Air turboprop plane that seated about 50 people. The booster club bought the extra seats that we as a team didn't use and they traveled with us to make up for the extra cost. It was fantastic.

We flew to places like Lethbridge, Medicine Hat, Calgary, Brandon, and Winnipeg—all cities that weren't much farther than an hour flight away. We also flew commercial once a year, taking our annual after-Christmas West Coast trip on Air Canada to Vancouver to play Victoria, New Westminster, and Kamloops, and that was really a thrill. But this was junior hockey, so it was mostly long bus rides. Those were hell, especially the 10-hour bus ride to Flin Flon with the last 6½ hours on a grid road, no pavement. By the time we got there the shocks on the bus were shot and you couldn't have imagined how uncomfortable it was.

That wasn't the only hard part about traveling and being gone so much. We would go on the road for two weeks sometimes and those long trips made it extremely difficult to get your school work done. We were fortunate that all the teachers worked with us to make sure that all of our assignments were prepared ahead of time, so we wouldn't fall behind in our classes. We also didn't have our long underwear laundered every day. You'd play a game one night and then drive three hours to the next town with your wet equipment under the bus, and when you pulled your long underwear out of your equipment bag the next day, they would be frozen solid. You had to let it thaw out before you could even hang it up to dry. They only washed our stuff once a week, and on a bus full of teenagers you can imagine the germs that spread. You had zits on your face, your neck and your back, and when you're trying to attract female companions, that's not a very attractive thing.

Meanwhile, after being better than most of the kids I had been playing against, I now realized that everyone was as good as me and I had to prove myself. I definitely got some confidence from making the team, but then I figured out that I was new and at the bottom of the totem pole. Soon, though, everything was starting to feel like a good fit, including my skates.

Remember those skates Mom bought me for playing my saxophone at the luncheon? The ones that she bought a couple of sizes too big so that I didn't outgrow them? They were size 10½ and those were the ones that I was wearing when I got to Blades camp. Alex Kuzma was the trainer, and he laughed his ass off because I went from a 10½ to 8½. The Bauer skates were also hurting my feet like crazy, so Kuz switched me to CCM. He said, "All of a sudden you know what skates are supposed to feel like." It's funny because when I later turned pro, Bauer wanted me to start wearing their skates again. I tried them on, but my feet are so flat they gave me bad blisters. People couldn't believe I actually played in Bauer skates growing up, but they were cheaper than CCM. Comfort comes at a cost. It was the same with my sticks. I didn't have a great slap shot until I got to the Blades because I didn't want to take a chance of breaking my stick, but now they were free so I wasn't afraid. We also were able to torch and curve our own blades and it was nice to be able to experiment with a stick that you didn't have to pay for until you got the curve you really liked. It made a big difference.

I had a decent year my first season with the Blades. They had four centers returning that year with Bob Bourne, Ralph Klassen, Garth Dietrick, and Fred Williams, so as a 17-year-old rookie I had to somehow find a way to play ahead of one of them or become a winger. It was an eye-opening experience. There were certain buildings that you had to go into and prove your manhood. Mom used to get mad at me when I got penalized in minor hockey in Foam Lake, but I quickly realized that this wasn't minor hockey anymore and if I was ever going to play in the pros, I had to learn how to fight.

I had won the scoring title in senior hockey in Foam Lake, but back then I never had to worry about getting touched. Now I'm playing against kids my age, and if you don't fight, you're a chicken shit. I had no idea what I was doing the first time I dropped my gloves. It was against another rookie from Flin Flon, and I just knew I had to drop my gloves and swing as hard as I could and hope I made contact. But I also knew that the best thing to do in a fight was to grab onto some of your opponent's equipment, and that's what I tried to do. When I went to grab onto the side of the guy's helmet, it came off, and as I desperately reached for his hair, I found that he didn't have any. As it turned out, the Flin Flon veterans had hazed all the rookies that day, shaving their heads, so that's why he didn't have any hair. I had nothing to grab on to and consequently, I got knocked on my ass. The elation that comes with surviving your first fight never gets you over the fear of fighting again, but at least it gives you the feeling of what to expect. I never fought a lot in my career, but from that moment on, I knew that I could handle myself if I ever got in that situation again and I knew to grab something lower, like the side of the sweater.

I was feeling more and more comfortable playing junior hockey with the Blades, and I'm not going to deny it, I probably got a little cocky. I think Shaky noticed that and started pulling me back, playing me less. He kept me in check, but that's when I learned that coaches were an entirely different breed. Shaky would sit you down but not tell you why he sat you down. Just when you think you're playing good, you're not playing anymore. I guess it's part of being a coach; they play mind games with you just because they can. But it was something I had to get used to because he certainly wasn't the last one like that. The year ended with us losing in the playoffs to Regina, who went on to win Canada's junior hockey championship the Memorial Cup, that season. I thought it was a successful year for me. For a rookie that had never even seen a junior hockey game before playing in one, I finished with 22 goals and 50 points. Mostly though, I survived it, and I mean that quite literally.

There were still six weeks left in the school year when the Blades' season ended, but my days at the boarding house ended immediately, as I moved into Miami Apartments with my brothers Ron and Don. It was hardly Miami on the south side of Saskatoon, but it was a great two-bedroom apartment. I got delegated to the couch, but I couldn't have had more fun finishing high school, living the college lifestyle and going to all the parties with my brothers. After all those years of them pushing me aside, I was finally part of the deal. I turned 18 in May and now it wasn't really a gamble to go into the bars anymore because I was legal, and because the season was over I didn't have to worry about Shaky finding out. Life was great.

I graduated in early June and my folks were extremely proud of me, not only for what I did in the classroom but also for what I was doing on the ice. But then reality hit when it was time to head back to Foam Lake for the summer. It was great to be back in my hometown with all of my old friends, but the summer went a lot slower because I really missed being in Saskatoon. The highway through Foam Lake was being redone, so I was able to get a job for the department of highways as a gravel checker. It was long hours but extremely easy and boring, so I was basically thinking about hockey all the time. Any free time I had though, I exercised. I was going to make sure I was in better shape than I'd been in my rookie season.

That's why I was so excited to get a call in early July, asking if I'd be interested in being a hockey school instructor. I had never been to a hockey school as a student because my folks never wanted to spend the money. But now that I'd played a year in Saskatoon with the Blades, a friend of my dad's, John Dunlop, and his good friend, Wally Sotski, wanted to know if I would be interested in making some money teaching kids at a school they started in Yorkton, Saskatchewan. Yorkton was the big city in our area, population maybe 15,000–20,000, and it was 60 miles from Foam Lake. Another local kid named Dennis Polonich, who was three years older than me, had been playing junior hockey in Flin Flon and was drafted by the Detroit Red Wings, and he was helping John and Wally run the hockey school. So when they asked me, that was an easy answer. I got to spend two weeks on the ice getting paid to teach hockey. It turned out to be one of the greatest experiences I ever had. It was the perfect way to end the summer and then head back to Saskatoon for the start of my second Blades training camp.

Ron and Don, who were studying for their physical education degrees, were going into their senior year of college and moving out of Miami Apartments. I signed up at the University of Saskatchewan, so I was now a college student, but the Blades were still responsible for my housing, so they were looking for a place for me to board. It was just a shot in the dark, but I mentioned to Shaky that my brothers had an extra room and I could live with them. I thought there was no way he would let me, but I must have caught him at a crazy moment because he said yes.

That was 44 years ago and I still can't believe it. Ron, Don, and I moved into our new apartment, and I even got my own room. It was a great setup for me. With all of our games and all the travel, it was nice to have a place that was real comfortable, and having the twins there to dissect my play was always appreciated. I took a half-load of classes to make sure that I could handle the responsibility of college life, and looking back, it was the right decision because with all the travel, it would have been literally impossible to take a full load with my hockey responsibilities. My parents were really excited that we were all living together because they knew that the twins were very responsible and they would make sure that I'd go to class.

It was perfect for Mom and Dad, too, because when they came in for my games on the weekend, they always had a place to stay. As the year started, Shaky's biggest concern about me was curfew because we always had to be home by 11:00 the night before games. Like any normal 18-year-old, I thought about staying out late a few times, but Shaky's house was not that far from our apartment and I was afraid that Shaky would come by and check on me. I liked living there so much, I didn't want to jeopardize the position I was in, so it wasn't worth the risk. Plus, it never was a factor because Ron and Don had way too much respect for what I was doing to let me miss curfew.

4

BERNIE & BERNADETTE

THAT SECOND SEASON with the Blades is when everything started happening for me. I'd worked so hard because I knew two centermen, Bobby Bourne and Garth Dietrick, had turned pro and were moving on. Ralph Klassen was going to be the No. 1 center-iceman and I was confident that I was going to be the No. 2. Training camp started and I could sense that things were coming together. I thought I had a real good camp and as the regular season opened, Shaky started giving me more ice time and I was building some confidence. Ralph was supposed to be the guy, but I was leading the team in scoring almost immediately. I had 10 goals in the first 11 games and I was one of the top 10 scorers in the league. I was not just playing a regular shift; I was playing on the power play and killing penalties. Shaky kept giving me more responsibility and not only was I responding, but our team was becoming one of the best in the WCHL.

It's a 150-mile drive from Foam Lake to Saskatoon, and with winter weather the way it is in Saskatchewan, it can be treacherous. But every game that we played at home, Mom, Dad, and Kenny would come in for the game. In fact, in my three years of junior hockey, my folks never missed a game, which is amazing. They would drive back home that night and Dad always made it to work the next day. It was really great to see them so supportive, after all the years of not wanting me to leave home. Plus, I knew when they came, Mom was always going to stock our apartment with all kinds of our favorite culinary delights: pierogies, cabbage rolls, and plenty of desserts. To have her cook the pregame meal was always so much better than when I did it myself.

My goal that year was to try to surpass the 100-point plateau that everybody always talked about. Only five players in the history of the Blades had done that, and with the start that I had, I really felt I could achieve that goal as long as I stayed healthy. But unfortunately, in late November, I got hurt screwing around at the end of practice. Bob Hoffmeyer and I dropped our gloves to throw some fake punches, and as we both threw rights, they collided and I broke my third knuckle on my right hand. Obviously, Shaky was not happy, but with such a stupid move I had no choice but to at least try to play through the pain of the injury. I thought, *What the heck, it's my top hand on my stick, so it shouldn't bother me.*

The next night, the doctors froze my right hand for the game and I suited up. It was a real bad decision. Even with the freezing, I just couldn't get comfortable. Then I missed a check and hit the Plexiglas, bruising my right shoulder. It got even worse when, later in the game, I strained my knee when I ran into the goal post. I went from relatively no injuries to three injuries all at the same time. I guess if you're going to get hurt you might as well do it all at once. Luckily, the injuries weren't that bad. I was only out for two weeks. Of course I wasn't 100 percent when I came back, but that's what you do in hockey because you know that there's always somebody there to take your job. As good as things were going for me, I couldn't take the chance of letting that happen.

Meanwhile, Ron and Don were working toward careers as P.E. teachers and that year being their last year, they were assigned to teaching internships. Don was assigned to E.D. Feehan, my old high school, where he also was tasked with helping coach the varsity football team as well as the girls varsity volleyball team. There were a couple of sisters on that volleyball team named Bernadette and Loretta Stadnyk. Bernadette was a couple of years younger than me, but I had met her in passing in my only year at the school. The previous May, just before graduation, I happened to be leaving school at the same time as she and her cousin. Her cousin asked if they could have a ride to their house and I obliged because I really liked what I saw in Bernadette. She was cute. She sat in the back, so I was able to adjust the rearview mirror so that I could keep an eye on her the whole ride. When I dropped them off, I don't remember how exactly I asked for it, but I managed to get her phone number. Somehow I lost it, though, and never called her. I was never good at making those date calls anyway.

Now it's seven months later and Don decided to have his volleyball team over for a get-together around Christmas time and he made sure that it was on an off night for me. The entire girls volleyball team was over at our place. How could that not be good? Don encouraged me to talk to Bernadette. He just felt that she and I would hit it off if we spent a little time together.

After everyone left that night, he said he could see some magic between us and told me I was crazy if I didn't ask her out. I did get her number again and this time I didn't lose it. It took a couple of months, but in February I finally had the balls to call her and ask her out. I remember our first date; we went to see *The Longest*

Yard. I rang the doorbell and her dad, Bill, who was the nicest man you ever met, answered the door. After a quick introduction to Bernadette's mom, who was also very nice, he proceeded to pour me, of all things, a shot of scotch as we waited for his daughter to come downstairs. I had tasted scotch before and knew I didn't like it, but how could I say no? We toasted, I shot it back, and he had to have seen the look in my eyes. I asked where the bathroom was, excused myself, and it took everything I had not to puke it all out. What a way to start a new date!

Bernadette's parents loved me. I was a Ukrainian Catholic boy, and her family—one older brother, then six girls, and two younger brothers—was Ukrainian Catholic as well. My mom used to tell all of us boys to date a lot of girls. "Don't pick one right away but make sure the one you marry is both Ukrainian and Catholic." We used to say, "Oh yeah, Mom, we're going to walk into the bar, walk up to a girl, and ask her if she's Ukrainian Catholic." There is a large Ukrainian community in Saskatchewan, but to find a girl like Bernadette that you really like and then find out that she's also Ukrainian Catholic, Mom was pretty impressed.

Bernadette was everything that I was looking for. She was good-looking, she was friendly, had a great family, and when we found out how much we had in common, we just laughed. Her birthday is May 21st, mine is May 12th. Her mom and dad and my mom and dad were married on the same day in the same year: July 15, 1951. Then, of course, there's our names: Bernard and Bernadette. Everyone else thought that was a bigger deal than we did. To us, it was just Bernie and Berna, but everybody else thought it was such a novelty.

We started hanging out all the time. I would go to her volleyball games and she would go to my hockey games, and it just took off from there. But from that day on, whenever I stopped by the house to pick her up, her Dad was always there to entice me with a shot of scotch. Thankfully, he didn't get mad at me when I told him I really didn't like scotch, so he would pour me a shot of rye whiskey instead. It took some time, but he gradually nurtured me into a scotch drinker and the fact that I have acquired a taste for good scotch is all on his shoulders.

That December, the World Junior Championships were in Winnipeg and I really wanted to go. I was leading the team in scoring and I thought I was playing the best of anybody on the team, but Shaky sent Ralph Klassen and Danny Arndt to represent the Blades. They were in their last year of junior, so I understood his thinking, but then he told me that the guys in their last year of junior were the only guys who were allowed to go. I knew that was bullshit because Brian Sutter and Bryan Trottier went and they were the same age as me. It was pretty loyal on his part to say, "I want our older guys to go," but I just hated being overlooked because I worked hard for this. I wasn't the only one that thought that way because there were a few articles written about my absence from that team. But it was one of those things that I had no control over.

I had set two other goals that year, and by early March, both had come to fruition: we clinched first place in the Eastern Conference of the WCHL, and I scored 100 points, reaching my goal on a night I got a hat trick. Even though I missed two weeks, I finished with 107 points, moving into an elite group of only six players in Blades history to post 100-plus points. The others were Orest Kindrachuk, Laurie Yaworski, Bernie Blanchette, and Gerry and Herb Pinder—and I became the first one to do it since Kindrachuk and Yaworski in 1970–71.

But none of that mattered when the playoffs started. There were two divisions in the WCHL, the Eastern and the Western, and we ran away with the East in the regular season. But now it was "game on." Our first opponent was the Brandon Wheat Kings, and after losing the first game, we swept the final four and eliminated them. I had a decent series, scoring five goals and eight points, and Shaky was pretty happy with the way things were going. But our next round was against our most heated rival, the Regina Pats.

The year before, my first season with the Blades, we had a playoff game in Regina and for those people who remember former NHL referee Kerry Fraser, he started his officiating career in the WCHL. In Game 6 of that series, Fraser made a call against the Pats and discovered the hazards of working a game with a crazy crowd in Regina, being hit in the shoulder by a cowbell thrown from the stands. The game had to be delayed 15 minutes while Fraser was being tended to. He did return, and years later when we were both in the NHL, we laughed about the incident. We lost to Regina my first season, but we got our paybacks this time, beating the Pats and their goalie, Ed Staniowski, to advance to play New Westminster in the Western Final.

You have to understand, New Westminster was in the final for more reasons than being a pretty good hockey club. Their game was not a finesse game, it was a game of physicality and intimidation, and to put it mildly, they were a goon squad. There was an article in the paper before Game 1 that basically said that New Westminster was expected to be physical and Saskatoon was expected to be roadkill. They had home-ice advantage, so we started the series there, where they had lost just one game all season. Going into that building was like going to the dentist. You just dreaded it. They had big bruisers, but it was their group of little shit-ass players that ran around and pissed everybody off. They were ready to run over anyone and everyone in their way. Were they going to play hockey or were they going to break your face? We really didn't have anybody that was an "enforcer," so basically we were scared shitless.

If we'd bet on ourselves, Las Vegas would have lost all of their money because to everyone's surprise, we won the first two games in New Westminster. We were up 2–0 in the best-of-seven series and were clearly in the driver's seat going back to Saskatoon for Games 3, 4, and 5, because our home record was almost flawless as well. The excitement on that plane going back to Saskatoon after those two wins was unbelievable. The Blades had never been to the Memorial Cup—that's Canada's junior hockey championship—in their history and we could taste it. The city of Saskatoon was abuzz. I remember at Mass on the Sunday before one of the games the priest giving us an extra prayer. But New West wasn't ready to give up, and to the shock of us and our fans, they beat us in two of the three games in Saskatoon. So we headed back to British Columbia for Games 6 and 7, and although they were both close games, after losing Game 6, we also dropped Game 7 in heartbreaking fashion and fell short of going where no Blades team had ever gone before.

At 18 years old, and after working so hard the entire season, it was devastating. But we did what every group of kids our age would do: we went to drown our sorrows. Our team found the closest watering hole near the hotel we were staying at and let the beer flow. It was late when we finally left, but a few of us, including teammate Glen Leggott and myself, stopped in one of the few restaurants that were open on the way back to the hotel. Well, we had a snoot full of beer in us and we started giving the waitress a rough time. Let me tell you something, cops showing up at a restaurant is usually not a good thing, especially when you dared the waitress to call them. They took us outside and I started trying to make my case, but to no avail and, shockingly, they told us they were taking us downtown. Legs pleaded, "If you're going to take him, you're going to have to take me," so they obliged. What a stupid statement by him, but that's a good friend.

It was a very humbling experience and I'm not sure if I could have went downtown by myself in the back of that paddy wagon. No seatbelts wasn't a big deal, but there were no seats. We went from New Westminster, which is a suburb out by the airport, all the way downtown to the drunk tank, and they threw us in two separate drunk tanks. I've never been so scared in my whole life, because after that ride I'm sober as a judge and I'm sitting in a cell with 20 guys who are just hammered. This one guy had been in a fight and took off his suit to clean it, so he's standing there in his underwear. I'm going, "Wow, what was I thinking and how long is this going to last?"

I actually sat right beside the door on the floor and was scared to death to even close my eyes, never mind sleep a wink. It was the slowest 4½ hours ever, and it was the same way for Legs on the other side. As if it wasn't bad enough that we were in the drunk tank, we had an early-morning flight back to Saskatoon with the team and the bus was picking us up at the hotel at 8:00 AM. I prayed all night that we were going to get out in time to be on it. At 6:00 AM, the door opened and I heard my name called, and as I walked out I saw Legs leaving his cell as well. I'm not sure if we laughed or sighed, but boy were we relieved. We had just enough time to jump in a cab and get back to the hotel to grab our luggage by 7:30. We changed into a new set of clothes and walked onto the bus like nothing ever happened. We were sure that none of the other guys would squeal on us, but we were scared that Shaky was going to find out. Luckily, he never did, or at least if he did, he never said anything.

The missed opportunity to go to the Memorial Cup was certainly disappointing, but it was the breakout year I'd been hoping for. Not only did I lead the Blades in scoring during the regular season, but I led the WCHL in goals in the playoffs. I always felt if you're going to play well in the regular season, you've got to make sure you can play when the pressure is on, and I did.

I was 18, turning 19 in May, and the draft back then was always for players that would turn 20 in that calendar year. But in the previous couple of drafts they had made exceptions for exceptional underage players, like the year before when Bryan Trottier had been drafted by the New York Islanders. With that in mind, I was pretty pumped when my name came up as a possible pick in the upcoming draft. But then the NHL and the World Hockey Association decided against the underage draft that year, saying it was unconstitutional or some bullshit and proclaimed that only 20-year-olds would be eligible. I was disappointed, but it was probably a good thing because I believe underage kids could only be drafted in the first or second round. So I probably would have been a second-round pick and gone somewhere else for less money. Regardless of what rules they were making up on the fly, I now knew that there was a strong possibility I was going to get my chance to play in the NHL and that it was time to begin the process of hiring an agent.

Shaky didn't like agents and he was always really vocal about it. Things were so different back then and it was such a hard decision to make. Every agent fed you the same bullshit, always stroking your ego to try to get you to make up your mind quickly. My choices came down to Alan Eagleson, the top agent at the time, or David Schatia and Larry Sazant, who both ran one of the big-name agencies. Eagleson wanted me badly, but I just thought he was too big. He had Bobby Orr and all the big stars, and I wasn't sure if he would have the time for a young prospect like me.

Eagleson had a local guy, Bud Quinn was his name, who was really involved in the hockey community and worked in recruiting junior players and Bud tried to convince me that "Eagle" was the right choice. In fact, Bud told me that if I didn't choose Eagle, it would be the biggest mistake of my life and it would cost me dearly. It turned out that he was probably right, but I didn't realize that for about a year. Schatia and Sazant had called Shaky, and invited both Blair Chapman and me to visit their offices in Montreal to meet with them. They paid for our flights and hotels while we were in Montreal for a couple of days and really wined and dined us. We even had dinner with the great Bernie "Boom Boom" Geoffrion, who was working with them at the time. Are you kidding me— Boom Boom Geoffrion—that was the thrill of a lifetime!

The meeting went well and I was impressed with everything they showed us. I left Montreal with a really good feeling. Maybe it was Boom Boom or maybe I was just clueless, but I needed an agent and after talking to my folks when I got back, we made the decision to go with Schatia. I had an agent now and was getting even more excited about being drafted because agents don't really want you unless they know you're going to make some money. But not being draft-eligible that year, I had a chance to become a bona fide first-round draft pick and potentially the No. 1 overall pick. I knew if my second season with the Blades was a breakout year, my third season had to be even better. We had a really good nucleus coming back and I knew that I had a great chance to be the captain. I wanted this to be my team.

I stayed in Saskatoon that summer. My dad was friends with a guy who ran a paper-supply company called Crown Zellerbach and got me a job filling shelves in the warehouse and unloading boxcars when the trains came in. It was a great job, and since I played for the Blades, the management at Crown treated me like gold, letting me work at my own pace as long as the job got done. When I was off, I was able to hang out with my friends in Saskatoon, and just being in the city meant spending a lot of time with Bernadette. We were in the bars or at a movie almost every night during the week and on the weekends we drove a couple of hours north to Emma Lake, where her parents had a summer cottage.

Ron and Don had just graduated from college and had gotten teaching jobs in the city, so both of them bought fancy new dream cars, Camaros. They were beautiful. Ron's was white with a red ragtop and Don's was all white. I was still driving my 1962 Viva

Vauxhall, and because Ron and Don got new cars, maybe I thought Dad and Mom felt that it was time for them to buy me a new car. That turned out to be quite a humbling experience. There were a lot of cars out there that I would have loved to have, but since it wasn't my money, Dad wasn't going to let me make the decision. After spending a whole weekend shopping, he decided that I was going to get a Ford Maverick, and if that wasn't disappointing enough, it was canary yellow. It was not the car that I wanted. Some of my teammates were driving Mustangs or Camaros and I was getting a Ford Maverick. I threw a temper tantrum. I felt like, *How dare you do this to me? Don't you know what I just accomplished with the Blades?* It didn't faze my dad one bit. Looking back, instead of the immature way I responded, I should have been so much more appreciative. I didn't get my way with the car, but it was way better than what I was driving before, and it was Dad's way of giving me what he thought was right. And Dad was right a lot.

A fancier set of wheels would have been nice, but I still felt on top of the world. Then on the first day of training camp with the Blades, Shaky ruined that, or least I thought he did. He called me into his office to give me his outlook of what the year was going to look like and the first thing he said was, "You're not going to live with your brothers this year at the apartment. You're going back to board with a family just like you did in your first year." I was shocked because I had had such a great year, and now my brothers were actually teachers. I thought, *Why would I not be able to live with them again?*

I guess the answer was that he either didn't trust me or he could see the potential that I had and he didn't want to chance anything, or maybe both. Shaky had said many times in interviews to the press that if I put my mind to it, I could be the best player in the league. His word was final, so there was no argument. I moved in with a new family, not very far from my brothers' apartment. It was a nice household, and the great thing was, besides the two kids they had, there was another college student boarding there. His name was Gordon Dean, and we immediately hit it off and became great friends. It was great having Gord around because he was a dentistry student and having someone the same age as me who wasn't playing hockey was a good change. Meeting Gord was one of the pluses of moving out of the apartment. Maybe Shaky knew what he was doing after all.

That wasn't the only good move Shaky made going into that season. He put Blair Chapman on right wing with me, and from the beginning it was as if we had been playing together for 10 years. We just seemed to have that magic and that sixth sense, knowing where the other was going to be on the ice at all times. Whether we had Bruce Hamilton or Neil "Bunny" Hawryliw on the left side with us, no one could stop us. I was leading the league in scoring with 20 points in the first four games and I was like, "Wow, this is unbelievable." I was riding a wave that I had never seen before. We were tops in our division, and Saskatoon was abuzz with the Blades again. I didn't think it could get any better, but then it did. For whatever reason, we didn't have a captain at the start of the season, but about a month in, Shaky decided that it was time to name one. He put four names on the board and asked us all to vote. I was extremely proud when at the end of the vote I became the captain of the Saskatoon Blades. That was truly an honor.

There were a lot of perks of being the captain and leading scorer of the Blades. Every home game, there was a "Player of the Game" award, and I had won it a few times in my first two seasons. But when you're putting up four or five points every game, it seemed like I was receiving the award almost every night. I would do all the interviews and Bernadette would always be the last one in the building, sitting at a table, waiting for me. If you were the "Player of the Game," they gave you a gift certificate to a store called The Army and Navy, which was run by a man named Sonny Ludwig, and you could pick out almost anything you wanted. Every time you went in there with a gift certificate, it was like Christmas because it was a department store that had almost everything. Whether it was camping equipment or a new leather jacket, we would just go in there and pick it out and take it home. Even if I didn't have enough value in the gift certificates, they would say, "Whatever you want, just take it."

Another one of our big supporters was a gentleman that we called "Gus," who owned two restaurants, Mr. Steer's and Cousin Nick's. Gus never missed any of the games at the old barn in Saskatoon. He was such a rabid hockey fan that when the game turned into a boxing match, you would see him standing right behind the glass, yelling obscenities at the other team and tossing a beer or trash over the glass. We were lucky to have him around the arena and it was standard procedure for most of the team to go over to Mr. Steer's after the games. He and his wife didn't have any kids of their own so he treated us like we were his own. The drinking age was 18, and even though Bernadette was only 17, Gus never worried that she was sitting there drinking screwdrivers while we were pounding beers. And he never let us pay for anything. He always said, "Just make sure you take care of your server."

We were having so much fun and we were hardly spending any money at all. With what I was making playing hockey, and what I was saving at the stores and bars, I felt rich. Shaky was giving me the league maximum pay, which was $300 a month. My only real expense was $110 for room and board, but my parents were paying my landlady, so I had the full $300 a month to spend. It sounds funny now, but in 1975, I felt rich. Draft beer was five for a dollar—what more can I say.

But in order to boost my draft status in the NHL and make the big bucks, I knew I had to be viewed as one of the best players in the world. It's one thing to do well against your peers in the WCHL, but it's another thing to do it on an international stage. Fortunately, that year a Russian select team was touring Canada, and the league put together a WCHL All-Star team to play them at the brand-new 17,000-seat Edmonton Coliseum. This was a huge deal for all of us, playing a Russian team that everybody in Canada hated in a venue that we could have only dreamed about, and to make it even better, every NHL scout was going to be there watching.

It was such a thrill to experience the excitement and pressure of playing for your country and it was an atmosphere that I had never seen before. There was sheer passion on every shift, like it was the last one of your life. The game was absolutely fantastic and we ended up beating the Russians 5–4, and I remember we cele- brated like we had just won the Stanley Cup. My teammate Blair Chapman and I were a big factor in the win. We had a ton of ice time playing our regular shifts, killing penalties, and playing the power play, and through it all, Chappy had a goal and I had two assists.

I knew from that game on that Chappy and I were destined to be high picks in the upcoming draft, and I got a clue of that the next morning on the flight back to Saskatoon. A scout by the name of Gerry Ehman, who had been at the game and was the head scout for the St. Louis Blues, approached me and said, "Great game, Bernie," and then he asked me a really strange question. The question was, "Who do you think the best player on the ice was last night?" I never really could answer that question. But a few months later, he would answer that question for me.

After the great experience playing against the Russians, I was back in the spotlight a couple of weeks later in the WCHL All-Star game. Those games are usually not very competitive, but this one was different. All of us were eyeing NHL careers, so the game was played a lot harder than the All-Star games of today. I was on the East team with Brian Sutter and Blair Chapman and interestingly enough we were all on a line together. I had a goal and an assist, Brian had a goal, and Blair had an assist, but we lost 9–7. Who would have ever guessed that five years later we would be playing on the same line together in St. Louis?

5

BREAKING BOBBY CLARKE'S RECORD

THE REGULAR SEASON resumed after the All-Star game and with the scoring pace I was on, I started thinking about the WCHL's single-season scoring record. Flin Flon's Bobby Clarke, who of course went on to a long and prosperous career with the Philadelphia Flyers, had set the record in 1968 with 168 points in 59 games. Every game I got closer and closer, and the anticipation grew that I was going to rewrite history. I tied the record in a 13–3 win over Edmonton with two goals and three assists. That gave me 168 points in 65 games, which meant that I still had seven games left to break the record. I broke the record in Brandon, Manitoba, against the Wheat Kings on March 12. The magnitude of the accomplishment was overwhelming. After all, Bobby Clarke was an NHL star, captain of the Philadelphia Flyers. The record was one that few people thought would ever be surpassed.

That night, Shaky surprised the hell out of all of us by bringing a few bottles of champagne into the locker room and proposing a very special toast to commemorate that moment for me. This was totally out of character for Shaky to buy us booze. We used to have to sneak our beer on the bus in our bags. It was kind of a daring event to open a bottle on the bus, so we'd cough or sneeze real loud whenever we popped one open to hide the sound. If you got caught with empties, you'd be in trouble, so we'd slide open a window on the bus, even when it was 40-below outside, and drop the bottles on the road.

Anyway, I think Shaky was probably relieved that I had finally broken the record because of the distraction of the thing, but I thought it was pretty cool that he respected the accomplishment enough to make that big of a deal about it. This was a moment when you understand how much a coach respects and cares about you, even if he never told you. As much as I got along with him, he was one of those guys I had a love-hate relationship with. I think every player who has ever played this game has probably had a love-hate relationship with their coach. It's not until you finish your career that you look back and figure out who taught you what and who was responsible for your success. I believe there was no better coach than Jackie McLeod to teach you the game of hockey the way it's supposed to be played. He gave me the blueprint to take my game to the next level as a professional. He had a system to counteract every system that we faced. No one knew the finer details of the game like he did, and I feel very fortunate that I was able to have him coach me for my three formative years of junior hockey.

Once again the regular season was a great success, as we won our division, and we had home-ice advantage to open the playoffs. Our first-round series was against the Lethbridge Broncos and Brian Sutter, who was the captain of the Broncos and who I didn't know was going to become a big part of my life going forward. The series was hard-fought, but we beat them in seven games.

The next series was a matchup against the Kamloops Blazers, and we won that series in six games. All that hard work got us the distinct pleasure, if you can call it that, of playing the New

Westminster Bruins in the WCHL final for the second straight year. Once again, it was Beauty vs. Brawn and once again we had to start the series in New West, which had set a new league record with 54 wins and 112 points. It was a nasty series that went back and forth, and like the year before, we fell to the Bruins in the seventh game in front of a packed house at the Pacific Coliseum in Vancouver. Losing is always disappointing, especially losing to them twice in two years in the seventh game. We were proud of what we were able to do, but I'll always look back at it as two shots to get to the Memorial Cup in two years, and it hurts to think that we couldn't get there. At least this time I was smart enough to stay out of jail.

I finished my last season in Saskatoon with 72 goals, 115 assists, and 187 points, which was a new WCHL scoring record. I set a few other records that season, including a 31-game point streak and scoring 45 points in the postseason. I closed out my three-year career with 133 goals, 211 assists, and 344 points in 206 games. I still can't believe that, especially the goals. It's hard to fathom that I could score 72 goals in 72 games. I never shot the puck, I was a passer; I always was and always would be. I went from not knowing if I was going to make the Blades as a 17-year-old to setting league records and being the MVP in the WCHL. It was beginning to look like it would all pay off and that a pro hockey career could be my future.

Back then, though, my parents wanted me to be a doctor and I had somewhat of an aspiration of being that. I was a straight-A student, good in chemistry and physics. As a kid, I didn't really know what I wanted to do, but what teenager really does know?

If I hadn't made the Blades, I don't know what would have happened to my life. I think I would have been asking myself, "What do I want to be after I graduate next year?" and hockey probably wouldn't have been in play. I really believe that. If I wouldn't have made the Blades before my senior year of high school, I probably would have never played hockey again. I think I could have been that doctor, but making the Blades was the turning point and, I believe, destiny.

A week before the NHL draft, I went to Montreal for the Memorial Cup, where I was up for an award called the Canadian Major Junior Hockey player of the year. CCM sponsored the award and this was only the second year they had it. There's one representative from Western Canada, one from the Ontario Hockey League, and one from Quebec. CCM told me ahead of time that I wasn't going to win and asked me to not hold it against them. The reason was Ed Staniowski had won the award the year before, representing Western Canada, and they wanted to spread it around.

But it was still a great trip for me. The Memorial Cup was being played and the Canadiens were in the Stanley Cup Finals at that time, playing against the Philadelphia Flyers. I got to go to the Finals, which was the first time I'd ever attended a real NHL game. It was such a thrill to be at the Montreal Forum, watching the team that I'd idolized my entire life. All those years watching games played at the Montreal Forum on *Hockey Night in Canada* and now I was there in person. If that wasn't a big enough thrill, Bobby Clarke, whose WCHL scoring record I had broken, was right there in front of me. In my mind, I thought that maybe later that year I could be playing in that very same building. This was a perfect trip, as I was also able to meet with my agents, Schatia & Sazant, who were based in Montreal. I was in hockey heaven.

I knew at this point that I was going to be a first-round pick, but where I was going, nobody knew for sure. You want to be drafted as high as you can be, and when I put together the year I had in Saskatoon, there was no doubt in my mind—or in anyone's I talked to—that I had a really good chance of being the first-overall pick. Max McNab was the general manager of the Washington Capitals at the time and we had an interview with him in Schatia's office. When I left that meeting and flew back to Saskatoon, it was pretty clear, according to my agents, that Washington was going to take me No. 1.

I really had my fingers crossed that it was going to happen. It is pretty special to be the No. 1 overall pick in the draft. But the day before the NHL draft, the Capitals decided they wanted to take a defenseman. They felt the top defenseman in the draft was Rick Green, so Rick became the No. 1 overall pick. Pittsburgh had the second pick and the Penguins took my teammate and right winger in Saskatoon, Blair Chapman. I was extremely happy for Chappy. He was very solid, had a great shot, and worked hard to be picked that high. He was a big part of my success, but I winced when people said, "Chappy made you." I didn't think that, so when he got picked ahead of me, it gave me fuel to prove people wrong.

After Chappy went No. 2 overall, Glen Sharpley went No. 3 to Minnesota, and Fred Williams, another one of my teammates in Saskatoon, went No. 4 to Detroit. Williams was a client of Eagleson, so when his name got called, I knew it really cost me for having Schatia & Sazant as my agents.

Freddy was a big guy and his nickname was "Fats." He was a great skater, great penalty-killer, and a really good defensive player, but by most accounts, not a first-round pick. Our last year with the Blades, I scored 72 goals and he had 31. There was a lot of speculation about why the Red Wings drafted him that high. Alex Delvecchio was the general manager and his nickname was "Fats" too. There were people saying that was one of the reasons Delvecchio liked Freddy. He never did make it in the NHL, playing half a season with the Red Wings and maybe three more years in the minors before he was finished. When I saw him in the summer after the third or fourth year, he was over 250 pounds. We had always called him the "Fat Cat," and now really was. The No. 5 pick was a Swedish kid, Bjorn Johansson, that went to the California Golden Seals, and then No. 6 was Donnie Murdoch, who went to the New York Rangers. Murdoch was a sniper, a real good scorer, but later had some issues and fell out of the league.

The Blues were up next, and I had a connection with them. Shaky, my junior coach in Saskatoon, knew Emile Francis, who was the Blues general manager. They met through hockey, but got to know each other more through baseball in the mid-1940s to late '50s. Shaky played baseball for North Battleford in Saskatchewan, and Emile was the player/manager. They called Emile "the Cat" because he was a goalie and one of the newspapers wrote that he had "cat-like" reflexes, so it stuck. But he was a good shortstop, too, playing with Shaky with the North Battleford Beavers.

But now it's May 27, 1976, about 20 years later, and Mr. Francis is the GM of the Blues and he's calling Shaky to find out more about me, whether or not he should pick me. He was concerned and Shaky kept telling him, "Relax, you're getting the best hockey player of the whole bunch." The drafts back then were a lot different than what goes on these days. They were not held at the NHL rinks, so there were no sold-out crowds in attendance, and it was not on television. Our draft was a teleconference call originating from the NHL offices in Montreal, and it started at 9:00 AM Eastern, so it was 7:00 Saskatoon time.

About 7:30, the phone rang at our apartment and it was Gerry Ehman, who was the Blues' chief scout and, yes, the same person that had asked me who I thought was the best player in that All-Star game against the Russians. I guess Gerry was finally telling me who he thought the best player was, saying that he was delighted that the Blues were making me their pick. I remember I had to ask Gerry, "What number did I go?" because I didn't know the order of the draft. Jerry told me I was No. 7, which overwhelmed me with all kinds of thoughts. I was excited, but also disappointed that I wasn't the No. 1 pick after the year I'd had. But now I was property of the Blues, and they were extremely happy, so how could I not be happy?

The World Hockey Association draft had been a week before the NHL draft, and though my goal was to be in the NHL, this was something that we had to pay attention to. Chappy was the No. 1 overall pick by the Edmonton Oilers, who then also took me with the No. 6 pick. Since we had the same agents, Schatia & Sazant, we talked to them and they said maybe we should cut a deal with Edmonton, or at least use the Oilers as leverage. Edmonton did make a substantial offer to both Blair and me to go there, but the day before the NHL draft, Pittsburgh knew that Washington was going to take Rick Green, so the Penguins told Chappy they were going to take him and already agreed to terms. Chappy had no intentions to play in the WHA, and I didn't either, but at least we could have used Edmonton as a bargaining tool. All the leverage was gone though when Chappy signed with Pittsburgh, which I thought was the dumbest thing. I couldn't believe Schatia & Sazant didn't at least drag out the negotiations between the two leagues.

My contract with the Blues was a much longer process than Chappy's. My agents never told me why, but it was about a month and a half after the draft before I finally agreed to terms. Mr. Francis made arrangements so that we could meet him in Montreal to finalize the deal. All the hard work in junior hockey, the anticipation of the draft, and all the negotiations were finally over. I was now going to sign that first NHL contract. Mr. Francis invited my parents to come along. We were scheduled to leave for Montreal on July 12, but there was a problem.

Mom and Dad were going to celebrate their 25th wedding anniversary on July 15 in Foam Lake. We'd already sent out invitations for about 200 guests for a banquet and dance at the church hall. It should have been no problem for us all to meet Mr. Francis in Montreal on July 12, sign the contract on July 13, and get back to Foam Lake two days later for the party. The catch, though, was that Air Canada was going through a strike, and they couldn't guarantee us that the flights would be on schedule back from Montreal. I don't know how we came up with this crazy solution, but just Dad came with me and Mom stayed back so that at least one of them would be at the party in case we didn't make it back on time. When you think about that, it was pretty stupid.

There wasn't the same pomp and circumstance that there is today signing your first contract. We met Mr. Francis for dinner at the Queen Elizabeth Hotel in Montreal, had a nice conversation and basically that was it. That was my first face-to-face meeting with Mr. Francis and from that moment on, just from the way he treated Dad and me, I knew that I was in the right organization. He was the most sincere, intense man I'd ever met. My dad was so impressed with Mr. Francis that when we left dinner that night, he said, "This guy is a gem." He was the most honest and trustworthy gentleman. Both Dad and I knew that he was going to give me the opportunity that I needed to be the best player I could be. So it ended up being a fantastic trip for us, and thankfully, the flights were on schedule and we got back to Foam Lake in time for the party. To this day, I still feel bad that Mom didn't get to go.

My first contract with the Blues was a four-year deal with a $75,000 signing bonus. I thought I had died and gone to heaven. I got a check immediately for $25,000 when I signed the contract. I would receive another $10,000 when I reported to training camp and an additional $15,000 the following July. The final $20,000 would be paid in two installments, $10,000 after playing 40 games in the NHL and the other $10,000 when I played 80 NHL games.

I felt that I now had some real money. I'd bought a new suit before we went to Montreal to sign the contract, but the one thing I wanted to buy the most was a new car for Mom and Dad. My brothers and I had talked about that in the many conversations through my junior career, that if I ever made it to the NHL I was going to buy our folks a new car, so we were all excited this was happening. Our first choice was to buy Dad a Thunderbird, so we walked into the Ford dealership in Saskatoon, and it was kind of funny because when you're a 20-year-old looking at a car with that kind of price tag, nobody gives you the time of day. I had the money to buy the car, but they just thought we were browsing, so nobody paid attention to us. After a few minutes, with nobody paying attention to us, we got pissed off and walked out. We shopped around, found a lot better service at the Oldsmobile dealership and decided on a new Olds Ninety Eight. Dad wasn't there, but we all agreed that this was a beauty and bought it. It took up most of the signing bonus I got, but for Mom and Dad it was well worth it. I wrote a check and it felt so cool to be able to do that.

Dad was so proud of the car. Not only that, but the purchase came at a good time. My dad's sister lived in Detroit and her daughter was getting married that summer and our whole family was going. Kenny and I were riding with Mom and Dad, and Ron and Don were following in one of their camaros. It was a 20-hour drive from Foam Lake to Detroit and we were making a vacation of it, stopping a few times along the way. I remember the first night of the drive it was getting dark and we pulled over in the middle of Manitoba looking for a hotel. My folks always walked in to see which hotel had the best price, so we stopped and looked at the first one and Dad didn't like it. Then we pulled into another one and I said, "Dad, look, this one has a pool, let's just get it."

He said, "I'm going to check out the price." So he went in and came out and said, "No, it's too expensive."

I said, "Dad, for God's sake, I'll pay."

He looked at me and slapped me. He said, "You're not paying for anything, you're not a big shot." You know what, he was right.

Even though I had the money, I shouldn't have been the one who decided where we were staying. He was in charge and I should have never questioned his judgement. That was a lesson in humility and it was also a lesson in being smart with my finances. I had to remember that even though I had come into some extra money, Dad was making sure that I understood it may not be there forever and I needed to learn some responsibility. It was a transitional time in my life because I was on top of the world, but I was still young and immature.

6

BECOMING A BLUE

HONESTLY, I WAS also very nervous at that time. I had been drafted by the Blues and didn't even know where St. Louis was. Hell, I didn't even know where Missouri was. I thought to myself, *That's the South, right?* We knew where Chicago was, where the big cities were, but not St. Louis. Another thing, I had no idea whether or not the Blues were a good team because I never followed them. We watched the Toronto Maple Leafs and the Montreal Canadiens and I was a Habs fan. Years earlier I had watched Montreal beat St. Louis in the Stanley Cup Finals, so I knew Glenn Hall and Jacques Plante. Later on, Garry Unger was an All-Star, so we knew who he was. But other than that, I didn't know who any of these guys were. In those days, all your information came from the *Hockey News*, which was more focused on the Canadian teams. I didn't know who the Plager brothers and Red Berenson were, so I had to do some research. I wanted to find out who was on the team and especially who the center-icemen were, because Mr. Francis had said I was going to get an honest chance at making the roster, and if I was going to do that, I wanted to know who I was going to have to unseat? I wanted to know who my competition was.

The summer should have been the best of my life, but it wasn't without a couple of setbacks.

Throughout my junior career, I constantly had bouts with a sore throat and strep throat, and the doctor decided that it would be a good idea to get my tonsils taken out, so a week after the draft I was scheduled for surgery. Anyone who's ever had their tonsils taken out as an adult will probably tell you that it's not a fun thing, and mine was no exception. I can't believe I actually let the doctor talk me into doing the surgery under just local anesthetic. To sit there in a dentist's chair with your head back and mouth open is as nauseating as you could ever dream, and the pain afterward is some of the worst I've ever experienced. And to make matters worse, I had a bad reaction to it.

I had so much pain when I swallowed that I lost the urge to eat, so I basically didn't for a couple of weeks and lost 20 pounds. When I went to see Mr. Francis to sign my contract, I was 6–1 and no more than 155 pounds. I knew I was too scrawny to play in the NHL at that size. I played my last year of junior hockey at 178, and felt comfortable, so I knew that I had to put the weight back on. Trust me when I tell you that after the pain finally subsided, I ate everything in sight and the pounds did come back.

Just when things were getting back to normal after the tonsil surgery, though, I had another setback. It was mid-August and I was getting real excited about going to training camp. There was a boys school called St. Peter's College in Muenster, Saskatchewan, which is about 60–70 miles from Saskatoon. That's where Ralph Klassen, my teammate with the Blades, grew up. They had a hockey school every year and Ralphy asked me to come, so instead of going to Yorkton to do the school there like I had the previous two summers, I decided to help Ralph. It was great teaching the kids, but mostly I was also looking forward to the ice time because

I wanted to get my timing down and make a good impression at my first professional training camp.

We were in the third or fourth day of the hockey camp and everything was going great. We were on the ice all day, getting lots of skating and conditioning, and having lots of fun in the evenings. Then one night we decided to shoot some hoops in the gym and that led to a pickup basketball game. I went up to pull down a rebound and came down hard on my right foot. With the shot of intense pain I immediately knew something was wrong. I limped off the court and hoped that lots of ice would fix the problem, but that was wishful thinking because when I went to the doctor the next day, I found out, sure enough, that I broke the fifth metatarsal on the bottom of my foot. It was already the third week of August when they put a cast on it and camp was just a month away. How could this have happened? Calling Mr. Francis and telling him that I broke my foot, and that I did it playing basketball, was a very difficult thing to do. Thank God he said "no problem" and understood, but now I was in a position that was gut wrenching. There was no way I was going to be in shape for camp.

The Blues wanted to fly me into St. Louis a week before camp to check out my foot, so I packed up everything I owned into a couple of suitcases and off I went. I was so excited, yet so apprehensive. I was alone going to a new country, a new city, a new challenge. Looking out the window as I landed, I couldn't believe what I was seeing with my own eyes. The green on the trees in St. Louis, and I still believe this, is the most pretty shade of green I've ever seen. It was so lush and so different than what I was used to seeing in the plains of Saskatchewan, where it was wheat fields and sparse clumps of trees.

Still inside the terminal, the city couldn't have made a better first impression on me, but then I walked out of the terminal and got hit by a wall of heat and humidity. I said, "What the hell is this?" Welcome to summer in St. Louis. I had no idea what to expect and actually I was scared shitless. It was the culture shock. I was in a totally different world with big bustling freeways, cars, and a huge airport. We had a puddle-jumper airport in Saskatoon, so other than flying to Montreal that one time, I had never seen anything like this before.

Mr. Francis was at the curb to pick me up. He took me down to the Quality Inn on Oakland Avenue next to the Arena and checked me in. I dropped my bags off and he took me right to Jewish Hospital. I realized how special it was to be a pro hockey player when the Blues orthopedic doctor, Dr. Jerry Gilden, was waiting for me. He took the cast off my broken foot, did X-rays again, re-casted it, and then said, "Okay, everything looks like it's healing right. You'll be ready for camp in a week." I was so glad to hear those words.

In the meantime, it was time to see St. Louis. Mr. Francis had three of the guys—Chuck Lefley, Bobby MacMillan, and Dave Hrechkosy—pick me up and take me to the Cardinals' game and a few of the bars near St. Louis University. I had never been to a professional baseball game, so I was in total awe going to Busch Stadium and watching the Cardinals. Talk about fantastic guys. I learned that night that even though I was only 20, if you hang with the Blues, you don't get carded and you have a heck of a time.

What a great night that was, but other than that, I made sure that it was a quiet week for me leading up to the first day of camp.

I couldn't work out or even skate, so I just hung around the hotel for the most part. Mr. Francis did take me down to get a look at the Arena and the locker-room facilities. The owners, the Salomons, had done a great job, and in that day and age it was a really nice locker room. There were three whirlpools, a nice sauna, and much more than I had ever seen in our junior locker room. It was really impressive, but even more exciting was the rest of the guys arriving at the hotel. I was constantly meeting real NHL players and that was the thrill of a lifetime, to be getting ready to go on the ice for the first time together.

On the first day of camp, after our physicals, the doctors removed my cast, and it was game on. This was not boys now, this was men. This was not Saskatoon anymore, this was St. Louis. I learned that when I walked out of the airport, and it wasn't much better inside the Arena. It had to be 100 degrees outside, and the Arena had no air-conditioning. Talk about tough conditions for training camp. But nothing mattered to me because I was in an NHL locker room in an NHL arena in an NHL city. They had a press conference to introduce me and the rest of the current draft picks. It was nice to be with a familiar face as well. Brian Sutter was the Blues' second pick in the draft that year, and that was fantastic because Brian and I had played together a couple of times. We went head to head a lot, but I had played with him in the WCHL All-Star game and then I got to know him more when we played against the Russians. I didn't know him that well, but I knew him well enough to hang around with.

I was a little worried how I would play, but I had a lot of confidence in myself. Remember, no one expected me to win the scoring title in the WCHL and no one expected me to break Bobby Clarke's record, but I did. I scored 72 goals and had 115 assists, and then people said, "Well he'll choke in the playoffs," but then I ran away with the scoring title in the postseason. No one really gave me a chance to do anything, so that never bothered me. I knew that I was going to have to do it all over again in the NHL.

I would have been *really* confident if not for the fact that I was coming off a broken foot. I knew that my foot wasn't totally healed and I should have been in a cast longer, but it wasn't up to me. The doctors said it was healed enough that it would be fine in a boot, but they weren't the ones with their foot in the boot. Every time I tried to turn from forward to backward skating, I fell down because of the pain. It felt like I was stepping on a bump, like an acorn. After watching me struggle for a couple of practices, they finally held me out for the next few days. They realized I needed more healing time and they kept me home when the team went on the road to play in the preseason.

My first chance to play in an exhibition game was about 10 days into camp, and it was in Kansas City against Atlanta. The team was already on the road, so Derek Sanderson (who had been nursing an injury in camp) and I met them in K.C. We had an early-morning flight around 8:00 AM and to my amazement, immediately after takeoff, Derek ordered a cocktail from the flight attendant. Then he had another one. He had two screwdrivers on the short flight from St. Louis to K.C., and the best part was he didn't have any money on him, so he said, "Hey, kid, you want to pay for these?"

So I pulled out my money and paid. I was nervous that I was going to be playing in my first NHL game that night and here he was having a couple of cocktails an hour before going on the ice for the morning skate. Derek obviously had some issues and we all found out about those issues later on. That was a strange introduction to Derek Sanderson, but he was one of the neatest guys you'd ever want to meet.

The night couldn't come quick enough for me and it was everything that I had dreamed about. I scored my first NHL goal against Phil Myre and I must have been pretty damned excited because I called my folks immediately after the game to tell them. I know it was only preseason, but to score a goal in your first pro game, I was pretty pumped. After flying to the game with Derek, I was now able to travel with the team after the game. I was part of the team and that felt so good. We bussed back to St. Louis, and I quickly found the difference between being in junior hockey and the NHL. Remember, we had to hide our beer in junior. Not here. There were cases of beer and you could drink all you wanted all the way back to St. Louis.

Next on the preseason schedule was a trip to Western Canada and I was really looking forward to it. Although I had only been away from home for about three weeks, I was starting to feel really homesick, having no one around. This trip had stops in Winnipeg and Brandon, Manitoba, and then in Edmonton, so I was going to be in my own neck of the woods. Mom and Dad and Bernadette were going to be in Edmonton, so I was excited that I was going to get to see them. Because of my foot injury, I was only getting to play every second game, so it just happened that I didn't get to play in either Winnipeg or Edmonton. That was disappointing, but I did get a nice visit with them and the chance to see Bernadette again was great. I did get to play in Brandon against the Winnipeg Jets, who were the best team in the World Hockey Association, and what a thrill that was to be on the ice with the line of Bobby Hull, Ulf Nilsson, and Anders Hedberg. It made me feel like I'd really made it.

The pain in my foot was starting to go away and I was beginning to feel my way around the ice, but I didn't exactly impress anybody at my first camp. I would be lying if I said I was surprised when we got back to St. Louis to get the word from Mr. Francis that they were going to send me down. He didn't bullshit me; he was very honest. He basically said, "The fact of the matter is you didn't come the way we wanted to see you. We have four good center-icemen right now: Garry Unger, Red Berenson, Derek Sanderson, and Larry Patey. We want to see what you can do in the minors. If you look at my management career, we don't let very many guys just come right in the NHL. You have to go to the minors and work your way into the job." He said, "You're going to get an opportunity to play for Barclay Plager down there and Barc is a great guy. You're going to get a lot of ice time and we want you to find your game and when you are ready, we'll have you back up."

I couldn't argue with that, but it hurt me because I really felt that I would be the best new rookie coming into the NHL that year. I had put up 187 points in 72 regular season games and that was no fluke. I thought I had proved that I could play. But here I was headed to the minors and Blair Chapman, my teammate with the Blades, made the team in Pittsburgh. My ego was devastated.

The only thing that allowed me to cope was the fact that all of us rookies, Brian Sutter included, went down too.

I didn't want to go to Kansas City, where the Blues' farm team was in the old Central Hockey League. But honestly, when I look back, it was one of the greatest things that could have happened to me. Barc was absolutely unbelievable. He was 35 and had played in 614 NHL games, and he wasn't washed up by any means. He could have kept playing in the NHL, but Mr. Francis had told him, "Barc, I'm offering you the job to coach the team. I can't guarantee that this opportunity to coach will be there next year. And if you're not ready to call it a career, you can stay and play in St. Louis or you can go down and be the player/coach." And thankfully the way it turned out for me, Barc felt he was ready for the move, so he became our player/coach that year.

He was not only a good coach but he was the best defenseman in the CHL that year and he led by example. Whatever it took, whether it was blocking shots or dropping his gloves or two-handing some crazy opponent, he did it. This was not the NHL. This was the minors and he never complained. He truly amazed me because I had never seen anybody play the game that way. We thought, "This guy is unreal," and it gave us all the incentive in the world. That is the work ethic we needed. It helped me adopt the attitude that I didn't deserve anything and that I was going to work hard and do everything I could to get called back up. You earn your stripes.

The Blues shared the minor league affiliate in K.C. with Detroit. The Red Wings, you might remember, drafted Fred Williams, my other teammate with the Blades, No. 4 overall. It was interesting to me that when the Red Wings decided to send Fred down, they didn't send him to Kansas City either. They sent him to the Rhode Island Reds of the American Hockey League so there wouldn't be any comparisons with me, which I thought was pretty childish. That was too bad for him too because we had a real good team in K.C. But even with that good team, we were lucky to get 1,500 fans a night. The only time we had good crowds is when they had nickel beer night, and it was packed on those nights. It was an older team but with a good young mix of new draft picks, like Brian and me. Barc sat both of us down and said, "Hey guys, you're the future of the Blues. You guys are our first two picks, you guys are going to kill penalties, you're going to play on the power play, you're going to be the nucleus of this hockey club. So when you're ready, you're going to be going back to St. Louis."

Like Mr. Francis had told me, Barc put me on a line with Brian on the left side and Rick Bourbonnais on the right. Bourby was a second-year pro who was a hard-nosed guy with a good shot, so we clicked immediately. I knew what kind of player Brian was and I knew we'd click. He had played junior hockey in Lethbridge with Bryan Trottier. Trottier was a playmaker and Brian was hard-nosed, and they really gelled, so I knew Brian and I would do the same thing. It was like, "You get open and I'll get you the puck." Plus, I knew if any shit happened, Brian was going to be right there. Bourby was the same way. If somebody messed with him, he didn't mind dropping the gloves.

Most people don't know this, but I began my career with No. 7, not No. 24. Barc gave me No. 7 in the minors because Garry Unger was the No. 1 center on the Blues and Barc wanted to design the team the same way. I wish the jersey numbers were the only thing they passed down from St. Louis, but that wasn't the case. The Blues were also giving us their hand-me-down underwear, too. No one really knew at the time, but the Salomons were trying to sell the team and they were cutting costs. Back then, guys just wrote their number on the back of their underwear with a sharpie, so after they all went in the wash together, you knew whose was whose when they came out. Well, we would get our underwear and they would already have numbers written on them. We would have to cross it out and put our own number on it. They were all different sizes, so you found the ones that fit you, scratched out the number, and put your number on it. We got their old socks, too. It was crazy. I had just come from the Blues' camp, where you had new pants, new gloves, and any new equipment that you needed, and now in KC, it was all hand-me-downs. We all could have gotten pissed off about this, but instead I think the humor of it made us closer.

Other than dirty laundry and the fact that you were hoping to play well enough to get called up, there was really no stress in the minors. We had no family or close friends around, so we were independent. I came to Missouri with just my clothes, so for the first time in my life I was able to try to get set up as an adult, and I had the money to do it. I shared an apartment with John Smrke, who was the Blues' third pick in the draft. John and I spent lots of our time shopping, buying dishes, and furnishing our apartment with toasters, dishes, blenders, whatever. Team rules required us to wear a shirt and tie to all the games, so I bought a lot of clothes, too. And after driving whatever car my dad picked out for me, I was now able to buy the car of my dreams. I shopped around and finally decided on a Pontiac Grand-Prix. It was beautiful: white, two-door with glass T-tops and red interior with an eight-track player, upgraded speakers, and a CB radio. I did have a handle, but I was afraid to talk to anybody so I can't even remember what it was. I just listened to the chatter. I still look back and it was the nicest car I ever bought, and I've had a lot of nice cars. Maybe because it was my first one is why it was so special.

Brian Sutter and his wife, Judy, who got married earlier that summer, had an apartment in the same complex as John and me. We were all young kids and we just wanted to hang out. There was quite a bit of down time, so like most kids our age we went to all the bars together. The drinking age in Missouri was 21, but it was 18 in Kansas and we lived on the Kansas side of the border. I had a fake ID to get into the Missouri bars, thanks to Bruce Affleck, who had given me his driver's license in training camp. The Canadian driver's licenses didn't have pictures on them, so we got away with using them pretty easily, but for the most part we stayed around our apartment so we didn't need the false ID that often. It was fun times for us. Yeah, we were on our minor league salaries, but beer was cheap, so when we were together with the guys it was always a blast.

Living the professional hockey life was a different world, too. Half the guys smoked and it wasn't just at lunch or dinner, it was in-between periods, and it wasn't just one cigarette, it was two or three. If you had to go to the bathroom between periods, you had to walk through a cloud of smoke. What always amazed me was that the guys who smoked the most were the fastest skaters. Thankfully, I never got into the smoking deal, and trust me, I would definitely have been slower because of it. Living on your own was pretty neat. Nothing really to answer to except what was going on at the rink, and everything was great out on the rink in K.C. But in the back of my mind, I didn't want to be there. I knew I was going back to St. Louis, or at least I was hoping that would be the case. Mr. Francis had told me as soon as I got back to my game, he was going to call me back up.

Well, I had a great start to the season, but Brian got called up first in late October. When that happened, it was kind of an embarrassment to me because the second-round pick was getting called up before the first-round pick. Barc must have known I was going to get upset because he immediately grabbed me and said, "Hey Bernie, Brian is not going up because he's better than you. He's going up because they need a left winger and he will only be up for a couple of weeks. Just keep biding your time and you're going to get your chance."

Barc was always so sound in his reasoning. We had a great relationship because I could yell at him, and he could yell back, and it was okay. I was never disrespectful to him; you couldn't be. If he just looked at you wrong, you just shut up because he was going to kick your ass. But after talking to Barc, I realized that if I kept working hard, things would work out. I had total faith in him and he was right as usual. Brian was back in two weeks and my hard work paid off when the call came on December 20, 1976.

We had a morning skate and Barc called me in and said, "Good news, you're going up today."

"What?"

"Yeah, you're going up. You and Bourby, you're both going on a road trip with the Blues to Colorado and Vancouver."

I'm thinking, *Wow, dream come true, finally a chance to go up and play for real. The NHL.* Then I had to stop and think for a moment. The bad news was that Bernadette was coming to visit me in Kansas City for Christmas. She'd jumped on a plane that morning with two connections: Saskatoon to Winnipeg to Chicago to Kansas City. There were no cell phones back then, so there was no way to get ahold of her. It was very stressful because I had to jump on a plane to meet the team in St. Louis and then head to Colorado and she was headed to Kansas City. As excited as I was, I was frantically trying to arrange for my roommate, "Smrkie," who she's never met in her life, to pick her up at the airport in K.C.

Luckily, Smrkie's girlfriend was there, so at least it wasn't just him. But when they got there, Bernadette thought it was a joke and that I was hiding around the corner. As the minutes went by, though, she realized that it wasn't a joke and that she was stuck in Kansas City until I got back. Once I knew that she got to our apartment that night, I called her and she said everything was fine, but I knew she was saying that to me because she knew how important it was for me to be finally getting my chance to play in the NHL. I felt so bad for her but that's the kind of amazing person she is.

7

FIRST NHL GAME

WE PRACTICED IN St. Louis the next morning, flew to Denver early in the afternoon, and on December 22, 1976, I played my first NHL game, against the Colorado Rockies, wearing No. 14. I had worn No. 7 in the minors, but when I got called up, of course, Unger was wearing that number. No. 24 wasn't being worn with the Blues at the time, but Doug Palazzari had worn that number when he got called up the year before. So even though he was playing in Kansas City, maybe they were holding it for him in case he got called up. That's the only explanation I can recall, but quite frankly they could have given me any number and I would have been happy.

It was a long day of preparation and nerves. This was the day that I had waited for from the time I had been drafted in June. This was the carrot dangling in front of me and I was finally going to be able to grab it. That night, I played on a line with Bourby and Chuck Lefley, who the team was trying to get on track. Chuck had 43 goals the year before and three months into the season he maybe had three. We won the game 2–1; unfortunately we only got to play a few shifts. But that was okay. We were in the show and Bourby and I understood that we were just getting our feet wet.

We flew to Vancouver the next morning, and what an amazing difference it was to be playing in the NHL. It was amazing yet intimidating playing in front of 17,000 people, not 1,500 like in the minors. This was going to be such a special trip and my first experience of a tough turnaround, crossing the border and going through customs and then playing back-to-back games. It was a long day, but I was excited because I was back in Canada for the first time, playing in Vancouver at the Pacific Coliseum, which I was familiar with from junior hockey. And to top it all off, I had relatives coming to the game.

I was extremely nervous when we took the ice for the pregame warmup, but I remember thinking, *This could be the night that I score my first NHL goal!* I could do it in front of some family and friends. But then the game started, and as it progressed our line sat at the very end of the bench... and sat... and sat. I'll never forget that because they had just held the circus at the Coliseum and there were a ton of flies still buzzing around. We were actually on the bench killing flies with our sticks. That was probably the most disheartening thing I ever experienced—relatives watching, I don't even get a shift, and I'm swatting flies on the bench. I didn't even get credit for the game on my pension because I didn't have a shift. But we won the game and everyone was happy.

That was the last game before the Christmas break, so we had a few days off coming up. We jumped on the bus with the team right after the game and headed to Seattle so we could catch an early morning flight back to St. Louis. I was planning to spend the holiday there, but Mr. Francis allowed Bourby and me to fly back to Kansas City. I was elated because Bernadette was there, all my teammates that had become dear friends were there, and to have dinner with the Sutters on Christmas Eve was like being with our family at home. Bernadette had gotten to know Brian's wife, Judy, during those three days that I had been on the road trip with the Blues, and they had really hit it off. I was so elated to get off the plane in K.C. and see Bernadette at the airport. It was maybe three days later than it should have been but we were now together and it was a wonderful time. Unfortunately, it went too quick.

On Christmas Day, Bourby and I and Bernadette had to get in the car and drive to St. Louis so that we could join the team for practice the next day. My folks were scheduled to fly to Kansas City to spend the week there with us, but because of the call-up, they had to re-route their trip to St. Louis. They flew in on December 26, so after practice Bernadette and I picked them up at the airport. We were staying at the Quality Inn on Oakland Avenue, just down from the Arena, and let's just say it wasn't the Ritz-Carlton. It was also a very awkward situation because my parents got a room next door, and they weren't very pleased that Bernadette and I were staying in the same room. She was 18 and I was 20 and being Catholic, Dad said, "You stay with me and Mom will stay with Bernadette."

I'm sorry, but that wasn't happening. I basically said, "Dad, you know what, she came all this way and we're not going to stay apart. We only have a few days and we're responsible adults." There were two beds in the room and we made sure that we messed up both of them. It didn't take a rocket scientist to figure it out, but whether they bought it or not, that was the way it was going to be.

It was great being in St. Louis and having Mom and Dad and Bernadette there, but we would have been more comfortable at our apartment in Kansas City. I still didn't know St. Louis. I'd been here for 10 days during training camp. I knew where the Quality

Inn was, knew where Musial and Biggies was, but that's it. We had a car, but where were we going to go, especially with it being windy and snowy? It was terrible because we ended up just sitting in the shitty hotel with the snow blowing into the rooms under the doors. But at least we were together. I guess being together for the holidays can be somewhat overrated. We had two games that week and I was extremely excited because I was finally getting a chance to play at the Arena. But I barely played in the first game, on December 28, and I didn't even dress two nights later, instead sitting in the stands with my folks and Bernadette. The only good thing about it was that I was making extra money. My two-way contract was in effect and I was making $20,000 in the minors and $55,000 in the NHL, so I probably made an extra $1,500 that I wouldn't have made in the minors. That was a nice little Christmas bonus.

As tough as the week was on Bernadette and me, I think it was tougher on my mom and dad, and we made it even tougher on them. We decided to go back to Kansas City for our New Year's Eve party with all of my teammates at Kemper Arena. So on New Year's Eve, right after practice with the Blues in the morning, Bourby and his girlfriend, Bernadette and I, and Mom and Dad jumped in the car and drove four hours back to Kansas City for the party. We stopped by our apartment to at least show Mom and Dad where and how I was living in K.C., and then we went to the party.

It was a fun evening, but when you look back and put it in perspective, that was a long way to go for just a few hours of pleasure—though I still think it was worth it. We had to get back in the car at 1:00 AM and drive the four hours back to St. Louis because there was a morning skate for a game that night against Minnesota. Bourby and I were thinking we weren't even going to play in that game and luckily we were right. We were healthy scratches, but that sort of worked out fine. Mom and Dad and Bernadette decided that they were going to fly back to Saskatoon the next day because of the uncertainty of my schedule, so I at least got to spend time with them watching the game from the stands.

Later that night, the team chartered to Washington, D.C., because we had an afternoon game the next day, and when we didn't dress for that game either, we knew the writing was on the wall. We flew back to St. Louis from D.C., and Mr. Francis asked Bourby and me to come by his office the next morning before practice. He gave us the news that we were getting sent back to Kansas City. He said, "I just wanted you to get to know the players, get used to the practices, feel like part of the team and what life is like in the NHL because the next time we call you up, it'll be for good."

I think we were both really happy being sent back down to K.C. I think we both realized how much we missed playing. It's one thing to practice, but there's no fun in that if you're not playing real games with real competition. I was in K.C. for the rest of January, but the big news came in early February. Barc called all three of us in—Brian, Bourby, and me—and said, "Guys, this is it, you're going up. This is for real. You're packing up your stuff and you're going for good." To see the pride and thrill on Barc's face was something I will never forget. We were like his children. So we all packed up our cars the next day and drove to St. Louis. We had one practice with the team and then flew to Boston.

Unfortunately, Bobby Orr was gone by then, but the Bruins were a big, strong team and hard to play against. It was officially my fourth game in the NHL—not counting that game in Vancouver—and it was going to be our first NHL game as a line together. Barc had told us about making the best of this opportunity and Mr. Francis had told us the same thing. After the success we had had as a line in K.C., we were not going up to be a fourth line. I had scored 30 goals and 69 points in 42 games in K.C. and I had no intentions of being a fourth liner, so I was looking forward to the opportunity. We were there as an integral part of a team that was fighting for a playoff spot. We were anxious, but couldn't wait for the game to start. If you ever had to sit in a locker room next to a nervous Brian Sutter, you'd understand what I'm talking about. He couldn't stop twitching and moving and punching me in the side of the chest.

I will never forget that night, February 3, 1977, because I fulfilled a lifelong dream by scoring my first goal in the NHL. It was against future Hall of Famer Gerry Cheevers, and after scoring it, I had to give an assist to our goalie, Eddie Johnston. He had been a longtime teammate with Cheevers in Boston, and they were best friends, so Eddie gave me a scouting report on him before the game. Eddie told me that when you're coming down the off wing, which was the right wing in my case because I was a left-hand shot, Gerry will cheat and take a quick step. He said when he takes that step up, just shoot it right along the ice, which I did and sure enough it went in. It was funny coming back to the bench, seeing the smile on Eddie's face, and of course the I-told-you-so. What a great feeling! The guys grabbed the puck out of the back of the net and I sat on the bench knowing that I had the puck to prove that I had scored a goal in the NHL and actually had statistics now, something you could never take away from me. I even added my first ever assist on a goal by Ted Irvine.

Unfortunately, we lost the game 5–4, but that night was the thrill of my life. I called my dad and mom and that conversation was one that I'd only dreamed of. I don't think a postgame beer could ever taste any better than that. I'm quite sure I had more than one.

We flew back to St. Louis the next morning and went straight to practice to get ready for our Saturday matchup against the Buffalo Sabres at the Arena. This felt different after what happened in Boston. I had gone through training camp and practiced in the Arena in December during my call-up, but other than just a few shifts against the New York Islanders on December 28, this was really my first home game as a Blue. I had always heard from former junior teammates who had played at the Arena that the excitement of the crowd in St. Louis was as good as any in the NHL. I was about to find out how exciting it was that night.

Mr. Francis told us that we were going head-to-head against the "French Connection," the famous line of Richard Martin, Gilbert Perreault, and René Robert. That was a little nerve-racking because they may have been the top line in the NHL at the time. But we went head-to-head with them all night, and not only did we battle them hard shift by shift, I ended up having a hat trick and we won 6–5. It was like I had died and gone to heaven. I had many hat tricks in junior and a couple in Kansas City, but to be able to get one at the Arena in front of 15,000 or 16,000 people, I was ecstatic.

I scored the third goal on a backhander with a couple of minutes left, and the hats started flying onto the ice. That was something you watched on TV, but you can't believe when it's actually happening to you. I couldn't even dream that moment. How do you go from being in the minors on Tuesday to scoring a hat trick on Saturday and having four goals in two games?

As unbelievable as it was, though, I felt like it was a longtime coming because I'd hoped to be in St. Louis from the start. Being a first-round pick, I expected to march right in and be a big part of the Blues, beginning with the first game. It took me five more months than I had planned, but that kind of made it more fulfilling because of all the hard work that I put in. I never really thought that I'd have to spend time in the minors, but after I did it, I was thankful that I got a chance to mature and develop. I was 165 pounds at the start of camp and now I was close to 190 pounds. You're skating everyday and you're eating healthy. It's not like you're going back to your landlady's house and not knowing what you're going to get to eat. Now, you're going out for steak dinners with high protein, and the diet itself makes you put on the weight.

This was now the NHL and things were so much better. Instead of hand-me-downs, it was now gloves and pants and, yes, new underwear. I even got to finally order my own stick pattern. I chose to go with a Sherwood featherlite stick and I was so proud to know that I had my very own name on my stick.

Now almost 21 years old, I had to grow up fast. I remember my first trip into Philadelphia to play the Flyers. There had been a fierce rivalry between the Blues and Flyers since the beginning of expansion in the late 1960s. The Blues had not only beaten the Flyers on the scoreboard in the early days, but they had also knocked them silly. But things had changed by the time I got into the NHL, with the Flyers turning into the "Broad Street Bullies" and winning back-to-back Stanley Cups in 1974 and 1975 and coming up just short to Montreal in 1976. It was scary for a young player to hear all the horror stories about the Flyers' tough guys like Dave Schultz, Bob Kelly, Don Saleski, and Moose Dupont. Of course, they had stars, too, like Bobby Clarke, Reggie Leach, and Bill Barber, and then Bernie Parent in goal. The Spectrum in Philadelphia was one of the most intimidating buildings in the NHL and the noise from the raucous crowd sure lived up to its reputation in my first game there.

We had a tough team, including the guy who we all believed was the toughest player in the league, Bob Gassoff. I had been in some crazy brawls in junior with Flin Flon and New Westminster but this was NHL hockey with real men. Midway through the third period, it was Brian Sutter who triggered everything that night. If you can believe this—and if you know Brian you will—he stood in front of the Flyers' bench and challenged the entire team. He had a couple of takers and I believe it was Don Saleski that he fought. Brian had no fear in him at all, so that was fine, but the problem in those days was that when one fight started, everyone else on the ice had to square off with someone else. The good news for me was that I ended up with Bill Barber and there weren't any punches thrown. We ended up losing the game by a couple of goals, but by us not backing down, I think our line gained a lot of respect.

Every day in the NHL was a new building and a new adventure: New York city and Madison Square Garden; Los Angeles and the

Pacific Ocean, where I actually got to see my first ever palm tree; and then the Montreal Forum to play the Canadiens, the team I had grown up idolizing. Hockey is a religion in Montreal and we were in the center of the hockey universe. I couldn't sleep all night and I was in awe walking into the Forum for the morning skate on March 23, 1977, knowing I was actually going to play a game there.

The Blues had beaten Montreal 7–2 in January before we got called up, so everyone was anticipating that the Canadiens would be seeking sweet revenge. It was quite comical because when you looked around our locker room that morning, it seemed like some guys thought we might not even get a shot on goal. The start of the game couldn't come fast enough for me. This was it: the Montreal Forum. I'll never forget skating onto the ice for the pregame warmup, and if that wasn't amazing enough, Mr. Francis put our line on the ice to start the game. There we were, Brian, Bourby, and me, standing on the blue line in front of 18,000 screaming fans ready for the national anthem. We were used to "The Star-Spangled Banner" playing, but in the stress of the moment, we forgot that we weren't in the U.S. and that "O Canada" would be sung, too. Well, Brian, in his usual crazy trance, always skated back toward our goalie to whack him on the pads before the anthem ended, and on cue as the U.S. anthem was ending, he started skating back toward the goalie. So instead of silence before the Canadian anthem, there was laughter throughout the entire building. Luckily, Bourby and I hadn't moved, but Brian, the poor son of a bitch, had to skate back to the blue line and take his helmet off again. Thankfully, it was a Wednesday and not a Saturday, or it would have been on the *Hockey Night in Canada* telecast. That was the only unexpected development of the night, though. The game went as all our guys thought it would—we got our butts kicked 6–1—but playing at the Forum for the first time is something that I'll always cherish.

I finished my first season on a decent run. I scored 14 goals and had nine assists, so I had 23 points in the last 30 games, but I was very inconsistent. Out of the 14 goals, I had three hat tricks and one game with two goals, which meant I scored in only seven of the 30 games. I knew I had to be more reliable moving forward, but at least it gave me a base of what I could do. The only real disappointment was that I played in 31 games, and if you played 30, you were no longer eligible for the Rookie of the Year Award the following year. But at the time, it didn't matter because we finished first in our division and we were headed to the playoffs.

We got a bye in the first round, but unfortunately, the reward for that was playing Montreal in the second round. The Canadiens went 60–8–12 in the regular season and lost only once at home all year. But this was another opportunity to play at the Forum, and because it was the playoffs, all the games would be on television and all of my family and friends could watch back home in Saskatchewan.

But goodness gracious, this may have been one of the greatest teams of all time: Larry Robinson, Bob Gainey, Guy Lapointe, Steve Shutt, Serge Savard, Jacques Laperriere, Guy Lafleur, Yvan Cournoyer, and Jacques Lemaire. No big deal, just nine Hall of Famers. We had to beat them four out of seven, so it was like, "Good luck." Of their eight losses during the regular season, though, one was to us, so it did give us some hope. But in Game

1, it didn't matter how loose or uptight anyone was because we were no match for the Canadiens. Mr. Francis tried to use some new defensive approach against them and that went right down the tubes. We were only going to forecheck one guy and hope to shut them down and try to win 1–0. Unfortunately, they scored early and often; so much for that plan.

Montreal beat us 7–2 and 3–0 at the Forum and the series shifted to St. Louis. I remember my brothers came to town to visit and one day I brought them down to the locker room. I wanted to give them a couple of sticks that had my name on them and were autographed by the team to take back to Saskatoon. But the Blues had strict rules, fining anybody $100 if they gave a stick away. If they weren't broken, you couldn't take it, so we used to tape up the sticks to make them look like they were broken and then take them. The trainers would even help us, saying, "Oh it's broken, go ahead and take it."

But I didn't do that this time, and when I went to hand my brothers the sticks, Mr. Francis walked up and said, "Hold it, where are you going with those sticks?" I told him that I was sending them back to Saskatoon. He told me that it was going to cost me $200, so I hurried up and put them right back. Well, we played a game that night and there was a faceoff in front of our bench and Mr. Francis was bent over laughing. Here I was playing in a Stanley Cup game with a stick autographed by the team. He still says it's one of the funniest things he's ever seen in a hockey game.

That playoff experience was a real eye-opener for me. The level of play was so much higher than the regular season. The Canadiens swept us in four games and we only scored four goals in the entire series. I scored one of them against the great Ken Dryden, so there was some sense of accomplishment. Montreal went on to win the Stanley Cup for the 20th time in franchise history, so it wasn't just us that they beat. Even though they were my favorite team growing up, it's hard to like a franchise like that when you haven't won a Stanley Cup yourself. So from that time on, the kid that had adored the Canadiens from a very young age hated those bastards more than any other team in the NHL.

It was mid-April when we lost out in the playoffs, so I had four months ahead of me to do nothing but reflect on what happened and get ready for next season. I said, "You know what, I should go back to college." I had gone to college for two years, taking a half-load each year, so I had one full year under my belt. I only thought about it for a moment and then I said, "Nah, I don't really want to do that." I needed some time off both mentally and physically. I went back to Kansas City because I still had some stuff in my old apartment, and our minor-league team was in the CHL finals. I was ineligible to play, but I wanted to watch a couple of games. Based on what I had done before being called up to the Blues, I was voted the Rookie of the Year in the Central League, so Bud Poile, the commissioner, presented me with a plaque at one of the games. It was a real honor, even if it was the minor leagues. I had worked so hard, and to get 30 goals and 69 points in just 42 games was quite an accomplishment. I finished in the Top 10 in scoring even though I had played 34 fewer games than everyone else.

While I was in Kansas City, I decided to buy a boat. It was something that I had always wanted, and after looking at one at a dealership, I fell in love and had to have it. I had made some extra money that year because of the playoff bonus, and it was just enough to cover the cost of the boat. I already had my beautiful Grand Prix, and now all was perfect in the world because I had this beautiful metallic-blue boat, too. I loaded it up with all kinds of beer and headed back to Saskatoon. They allowed you to take two cases of beer into Canada, so I guess you could call what I did "smuggling" because I must have packed at least 20 cases into the boat. I pulled the canvas cover over the boat and headed across the border, hoping customs wouldn't open it up to check. If they check, they check, and you just have to pay duty on it, but I was young and foolish. They asked if I had anything they should know about, and I said, "Just my personal belongings for the summer, and some beer." They knew who I was, so they just waved me on through. So off I drove to Saskatchewan with a boat full of beer and whiskey and a great big smile on my face.

It had been an amazing year, full of drama and disappointment, and I was so just so excited to be headed back home to see my family and friends. It was fantastic to move back in with my brothers and spend time at their apartment again. It was great to just feel normal, be in a familiar environment, and just recuperate from the mental grind of the season. It was also nice to be back with Bernadette. As I mentioned earlier, her parents had a cabin at Emma Lake, about two hours north of Saskatoon, and we'd always go up and spend time with them. After a bunch of trips up there, my brothers and I decided that we should buy a lot and build our own cottage on the lake. Luckily we had Bernadette's dad because he knew exactly what to do. He was the best wheeler-and-dealer you could have ever met and he found us a fantastic lot right on the water. We paid $14,000 for it, and everybody thought we were crazy at the time, but in today's dollars, it was a steal. My brothers had just started teaching and didn't have any money set aside, so I cosigned on the loan and we bought it split three-ways.

Our plan was to build the cottage ourselves, but that might not have been one of our brightest ideas. I don't want to say we were terrible carpenters, but let's just say we didn't know what the hell we were doing. As I said earlier, thankfully we had Bernadette's dad. At the very front of the cottage there was a peak that went out over the deck. I mean, it was way out there. Everyone was wondering, *Who's going out on that beam to nail the first set of rafters?* My brothers were shitting their pants because there was no way any of them were going to do it. It was a two-story, and with the slope of the land, it was probably 45–50 feet from the beam to the ground. Well, her dad, all 260 pounds of him, without any hesitation, walked right out there and nailed the rafters.

We learned real quick that we had no idea what we were doing. I was putting on the siding and fell off the scaffolding about 15 feet to the ground. I thought I was dead, but somehow didn't even break a bone. We put more nails in that thing than you could count. We shingled the roof and everything, and I thought it turned out damn nice. We learned a lot building that cottage, and I'm glad we did, because I'm a lot handier today than I probably would have been otherwise. I also learned how to water ski that summer. We grew up only 12 miles from Fishing Lake, but Mom and Dad really weren't into boating, so we rarely spent any time there except for a week every year taking swimming lessons. But now we had our own boat, and being pretty good athletes, we caught on to water skiing pretty quickly. We loved it, and couldn't get enough of it. It was one of those summers that you wished would never end.

I was already back in Saskatoon when we heard that tragedy struck the Blues, losing the great Bobby Gassoff. Garry Unger was having a team party at his farm near Pacific, Missouri, on Memorial Day weekend, and Bobby died in a motorcycle accident. Diane, his wife, was pregnant with Bobby Jr., so it was just devastating. Bobby Sr. and I both played in the Western Hockey League, but I never played against him in the WHL. He played with Medicine Hat and they were one of the meanest teams of all time. This was like the Broad Street Bullies times two and they just annihilated everybody. Three or four years later, when I got drafted by the Blues, the first thing everybody said was "Well, you're going to a tough team." I said, "Great."

Gasser was the toughest guy in the NHL. He wasn't the greatest skater, but it didn't really matter because he was so tough that everybody respected him. No one messed with him, and nobody messed with any of us because of him. He would skate around and no one came near him. It was like Pig Pen in the comic strip "Peanuts," all this dirt around him and no one would get near him. You couldn't replace a guy like Bobby. He looked out for Brian, Bourby, and me because he liked the way we played and knew that we, like him, were the future of the franchise. Gasser was a big piece of the puzzle who was irreplaceable.

The Salomons were also selling the Blues that summer. Sid Salomon Jr. and Sid III deserved a lot of credit for putting together one of the best expansion teams in NHL history. St. Louis had never experienced hockey and the Salomon's built a winner, going to the Stanley Cup Finals each of the first three years. Without that instant success, I don't know if the franchise would've ever gained traction here. They treated the team first-class, too, taking the players and families to their hotel in Florida for a couple of weeks at the end of every season. In talking to Bob Plager and Dan Kelly, you could go down to the restaurant and order a steak or whatever you wanted and everything was on the house.

But, unfortunately for me, the Salomons were on the verge of going bankrupt, so my first experiences weren't very good. I didn't know how an NHL team was run until I got to St. Louis, and from what I saw that first year, I wasn't really impressed. As I mentioned, when I was sent to the minors, we were given the Blues' old underwear and we couldn't get patterned sticks. It was basically being run the same way as a junior hockey team, a far cry from what I was expecting. We didn't know what was going to happen with the ownership situation, but it didn't look good.

Then we caught a break—during a bathroom break—that led to the sale of the Blues to Ralston Purina. As Mr. Francis tells the story, he was at an event with R. Hal Dean, the CEO of Ralston, and they ran into each other in a bathroom. They were standing at the urinal and R. Hal Dean said, "If you ever need any help, give me a call." So Mr. Francis called him and somehow they worked out a deal.

The fact that a big company was buying the team was great news. We all felt like, *Wow, Mr. Francis will be able to start running the operation like it was supposed to be.* He would now have carte blanche to do whatever he needed to do. I'll never forget after the sale, every piece of equipment—the whirlpools, the weights—everything had a Ralston Purina sticker on it. The Arena became known as the Checkerdome. We even got to charter a couple of times on the Ralston jets. From what the older guys said, it was back to the way the Salomons had initially run the Blues.

The timing of the ownership change was perfect because I was poised to have a big role on the team. Mr. Francis was very complimentary of the season I'd had the year before and press-wise I was considered one of the up-and-coming stars of the Blues. Everything was looking up, but then Mr. Francis decided to focus on his GM duties and step down as coach. He brought back Leo Boivin, who had coached the club in 1975–76, the year before I was drafted. Nothing against Leo, but Leo was old school. He had been a defenseman in the NHL for 19 seasons, so with Leo you had to pay your dues. Whatever I had accomplished in the last few months of the season was a moot point. Brian, Bourby, and I came to camp thinking we were going to be on the second line, like Mr. Francis had told us, and instead Leo put us on the fourth line. Leo didn't play us much, and the more we didn't play, the more we pouted. Nothing was going right and then I separated my shoulder early in the season running into Philadelphia's Moose Dupont, so a miserable year got worse.

8

WILL YOU MARRY ME?

I HAD BEEN looking forward to Christmas because Bernadette was coming to St. Louis and I was planning on popping the question. And, because word spreads fast in a locker room, everyone else knew that, too—and that wasn't a good thing. It was my second year in the NHL, but since I was in the minors and not with the Blues much my first year, I never had to deal with any rookie hazing. So over the course of that second year, I expected something to happen, and in hindsight I probably deserved it. I was never a quiet guy and I had a lot of frustration because I wasn't playing much, so I probably said more than I should have said, and since they knew Bernadette was on her way to town, it was time to pay for it.

The young players used to always stay on the ice a little longer after practice than the vets and take extra shots. So when I finally left the ice and entered the locker room, I saw the dreaded skate lace tied in a noose up over the trainer's table. I knew it could only have been for Brian or me, and Brian never said anything, so I'm thinking, *Well, Bernie, let's get it over with. There's no chance to talk or fight your way out of this.* For those people who don't know anything about hazing, it's supposed to be something to make you feel part of the team. Yeah, whatever!

I don't know who came up with this idea, but they stripped you naked and taped your arms and legs to sticks like a crucifix. Then they laid you spread eagle on your back on the training table so that you couldn't move. The noose was tied around your dick and the skate lace was pulled taut, using a little pulley system on the ceiling. They pretended they were doctors, with surgical gloves and surgical masks, and proceeded to shave the hair off your body. And if you moved, well that's what the rope on your dick was for. They'd yank the rope and you'd get quiet real quick. Also, they were very, let's say "careless" shaving you, so that they cut you in a lot of places that you don't want to be cut. Then at the end, to make matters worse, they put hot balm on all the open wounds just so you burn more. Not to mention, you're blindfolded so you didn't know who was doing the damage. You'd have to recognize the sound of someone's voice through their giggling and laughter. You're mad as hell, but you're at their mercy until they cut you loose.

They finally let me go and I was cut pretty badly, but mine was a lot more minor than other guys that I heard about. I'd heard that a lot of times when they were shaving players the razor slipped and, as you can imagine, that can be really bad. I was told by our trainer, Tommy Woodcock, that in the early years some of the guys got a big chunk—well, nevermind, let's just say that I was fortunate—*really* fortunate.

Still I knew it was going to be a long healing process, and the trainers were going to have to check and make sure I didn't get infected. It's all fun for the players, but for the guy who's the recipient, it's not. You're thinking, *Why are they making me go through this pain?* I'm not a proponent of hazing, but there are a lot of guys who are old fashioned and say that it builds camaraderie. It doesn't make any sense to me, but when you look back on it, you think,

Hey, I was one of those guys that got it done and as much as it hurt, it's a story of a lifetime.

Anyway, after cleaning up my wounds as well as possible, I was off to pick up Bernadette from the airport. We hadn't seen each other for three months and this wasn't a nice way to get reacquainted. Let's just say she wasn't impressed. But just seeing her again convinced me that I was making the right decision to get engaged. I had run it by my brothers and they also thought I was making the right decision.

A few days later, Bernadette and I went to a team party at one of the player's houses on Christmas Eve. Of course, the wives, like the guys in the locker room, are always up on the gossip. I was hoping no one would ruin the surprise, but I remember Claude Larose's wife and Eddie Johnston's wife giggling and pointing our way, so I think Bernadette knew something was happening soon. We'd spent the whole summer together, so she probably knew that there was a chance we were going to get engaged. But when she heard the chatter from the girls that night, I think it was pretty obvious.

The next day, Christmas morning, I wrapped up the ring and put it in her stocking, and when we were opening gifts, I had her open them from the biggest one to the smallest one. When she opened the ring, I proposed to her. I don't really remember what her reaction was. I just know she said, "Yes."

I know we were young—I was 21 and she was 19—but I had been away for two years and it was time to move our lives forward. Brian and Judy were already married for two years, so it didn't seem too young. We called her folks and my folks to tell them, and I recall her mom and dad being so overjoyed that they had tears and were crying. My mom and dad were over-the-top excited. They loved Bernadette and they were so happy that I wasn't going to be alone in St. Louis anymore. Finally, one of their sons was getting married. We both checked off the boxes that both families were looking for: pleasant to be around, hard-working, and Ukrainian Catholic. Heck, our parents could carry on a conversation in Ukrainian for crying out loud. It was almost like a match made in heaven.

That was the hockey season that no matter what I did, it was depressing, so getting engaged to Bernadette did pick up my spirits. Every day that I went to the rink, I thought, *This is the day things are going to turn around.* But under Leo Boivin, we were relegated to fourth-line duty and that wasn't changing. We were struggling as a team that managed only seven wins at Christmas. We had a little resurgence at the beginning of January, but it was short-lived. I'll admit that under Leo I showed some immaturity, but I was pissed off that I had to fight for that job again. Leo was trying to put Brian, Bourby, and me on different lines and we were struggling and nothing was working.

We weren't getting the ice time, and if you don't get ice time, you can't prove yourself. It would have been nice to talk to Barc because we were all his boys, but he was still coaching in the minors. Every once in awhile, Jimmy Roberts, one of our defensemen, would say, "Show me something." I would, but it wouldn't matter because I'd have a great shift and then not play for the rest of the period. I only had four goals by February and we were bad. We went 0–10–2 in a 12-game stretch from mid-January to mid-February and something had to give. Finally, on February 16, Mr. Francis fired Leo, and to my greatest joy, he hired Barclay "Barc the Spark" Plager to be the new coach.

Barc was my savior. I was on the verge of disaster until Leo got fired and he came in. The first morning after Barc took over, he sat me down and said, "I want you to play. We're going to do this together. This is not going to happen overnight but we are going to fix this." Barc was like my dad or older brother. Any question I ever had, we always talked about it. Maybe that was because we were together in Kansas City, but I think it had more to do with the fact that he really cared. He also knew my game better than anybody. I remember he used to say that when I skated, I had a "chicken hop." That meant that I had an extra step and I could pull away from everybody. If I wasn't skating well, he would say, "That's the problem, you've got to get that chicken hop back." He knew my game inside and out.

Barc's first game behind the bench was February 18, against Vancouver, and that night we both saw something that wasn't part of my game—fighting. I didn't have to fight a lot, but it happened on occasion. Those were the days when as soon as one started, you had to grab ahold of somebody. That night in a scrum, I unfortunately got paired with Jack McIlhargey, who wasn't a big guy, but he was one of the tougher guys in the league. When he first grabbed me, it was just a matter of hanging on and staring at each other. But then he took it to another level, twisting my sweater so that I couldn't breathe. He was choking me and I felt like I was on the verge of dying. The referee stepped in and grabbed a hold of Jack, and when the ref had his attention, I punched him as hard as

I could. It might not have been the smartest thing to do, but the risk of punching him was better than choking to death. Thankfully he never came after me again.

We only won nine of the 25 games Barc coached to end the season, but it was a much better situation for the younger players. The season was winding down and we were clearly out of the playoffs, but with Mr. Francis in a rebuilding mode, Barc was playing us like we were going to be the future. We were playing hard because we wanted to show them that we belonged in the NHL, but I have to admit, we were also playing to reach the incentive bonuses that most of us had in our contracts. Bonuses were not like what they are today—tens and hundreds of thousands of dollars. I had a clause in my contract for a $1,500 bonus for scoring 40 points and I had 39 going into our last game of the regular season April 8 in Colorado.

We were at the end of a three-game road trip and had a couple of days off before the game, so instead of staying in Denver, Mr. Francis took us to the Broadmoor Resort in Colorado Springs. We certainly didn't deserve to be going to such a nice place with the season that we'd had, but USA Hockey was based there and the plan was to practice at their new facility and then bus into Denver the day of the game. Well, we spent three days there, but only practiced once and the rest of the time we hung out at a bar called the Busy Bee. We had five great veterans—Red Berenson, Claude Larose, Bob Plager, Jimmy Roberts, and Eddie Johnston—who would be retiring after that last game, so it was great to sit and listen to all of their stories. But I remember we talked about who had a chance to earn their bonuses with goals, points, plus-minus, and all that stuff. There wasn't anybody as close to a bonus as I was, so when we arrived in Denver, everyone was aware that I needed just one point. The older guys would have helped all night to get it—that's what was great about them—but thankfully it didn't take long to cash in. On my second shift, I got my 40th point, triggering my bonus.

The regular season ended and it was only the second time in Blues history that the team didn't make the playoffs. It was the first time in my career, going all the way back through junior that I didn't play in the postseason. That was really disappointing, but thankfully we had gotten an opportunity under Barc and that was really encouraging. I finished the year with 17 goals, 13 of which came after Barc became the coach. If we hadn't gotten that chance, I don't know what would have happened the next year. But now we knew that we could play, and with some of the older guys retiring and Mr. Francis shipping out others who he'd brought in from Montreal and New York, there was going to be more opportunity. We went home for the summer and I remember Mr. Francis told us, "Don't ever get used to the rotten feeling of not making the playoffs."

9

BONDING WITH BRIAN

THAT YEAR, BERNADETTE and I really started bonding with Brian and Judy. We rode everywhere together, we went to dinner together, we were as tight as can be. Then when Bernadette came down, same thing, the girls were always together, and the four of us became very close. So since the season ended in April and our wedding was still four months away, we all thought, *Why go back to Saskatchewan in April? It's still freezing.* So we made plans to go to Florida for a couple of weeks. Claude Larose mentioned to us that his brother-in-law was the general manager of a hotel right on Daytona Beach, and Rosy said, "You guys go down and he'll take care of you." The night before we left, we had a few beers with Red Berenson and his wife, Joy, and then we spent the night at the Cheshire Inn by the Checkerdome, so we were super hungover the next morning. I remember I wanted to drive my car and Brian wanted to drive his car, so we flipped a coin. I lost the flip, so we took his car. We took turns driving and made it all the way to Lakeland, Florida. I'll never forget that, because the last hour was hell. It was so foggy the headlights were coming back in your face. We should have gotten hotel rooms hours before, but we made it.

We thought we were rich. We were making $60,000 a year and, back then, it probably was a lot of money, especially for a couple of 21-year-old kids. Florida was fantastic. We spent three days at Disney World and then went to Daytona Beach and had the time of our lives. We checked into the hotel in Daytona Beach that Claude had set up and asked for the manager, but he was busy, so we got our keys and went to our rooms. They had put us on the main floor right next to the laundry room. We looked at each other and the girls said, "We're in these dingy rooms next to the laundry for four nights? We can't do this."

So we went back to the front desk and the attendant asked, "Is something the matter?"

We said, "Yeah, we're not happy. This is not what we expected when Claude booked it. Can you find the manager for us?" The manager overheard the comments and came over to the front desk. He introduced himself and asked how we knew Claude.

"We're on the Blues with him."

"You guys play for the Blues?" he said, seeming pretty surprised. "I'm so sorry." I guess at the time we looked too young to be playing in the NHL and maybe he expected older players. Nonetheless, he apologized, and within minutes we went from the shithouse to the penthouse—the top floor overlooking the Atlantic Ocean!

Keep in mind that you're talking about four kids from Alberta and Saskatchewan, kids who were excited to see palm trees. The girls were taking a bunch of pictures because they'd never seen one before. We were also excited to see the ocean, but we should have been a little more prepared for that. We were used to the sun back home, which was less intense, and these were the days of baby oil, so sunscreen was out of the question. They warned us that this was Florida and you needed to wear some sunblock, but hey, we were kids. So we drove our car onto Daytona Beach at 9:00 the next morning, and after a day of baby oil and beer, we left at 6:00 that evening. Well, needless to say, we got fried so bad that we spent the next three days in miserable pain. We laid on a sheet with the air-conditioning running full blast. But we continued our trip down to Miami, then across to Treasure Island. When Brian and I played tennis there, the sweat got underneath our skin from the burn and we blistered. What a mess!

But through all the pain, the trip was pure bliss, clearly the best time we had ever had, and the four of us became inseparable.

We arrived back in Saskatoon in early May and we were busy right away. Bernadette had tons to do to get ready for the wedding, and I was putting the finishing touches on the cottage that we had started building the previous summer. We spent a lot of time there, water-skiing and fishing and drinking beer. My brother Ron got married that July, so we were back and forth between the lake and Saskatoon.

As they say, time flies when you're having fun, and our big day came quickly. Bernadette and I were married on August 5, 1978, in Saskatoon, and Brian and Judy were part of the wedding party. We had 500 people at the reception and Bernadette swears she didn't see me the whole night. We had a receiving line before the reception and I swear I kissed everybody at the door, even people I didn't know. And you know how it was back then, of course, you had to dance with Aunt Rosie and Aunt Emily and every other aunt in attendance. We did have our first dance—Barry Manilow's "Can't Smile Without You"—but Bernadette was right, we were kind of on our own all night. I guess that's the hazard of a big wedding. Everybody else stayed at the hotel and partied till the wee hours, but we were so tired, we went straight to bed.

The next day, Bernadette's dad had a party at the house in their backyard, and that's where we opened the gifts. Can you imagine how many gifts we had with 500 people? We had to hurry, too, because we left on our honeymoon to Hawaii at 5:00 that afternoon, which in hindsight was stupid. We should have waited until the next day, but were so excited to be going. We went for two weeks in mid-August, and I didn't do shit. It was all R & R with a lot of great food and fancy drinks. I'd played my second season in St. Louis at 193 pounds, and when I stepped on the scale after the honeymoon, I was pushing 210 pounds.

In those days, training camp wasn't like it is today, you didn't come in shape like they do now. In fact, half the guys never even skated in the summer. But I had never hit 200 before, so I knew that 210 was ridiculous and I had to get down in a hurry. I had a lot to do in a short time, so I started running and I was on a strict diet, eating only steak and salad. It was all protein, no carbs, and thankfully my body cooperated. I got my weight down very quickly.

This was going to be the third year of my three-year contract—my contract year—so it had to be a big year. I came back with the attitude that this was my make-or-break year. I had a wife now and I wanted to make sure that I made a good living for her. It was either do it now or look for a new career, so the pressure was on me, but I thought of it like my third year with the Blades when the pressure was on. I came out of nowhere that year in junior, a kid from Foam Lake who wasn't supposed to make the Saskatoon Blades, and I did it. I felt like, *Why can't I do it again?* I set goals in my mind and I knew that I was going to reach them. Plus, Barc had total confidence in us and we would have done anything for him. This was going to be our time.

Because of the miserable season we had the year before, the Blues were picking No. 3 in the 1978 amateur draft. Mr. Francis wanted a right winger who was a perfect fit for Brian and me, so they chose Wayne Babych from the Portland Winterhawks. We immediately became known as the "Kid Line," and right from the start of training camp, everything seemed to click. After two years of playing with Brian, he and I had that connection where we could read each other. I knew where he was going to be and he knew where I was going to be; we had that sixth sense. Brian was hard-nosed, he had a good shot, he could score, and he was crazy, too. Anything would piss Brian off and he would fly off the handle. If something was going on, he wanted to be in the center of it, and he always made sure that no one fucked with me.

Babs was a perfect fit, just what Mr. Francis was hoping for. He was big, tough as nails, and had a big shot. It wasn't a finesse shot, it was overpowering. And me? I was the playmaker. Give me the puck, get open, and I'll find you. I loved being the playmaker. I wanted the puck, and once I was inside the blue line, I found them and then they got the puck. I don't know how to describe it, but with the opportunity to play together regularly, our confidence as a line became overwhelming and we became the go-to line. Right from the first game of the year, we seemed to have that chemistry that allowed us to create scoring chances on almost every shift.

Babs was having a sensational rookie season and ended up scoring 27 goals, and Brian went from scoring nine goals his second year to a whopping 41 goals. I was among the Top 10 scorers all season long, and if there would have been an NHL All-Star Game that year I would have been a shoe-in. But as my luck would have it, the league hosted a Summit Series game against the Russian national team at Madison Square Garden in February that year. So with needing to fill only one NHL All-Star roster instead of two, I got overlooked. But I couldn't be too upset because this was my first taste of success, the breakout year that I needed. Finally, the consistency I had been seeking in my game the previous year, I now had it. I think a lot of it had to with who the coach was.

Barc and I were close, but we had a few confrontations. I remember one time we had a blow-up at practice at Brentwood Ice Rink, a small municipal rink in the St. Louis suburbs. First of all, I never liked practicing at Brentwood because the dressing rooms were horrible. We had to dress at the Checkerdome, grab our skates, and drive 10 minutes to Brentwood. Well, we got there and I was pissed off about something, and Barc was doing a drill where he would blow the whistle and then we'd break between the blue lines. The mood I was in, I just said, "Fuck that!" We were skating around and everybody was breaking blue line to blue line except me.

Barc blew the whistle and yelled at me, "If you're not going to fucking practice with the rest of the guys, get the fuck off the ice." So I did. I jumped off the ice, took off my skates, and drove back to the Checkerdome to shower. As I was getting dressed, I turned around and there was Barc. I thought, *Oh boy, I'm in deep shit.* But he said, "Come on, you and I need to talk. We're going to the bar."

We went to this favorite little spot of his, the Coal Hole in Clayton, and drank beer all afternoon and all night and we had a really good talk. With his famous index finger pointed in my face, he said, "You can't do that to me." I apologized and told him I was just frustrated. He knew I hadn't intentionally disrespected him, but he wanted me to understand that I had, and that I was never going to again. And he was right; I never did that shit to him ever again. I was so lucky to have that relationship with such a great person. We had to prove each day that we were going to be the players who were going to make this organization continue to grow and that's what Barc drilled into our heads. Barc was the best because he kept reassuring guys, "Let's not worry about the score, let's worry about what's going to happen in the future."

We were getting toward the end of the regular season, and we ended up only winning 18 games, so it was a very frustrating season. But it was exciting for me because I was closing in on 100 points, which was the magic number for offensive players like myself. I had 31 goals and 95 points with four games left, and I thought if I could just stay healthy I would surpass the century mark. But on April Fool's Day, of all days, we were on the road in Colorado and I was carrying the puck into the Rockies' offensive zone and I got hit by their big defenseman Barry Beck. As I fell to the ice, he landed right on top of me with my left wrist underneath him, and I knew right away that something was wrong. I tried to play a couple of more shifts, but I couldn't hold my stick.

We were flying back to St. Louis in the morning, so our trainer, Tommy Woodcock, just had me ice my wrist for the night and said we'd get a look at it when we got back home. But when Tommy saw me the next morning, he knew by the swelling that things were not good. I should have never even put my wedding band back on after the game because we ended up having to cut it off. The X-rays confirmed that I had broken the Navicular Scaphoid in my left wrist and I was out for the season. If only I could have avoided that hit. It wasn't meant to be, I guess, but personally, I couldn't complain after having a sensational season.

It was a strange summer going home with my left wrist in a cast and being without a contract. The plan was for the cast to come off at the start of training camp, but there was a chance that if it didn't heal properly, I would have to have surgery on it in the fall. It wasn't going to stop me from playing golf that summer, but I had to play one-handed. I could chip around the greens and putt with two hands, but I just couldn't use both hands on a full swing. Still, I was hitting the driver dead straight almost 200 yards with one arm! It was great because everybody was giving me strokes and I was taking their money. That was nice to make a few extra bucks on the course, but I wanted to get paid for what I was doing on the ice.

I had fired my first agents, Schatia and Sazant, because once I didn't make the team my first year, I never heard from them. So I was looking to hire an agent to negotiate my new contract, and a few of the guys turned me on to Norm Kaplan, so I went with him. Norm and Mr. Francis had had numerous conversations over the course of the summer about my contract, but neither side wanted to give in, so the negotiations continued. Before I knew it, it was time to leave the lake that summer and head back to St. Louis to get my wrist looked at and figure out my contract situation. Thankfully, my visit to our team doctors showed that my wrist had totally healed. They told me that there's only one blood vessel that feeds that little bone I broke in my wrist, and sometimes that doesn't heal, but mine did and the cast came off. What a relief!

Both Brian and I were itching to get back on the ice, but we certainly weren't going to show up for training camp until we got the contracts we wanted. Holding out was starting to look more and more like the reality. I remember in early September, with camp only a week away, we saw Susie Mathieu, the Blues' public relations director, and she was crying, saying, "You guys are going to ruin the whole organization if you don't sign. This is bad for everyone."

I guess that made sense. We were the nucleus of the team now and without us on the ice, ticket sales may have been a problem. But with the year I'd just had, I felt a big raise in salary was certainly warranted.

Brian and I went downstairs to Barc's office and he was all pissed off. He said, "You guys, I want you to think about what you're doing." We told him that we understood what we were doing. We weren't doing it because we wanted to. It was just business. Then Barc said, "Well, Mr. Francis wants to talk to you. Go upstairs to his office."

So we went upstairs to Mr. Francis' office and he called us in individually. I remember he looked straight across at me, staring me right in the eye, and trust me, he had the most intimidating stare of all time. I have never had more respect for anyone ever. We were separated by maybe $10,000 per year, and he asked me, "Why do you think you're worth this?"

I answered immediately, "I know I'm worth it because I know I'm going to be better and I know we're going to be better and I'm going to be a big reason why we're better."

"That's all I wanted to hear," he said. That was it. He told me, "Contract is done." He did the same thing with Brian. He just wanted to hear it from us. He didn't want to give in to Norm Kaplan. But when he talked to us, he believed in what we said and gave in. What a wonderful feeling that was!

Brian and I immediately left Mr. Francis' office and went back down to Barc's office where he was waiting for us. He must have known what was going to happen because he had the biggest grin on his face. "Okay, the contracts are done and you earned them. Now it's time for you and Brian to buy houses." We had always talked about how nice it would be to someday buy a house, but hockey is such a volatile business—heck, I had been on a two-way contract—the most we ever bought were cars and personal things. I guess our recent personal success and the brand- new contracts should have given us some sense of security.

I had just finished in the Top 10 in the league in scoring with 95 points and Brian had scored 41 goals, but we still didn't feel secure enough. But Barc was so sure that we were the future, and he treated us like his own kids, so he wanted to give us the down payment for our house. I hemmed and hawed, but Barc didn't care what we said, he would not take no for an answer. So Brian, Judy, Bernadette, and me went in search of a couple of homes. This was a dream for all of us, but the girls were so delighted. We found a builder and picked a couple of lots in a brand-new subdivision that were two doors down from each other and construction began.

Meanwhile, Mr. Francis was re-constructing the roster. The team got the No. 2 overall pick, which was the highest pick the franchise had ever had, and Mr. Francis drafted Perry Turnbull from the Portland Winterhawks of the Western Hockey League. Then, before the end of training camp, he traded Garry Unger, who had been the face of the team since 1972. Ungie might have been the face of the team, but I think his days were numbered after he hit Mr. Francis in the head with a puck at practice the year before. I'll never forget that day because we were in the middle of a drill and Ungie said, "Watch this guys," and he flipped the puck way up in the air towards where Mr. Francis was standing up by the blue line. To everyone's horror, it hit Mr. Francis in the head. He wasn't trying to hit him, and I know that he thought there was literally zero chance that he could be accurate enough with a flip, but nonetheless, Mr. Francis went down and was bleeding like a bastard. It was amazing though, Mr. Francis was tough as nails and he wasn't going to let this knock him out of practice. He grabbed a towel, stayed right where he was and didn't get stitched up till after practice. He didn't see who had done it and he was never going to ask anyone, but there is no question in my mind that he knew it was Ungie.

The day the Blues traded Ungie, we still had Larry Patey and Mike Zuke, but I knew that I had already proven that I was the No. 1 centerman. Mr. Francis then made deals for Ralph Klassen, Blake Dunlop, and Joe Micheletti. He called me and said, "What do you think about Blair Chapman?" Remember, Chappy had been my winger in junior and started in Pittsburgh, but now he was available. I was all for it, so Chappy became a Blue. Then we got Bryan Maxwell, Rick Lapointe, and we signed Jorgen Pettersson. When you looked at our roster, Chappy was No. 2 overall in 1976, Ralphy was a No. 3 in 1975, Lapointe was a No. 5 in 1975, and

Maxwell was the No. 4 pick in 1975. It was unreal. All these guys were a bunch of first-round draft picks and Mr. Francis knew that he wouldn't have to give up a lot to get them and give them a second chance. You could tell what he was trying to build.

Training camp was in Port Huron that year, and the big buzz was that Mr. Francis and Barc named Brian our captain right out of camp. They called me in and Barc basically told me that just because I wasn't the captain doesn't make any difference. Brian is the captain, but you're there to help, this is your guys' team, which was fine. I thought Brian was a great choice. I was captain of the Blades my last year of junior, Brian was the captain of Lethbridge, and we played against each other all the time, so I knew all about his competitiveness. He came to play every night and never backed down from anyone. He would never say much unless he had something to say, but he would go crazy and drop his gloves. To me, Brian was the captain because of the respect he demanded. So when they named him the captain, I didn't feel slighted. He was my best friend.

Like Barc said, I was part of the nucleus, too, and I was a leader in a different way. I was so used to having the pressure on me all the time and I loved it. It didn't faze me in the least bit. I wasn't expected to be a big scorer in juniors, but I was and I proved it. That's why I was very disappointed when I went No. 7 in the NHL draft. I should have been the No. 1 pick that year. It gave me greater incentive. To me, it was the same pressure that I had in junior. I don't want to call it the "star of the team," but I wanted to be the guy that everybody counted on. I wanted it, I loved it. And when I had something to say in the locker room, I would say it. I didn't need to be the captain to say what I wanted to say. The great thing about Brian and I, as different as we were, we were best friends largely *because* we had totally different personalities. He never got to me and I never got to him. We both wanted to win and that's the way that it was. We did anything we could to help each other.

We started off the year slow, but we were a team that was together all the time. We were all either newly married or young single guys and we all got along. We were each other's families. The camaraderie seemed better than ever. On the ice, we were getting stronger and tougher and we were going from this poor team to a team that could now compete with anybody. The resurgence was starting to begin.

But then we got the devastating news that Barc had a brain tumor. It was obvious to those of us close to him that something was wrong, but we certainly couldn't have guessed the significance. He never complained, but you could see that he was losing weight. He was tired all the time and having headaches. You could see he was woozy; he lost his balance a lot. He was always jolly, but we knew something was wrong with him. It was a malignant brain tumor and they couldn't remove it because of where it was, but they were going to try and treat it. They started with radiation to try to shrink it, and he was a little slow while he was going through that, but like I said, he never complained. He was such an inspiration to everybody because he always put the team first. We were young kids then, but Barc certainly wasn't old, so that put everything in perspective. Why him? It wasn't fair.

Red Berenson had joined us as an assistant coach at the beginning of the year, but with Barc getting sick, Mr. Francis promoted

Red to head coach in December. We really missed not having Barc around, but it was kind of a rallying cry for us. We wanted to make sure that we were winning games for him. It was quite a change going from Barc to Red. Barc was a traditional coach. Red was what we considered "new wave." I was in my fourth year pro and he was bringing in different stuff, like power skating, that we all really didn't want to do.

Red still thought he could play, too. He was always in the greatest shape and could skate for miles. When we'd go through the airport, Red would take the stairs. That was Red. He was always serious and you never knew what he was thinking because he had that intense attitude toward us all. But I think with me, it was a little different. Red was the kind of guy that never, ever wanted to retire from playing hockey, and the fact that I played with Red and then kind of took his job, I think it made our relationship different than the others. He wasn't the type that came to me when he was still playing and said, "Okay, Bernie, you need to do this and that."

Like Derek Sanderson, who said, "Kid, you're taking my job, you need to learn how to take faceoffs," and would spend time with me doing that. Red never gave me any advice. I don't want to use the word "resented," but he was the old pro and I was just a free spirit. He was a very proud man, as he should have been. He had a great career. I was the first-round pick and he wasn't going to let me just come in and take the job. He was going to make me prove myself. His ice time came down a little bit the year I got called up, and the next year it was the changing of the guard. He played less and less and then he retired. To me, I was pushing Red out and I think he had some animosity toward that when he started

That's me in eighth grade…

And again in 10ᵗʰ grade. This one's in 1972.

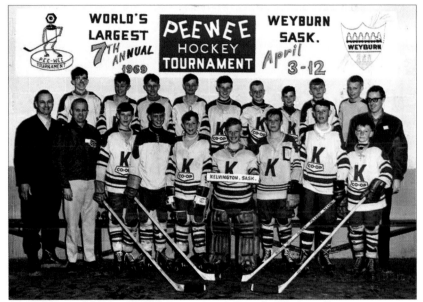

Team picture playing with Kelvington in 1969 at the Weyburn Peewee Tournament. I'm in the front row, left of the goalie, and Barry Melrose— wearing the "C"—is just right of goalie.

We're The Best

1971: Bantam Saskatchewan B Division Provincial Champs. I'm captain, in the middle row.

Sticks, gloves and helmets covered the ice at the Nipawin Arena Saturday night when the final whistle blew to end the Provincial Bantam B. Championship in favour of the Foam Lake Jets, and in their exuberance the Foam Lake boys tossed their equipment aside to cheer and congratulate each other and their coach, Jim Barr.

The hard-fought series start-

ed some four weeks ago with the Jets playing and defeating the Canora, Watrous, Maple Creek and the final played this past week against Nipawin.

The first game of the Nipawin 2-game total point series was at Foam Lake, Thursday, March 11th and saw the visiting club count the first goal at 5:29 and being answered by Foam Lake at 15:18 and 17:05 to

put the Jets ahead up to 18:34 when the Nipawin club tied th the score. The Jets trailed one behind most of the second with Nipawin scoring at 23:50 and the hometown boys not until 35:33 to tie the score for the balance of the period. Nipawin again jumped ahead one at 41:49, tied by the Jets at 43:10, Nipawin at 48:30, Jets at 53:32 and the Jets again in a spectacular goal by Ronnie

Chaykoski with only 44 seconds to go to win the game for the Jets 6 - 5.

Spectacular goal tending by Nipawin kept the visiting team in the game - shots on goal against Nipawin 48 and against Foam Lake 16. Five penalties were handed out to Nipawin and three to the Jets.

(Continued on Page 9)

Blade Blues triumph

Fedorko, Feschuk impress

By John Cherneski
of the Star-Phoenix

Bernie Fedorko has his sights set on a career in medicine.

"Tuesday, however, his instrument was a hockey stick and the operating room the Saskatoon Arena.

It was a clean operation, and the only pain inflicted by Fedorko was on Saskatoon Blade coach Jackie McLeod, and to a lesser degree gold and white-clad half of the Blade squad.

Fedorko was instrumental in leading the Blues to a 6-2 triumph over the Golds in the third annual Blue-Gold intrasquad game at the Arena before 615 fans.

Blades, of the Western Canada Hockey League, are preparing for the exhibition season, which opens Friday when they play host to Regina Pats at the Arena, 8 p.m.

The surprising thing about Fedorko is that he wasn't even supposed to stick with the club this long. The 17-year-old native of Foam Lake has been a real surprise to McLeod, who admits he was going to cut Fedorko three days ago.

"I was going to send the kid home a couple of times, Bernie would look bad on a

couple of shifts, and I'd have my 'mind made up," stated McLeod.

Then he'd come back on the next shift and make an unbelievable play, and I'd find myself reconsidering," added McLeod. It's like a bad headache with a good end result.

Fedorko is a centre, the toughest position to crack on the squad as there are three veteran centres returning, including Bob Bourne, Ralph Klassen and Garth Dietrich.

Fedorko helped set up Danny Arndt for the first two goals of the game early in the second period to get the Blue squad rolling.

On one goal, Fedorko was knocked down and off the puck, bounced back up and recovered to feed Arndt, who was standing alone in front of the net.

"He showed a lot of guts out there tonight," smiled an impressed McLeod.

Also scoring for the Blues were Roy Kemp, John Rooney, Darryl Roach and Dale Turner, while Rob Margoreeth and Ron Valade countered for the Golds.

The club battled through a scoreless first period when goaltenders Brian Hepp (Gold) and Greg Nordman (Blue) stole the show. Blues scored three goals in the second frame to all but wrap up the victory.

While Fedorko was the

up front, the same can be said about Marty Feschuk of the defensive brigade.

Feschuk, #71', 195-pounder from Meota, drew raves from McLeod, and at this point appears to have won himself a berth on the squad.

"Feschuk impressed more than anybody defensively," chirped McLeod. "He played well defensively, and that's something we're going to need this year, a defensive defenceman."

Other newcomers on defence who played well were lanky Bob Hoffmeyer from Prince Albert and Turner, who came to the Blades via Kelowna.

Hepp and Nordman played the first half of the game in goal, then were replaced by 16-year-old Randy Ireland (Blues) and Dean Vause (Gold).

Hepp was especially strong in the first period, stopping 15 shots, a majority of the difficult variety. Nordman, meanwhile, made four great saves from point-blank range to keeep Blues in the game.

Hepp was the victim of Arndt's first goal, while the remaining five were scored against Vause. Both gold goals came against Ireland.

The breakdown of saves was 33 by Nordman, seven by Ireland, 18 by Hepp and 19 by Vause.

Returning goaltender Brian Holdenerz didn't dress but

will draw the starting assignment Friday against Pats.

Ed Konihowski, a 19-year-old goaltender from Moose Jaw, joined the Blade camp Tuesday, giving McLeod six goaltenders to look at. Chris Annesley, an 18-year-old left winger from Moose Jaw, was another addition to the camp.

WHAT'S NEW DEPARTMENT: Blades, who try to run a first-class hockey club, which was just put back up Thursday after supposedly undergoing repairs, wasn't working at all as the game got under way. The clock, which was losing as much as two minutes a period towards the end of last season, was

finally put into operation for the third period. What a great start for a new hockey

SUMMARY
First Period
No scoring.
Penalties — Ashton (Gold) 3:14, McIvor (Blue) 8:25, Leggott (Gold) 11:56.

Second Period
1. Blue, D. Arndt (McIvor, Fedorko) 2:46.
2. Blue, D. Arndt (Fedorko) 10:01.
3. Blue, Kemp (K. Arndt, Belyk) 18:05.
Penalties — Owens (Gold) Colbourne (Blue) 10:20, Klassen (Gold) 17:30.

Third Period
4. Blue, Rooney (Hilkers, Roach) 1:38.
5. Roach (Rooney, Hilkers) 10:33.
6. Gold, Margoreeth (Williams, Fenson) 13:23.
7. Gold, Valade (Price, McKinnon) 16:36.
8. Blue, Turner 17:46.
Penalties — None.

Saves By:
Hepp (Gold)	15	3	x	
Vause (Gold)		x	10	— 29
Nordman (Blue)	3	4	x	
Ireland (Blue)		x	3	7 — 20

Newspaper article from The Saskatoon Star-Phoenix *during my rookie camp in September 1973, where they misspelled my name.*

Bernie Federko receives trophy for highest scorer in Yorkton tourney

Bernie Federko of the Provincial "B" Champion Bantam Jets received the trophy for the Highest Scorer in the Yorkton Bantam Hockey Tournament in the "A" Division. Bernie had seven goals and six assists in two games. Fourteen teams took part in the Tournament held in March. Congratulations, Bernie!

1971: Yorkton Bantam tournament writeup in The Foam Lake Review.

SASKATOON
BLADES
HOCKEY CLUB

1973-74

BERNIE FEDERKO

OFFICIAL PROGRAM

My rookie picture from the Saskatoon Blades program in 1973–74.

A record-breaking night in Saskatoon in 1976.

FEDERKO, BERNIE

CONTRACT BONUSES:

Player to receive additional $12,500.00 when he plays in 80 games in the National Hockey League. Thru 1977/78 Season has played 72 games.

1. Team finish First Place - $3,000   (3rd) $ -0-
   Team finish Second Place - $2,000   -0-
   Team finish Third Place - $1,000   -0-

2. 25 goals or 40 points - $1,000   (17 - 24 = 41)   1,000.00
   30 goals or 50 points - add. $500   -0-

3. If player is amongst top three (3) forwards on club as
   plus player he receives - $1,000   (no plus players)   -0-

4. If player is amongst the top three (3) candidates in
   voting for Calder Trophy - $2,500.   -0-

END OF SEASON TRAVEL:

Coach air fare to - St. Louis - Winnipeg   66.00
                    Winnipeg - Saskatoon   115.56 $ 181.56

A bunch of interesting documents from my life in hockey. This is my 1977–78 end-of-season bonuses and travel expenses.

St. Louis Blues   5700 Oakland Avenue ▪ St. Louis, Missouri 63110 ▪ Mission 4-0900

From the
Office of
EMILE FRANCIS
Executive
Vice-President &
General Manager

July 30, 1976

Mr. Bernie Federko
Box 130
Foam Lake, Saskatchewan, Canada

Dear Bernie:

As per our Agreement signed July 2, 1976 and Addendum signed July 20, 1976, you are entitled to a $25,000.00 Signing Bonus (less taxes in the amount of $4,457.35), which is arrived at as listed below:

$25,000.00   Gross

Taxes Withheld:

$ 2,812.50   Federal Internal Revenue - U.S.
     895.05   Social Security - U.S.
     750.00   State of Missouri Income Tax

$ 4,457.55

$25,000.00
  4,457.55

$20,542.45

Enclosed you will find Check No. 3731 in the net amount of $20,542.45.

I do hope you are enjoying your vacation. Look forward to seeing you soon. Be sure and pass on my regards to your Dad.

Kind regards.

Sincerely,

Emile Francis

Member
National
Hockey
League

EF/mh

enc. Chec, No. 3731 ($20,542.45)

cc: Mr, David Schatia

This is a letter documenting the first installment of my signing bonus from the Blues and Emile Francis, which I used to buy Mom and Dad a car.

CENTRAL HOCKEY LEAGUE

6060 N. Central Expressway, Suite 144/Dallas, Texas 75206/Telephone (214) 692-8585

April 7, 1977

Mr. Bernie Federko
Kansas City Blues Hockey Club
18th & Genessee
Kansas City, Missouri 64102

Dear Bernie:

Congratulations on your being selected Rookie of the Year of the CHL for the 1976-77 season as selected by the six Coaches of the CHL teams.

I personally believe it is an excellent choice and continued success to you in your hockey career.

Kindest personal regards,

CENTRAL HOCKEY LEAGUE

N. R. Poile
President

NRP/jlj

★ DALLAS *"Black Hawks"*
★ FORT WORTH *"Texans"*
★ KANSAS CITY *"Blues"*

★ OKLAHOMA CITY *"Blazers"*
★ SALT LAKE CITY *"Golden Eagles"*
★ TULSA *"Oilers"*

This is a letter from the commissioner of the Central Hockey League, Bud Poile, on my selection as the 1976–77 CHL Rookie of Year.

NATIONAL HOCKEY LEAGUE

960 SUN LIFE BUILDING • MONTREAL, P.Q., H3B 2W2 • (514) 871-9220 • TWX 610-421-3260

PRESIDENT'S OFFICE

January 22, 1980

To: All-Star Players —
     Clarence Campbell Conference

Re: All-Star Game — Detroit, Michigan
     February 5, 1980

Gentlemen:

This is to advise you that you have been selected to represent the Clarence Campbell Conference in the Annual All-Star Game which will take place at the Joe Louis Arena in Detroit on Tuesday, February 5, 1980.

You are reminded that there will be a financial remuneration to the players participating in the All-Star Game on the basis of $1,000 to each player on the winning team and $750 to each player on the losing team. To qualify for payment a player must be dressed.

Your Club has agreed to your participation in the Game and will be responsible for your transportation and other expenses going to and from Detroit and while you are in Detroit.

The Coach of the Team, Al Arbour, has requested that all players report to him at the Detroit Plaza Hotel prior to the Dinner on February 4th. Hotel accommodation has been reserved for you there.

Also, there are two tickets available for purchase by you to the All-Star Game but you are requested to notify the Detroit Club by January 30th whether or not you require these tickets.

....../2

And this is the information letter the NHL sent me about my first NHL All-Star Game, in Detroit in 1980.

Me on the ice in 1979. (AP Photo)

coaching. I thought he was very hard on me and I would never say that Red and I were really close.

Things, though, did start coming together slowly under Red. We got back to .500 with a 4–3 win over Pittsburgh on January 30. I had the game-winner that day with about five minutes to go and it was my 21st goal of the year. Like I said, I never considered myself a goal-scorer. I just felt like I was playing around the net, and for whatever reason, the puck was going in for me. My first couple of years in the league, I was watching everybody, trying to learn different traits. Ungie was a guy who did a lot of great things, including the way he got in position in front of the net. But Ungie played a totally different game than me. He always said he never had any good wingers. Well, he had lots of good wingers, he just didn't use them. No matter who they gave him, it didn't matter, he didn't use them.

I was a passer. I always prided myself in reading the play, knowing what might happen before it happened. Wayne Gretzky was the greatest at that. Wayne was not the fastest, or the biggest, but he's by far the smartest guy that ever played this game because Wayne went to an area. Wayne looked like he was sitting up in the stands and could see where those holes were. I kind of prided myself on the same thing. I never got any credit for being a good skater or a fast skater, but I never lost any races. When I got the puck, I already knew what I was going to do with it. I was going to gain the blue line and then slow the game down. If you're quick enough and smart enough, you can change the game in two strides.

I was probably more dangerous one-on-two than one-on-one because I would force one defenseman to back up. Once I gained the blue line, now I could turn around like "Gretz" and spin, and if Brian was going hard to the net, I'd give it to him. I was just as good and willing to make a pass on my backhand to my left winger as I was on my forehand to my right winger. I told Brian, "I'll find you." I prided myself in reading the play and I wanted the puck. If I didn't get that puck in the first five seconds, I yelled. Someone has to be in control and I was very fortunate that I was given that opportunity to be the guy that was in control. As soon as we went on the power play, it was, "Bernie gets the puck," and everybody knew that.

That wasn't me being overbearing, saying "I want it and if you don't give it to me I'm going to yell at you till I get it." I think everybody that's a No. 1 center on their team thinks that way.

10

ALL-STAR EXPERIENCE

MY ATTITUDE OF "I'm the center and it's my puck," that's how I had to operate in order to be successful. And the results proved it. In 1980, I was selected to my first NHL All-Star Game. It was at Joe Louis Arena in Detroit, and with it being Wayne Gretzky's first All-Star Game and Gordie Howe's 23rd and final All-Star Game, what a memory that was.

They had a banquet the night before and most of the guys were out partying until the wee hours of the morning. To me, this was such an honor, I was scared that if I stayed out too late. I would embarrass myself in the game. So I just took the evening real slow and only had a couple of pops. There was an optional morning skate the day of the game, and you'd think that because it was an All-Star Game, everybody would be there, but with everybody out drinking the night before, only about half the guys showed up. The spotlight was on Gretzky and Gordie Howe, but I was in awe of everyone: Reggie Leach, Larry Robinson, Phil Esposito, Guy Lafleur, Darryl Sittler, Jean Ratelle, and the list just went on and on. Everybody else was a bona fide star and I was just an up-and-coming player trying to make a name for myself.

I was so nervous before the introductions because they wanted you to skate out, stop, and look into the spotlight. It's one of those things that you dream of, but this was live TV, which was a lot more rare back then, and I knew everybody back home, including my folks, would be watching. So it was a thrill, but man, was it nerve-racking. I did have an assist, but we lost the game 6–3 to the Wales Conference. It was something I'll never forget, being on the ice with both Gordie and Wayne, and hey, I had one more point than Gretz and tied Gordie. So that's something.

I went back to the Blues totally invigorated after the All-Star Game. We won our next game after the break, 6–3 over Edmonton, putting us over .500 for the first time all season. I remember not long after that we went out to play in L.A. and stayed in Newport Beach. We were supposed to have three days off to relax and play golf, but they had torrential rain and mudslides, so instead of playing golf like we had planned, we were forced to hang out at the hotel. Perry Turnbull had been our first pick in the draft, so one of the guys decided that it was time for Perry's rookie hazing. Well, if you remember Perry back then, he was built like an Adonis, so it was going to be harder to get him than it was me.

I wanted no part in the festivities. I hadn't liked it happening to me, so there was no way I was getting involved in it happening to someone else—especially Perry. But they still had strength in numbers and got him in a room and down on a bed, and just like me, they used hockey sticks and trainer's tape to hold him down. They bound him down spread eagle and blindfolded him so he wouldn't know who was doing the damage. But as they started the process, one of the guys snipped a little bit of the hair on Perry's head, and he just went berserk. Perry's hair was so important to him that he just lost it. One of our goalies, Ed Staniowski, who was a little guy, tried to jump on his chest, but Perry just fired him off. He actually snapped the tape and chased everybody around the room. At one point, he grabbed the scissors and said he was going to kill somebody. It wasn't that much of a chunk of hair, but he thought it was. Thankfully, he didn't hurt anyone, but I'll never forget, we went back to Edmonton, which was close to his hometown, and he spent a bunch of money on a new cowboy hat so nobody could see his hair. That was Perry.

It wasn't the only naked body we saw that year.

One of the craziest things I ever saw happened on March 12, 1980, at Maple Leafs Gardens. We were beating Toronto 3–1 with about six minutes left and there was a faceoff in the corner to the right of the goaltender. I was taking the draw and all of a sudden I looked to the left and there was a guy—stark naked except for a pair of gray woolen socks—climbing over the glass. For a moment, he got hung up by his nuts, but amazingly, he dropped onto the ice and ran right through the faceoff circle. Everybody looked at each other and just busted out laughing. The crowd was going crazy, too, and no one knew what to do.

Finally, the linesmen chased him down and tackled him, and then two cops came on and took him off. I guess streaking was popular in those days, but the guy had a lot of balls—no pun intended—to do that in front of a packed house at Maple Leaf Gardens. We won the game 3–2 and Howard Ballard, who was the owner of the Leafs at that time, actually said afterward that it was the single-most exciting moment of their season—that's how bad they were. Ballard even ended up bailing the guy out of jail.

The only thing that ever compared to that in my career happened the year before, on February 21, 1979, at Madison Square Garden. We had a guy on our team named Steve Durbano, one of the biggest characters you ever met. The thing with Durby, he was a pretty good hockey player if you could keep him focused on hockey, but unfortunately that was easier said than done. He became distracted often, and when he snapped, you never knew what was going to happen. Well, one night we were playing New York at the Garden, and Durby went after the Rangers' Nick Fotiu. That caused a bench-clearing brawl, and by the end, it was pretty obvious that Durby was going to get a game misconduct. So he got ejected and left the ice through the Zamboni entrance, and as he was leaving, he pulled down his hockey pants and mooned the crowd. What a moment! I don't remember ever laughing that hard at a game.

We wound up finishing the 1979–80 regular season with 34 wins, which was 16 more than the year before. For me, it was another pretty consistent year, with 94 points, one short of the year before, so that elusive 100-point total escaped me again. But more importantly, we made the playoffs and what a feeling that was to be back in the postseason. Unfortunately, though, our first-round series against the Chicago Blackhawks was short-lived. We lost Game 1 in Chicago 3–2 in OT and then we couldn't muster any offense after that and got swept in three straight games. None of us had any real playoff experience, so even though we got swept, I think everybody said, "We took a big step forward this year and the direction is there." We could see glimpses, and most importantly, Mr. Francis was still really confident that we were on the right track.

That summer back in Saskatchewan was much more relaxing and enjoyable with no cast on my wrist, a new contract, two consistent offensive years, and a trip to the playoffs. We had moved into our new house in St. Louis right after the playoffs had ended, so we had a home base. Bernadette and I had been married for a couple of years, and with things going so well now with the hockey, we decided it was time to start having a family. We could not have been more proud when, in early August, we could tell our folks that Bernadette was pregnant. It was going to be the first grandchild for my folks, so they were especially excited. Once again, we had a great time at the lake that offseason, but I was looking forward to driving back to St. Louis for training camp the next year because my little brother, Kenny, was coming with me.

Kenny had played three seasons with the Blades immediately after I left Saskatoon. He was a really good player and some people said that he was every bit as good as me, just a little smaller. He'd put up great numbers, but in his last season, 1978–79, he seriously injured his shoulder and needed surgery. He was running first and second with Brian Propp in the Western Hockey League scoring race, so I was excited about the prospect of him playing in the NHL, but because of the injury, he missed the last half of the season and got overlooked in the draft. Even though Kenny wasn't picked, Mr. Francis and the Blues' scouts felt he was a good prospect and they signed him to a pro contract as a free agent.

He came to the Blues' training camp in Port Huron in the fall of 1979, but only lasted a few days and was assigned to the Port Huron Flags of the International Hockey League. He had 97 points in his first season with Port Huron, so the Blues extended his contract for two more years.

So now it was 1980–81, Kenny was headed to camp with me, and I wanted so badly for him to follow in my footsteps. But the talent that Mr. Francis had assembled for that season was so strong that Kenny was almost immediately penciled in to play with the Central Hockey League affiliate in Salt Lake City. It was a step up for him from the IHL, and once again he proved he could play, putting up nearly a point per game in the minors. But unfortunately for both of us, he never got called up.

It was great that Mr. Francis had signed him, but I always said, "Would it have been better if he would've went to another organization?" Maybe the Blues thought I would've been more worried about his well-being and that might affect my play. Whether that was true, I don't know, but that was probably the biggest disappointment I ever had, him not playing in the NHL with me. After those two years in Salt Lake, Kenny chose to continue his hockey career in Europe, where he spent the next five or six years. I had heard all the stories from the three Plager brothers about playing together in the NHL and I always wished that could've been us.

This year was Red's first full year as head coach and the good news was that Barc had a handle on his health issues and was back as our assistant coach. It was non-stop work with Red as the head coach. We worked out twice a day during training camp, with drills and conditioning in the morning and scrimmages in the afternoon. By the end of every day, you were so tired that you had a few beers, a bite to eat, and then it was time for bed.

Halfway through camp, you finally got over the hill and then there was always some time for fun. Weather permitting, Mr. Francis always arranged for a golf tournament with a bunch of beer and a dinner at a golf club. Well, it was a perfect day in Port Huron, and on the 18th hole, our fearless leader Brian Sutter had a brilliant idea. Tony Currie, who was by far the best golfer on the team, was playing right behind us. After we finished putting out, Brian decided that he was going to take a shit in the hole so that Tony's group could get a real treat when they were finishing up. But Brian wasn't able to squeeze anything out, so he asked the rest of our group to help, and in maybe one of the most amazing things I ever saw, Rick Lapointe pulled down his pants and, without any effort, filled the cup. You can imagine the laughter when Tony actually chipped his ball into the hole from long range.

Our team had a lot of sickos, but we liked to have fun, and the fun never stopped. After dinner, the bus arrived to take us back to the hotel, which was a good 15 minutes away. Everybody loaded onto the bus except for two of us, who were making a quick pit stop. The bus driver left the guys on the bus with it running to go get us, and when we walked back with him, the bus was gone. He was freaking out. Perry Turnbull evidently decided it was his calling to drive the bus, grinding the gears down the highway all the way back to the hotel. Thankfully, Perry got them back to the hotel safely, because when the three of us finally got there, the bus was parked nicely and still running. Mr. Francis was not happy when he found out about it the next day, but surprisingly, Red got a big charge out of it. The next day, Red asked Perry if he wanted to drive to our preseason game in Kalamazoo.

The regular season got underway and for the first time in NHL history there was going to be a totally balanced schedule. There were 21 teams and we still played an 80-game schedule, but you played each team four times—two at home and two on the road. There were no conferences, no divisions, and at the end of the year there would be 16 playoff teams, with No. 1 playing No. 16, No. 2 playing No. 15, and so on. We were really confident because we had a lot of talent and we could score. We knew offense wasn't going to be a problem, and we were right because we ended up having 10 guys score 20 goals or more that year. And with Mike Liut in goal, we knew that we could compete with anyone. We were wide open like the Oilers of the later years, and we'd count on Lutey to make a big save when we needed it, like Grant Fuhr did with the Oilers. We'd score seven or eight goals in a game and give up 25 scoring chances and Lutey would be the difference-maker.

There's no question in my mind, Lutey was one of the best goalies of our time. He was 6'2" and 190 pounds and one of the first big stand-up goalies. He was like Ken Dryden without the defense that Ken Dryden had in front of him. Lutey was also very well-educated, so we called him our clubhouse lawyer. He was one of the few guys on our team with a college degree and made sure we never forgot it. He was very focused but also very set in his ways, and we loved getting under his skin. I used to sing Jimmy Buffett songs and play the Bertie Higgins song "Key Largo" in the middle of winter to get in his head because he hated that stuff. When you know someone hates it, that's when you do it more, and that's the way we were. Lutey, though, was the most focused guy in practice and he did not let you score. So when we knew he was having a bad day and we scored, we let the whole world know. If you scored two or three goals in a row on him, he'd lose it and break his stick. When Lutey freaked out, he would go crazy, and we loved it. He was so competitive and that's why he was so good.

We used to play for beers during the warmup drills, shooting on Lutey and Eddie Staniowski in practice. In fact, I had whiskey bottle bets with Wayne Babych all the time. Babs scored 54 goals that year, but he was not a finesse shooter; he was overpowering, and you weren't going to overpower Lutey because he was way too smart. He knew where Babs was going to shoot, but he never knew where I was going to shoot because I really had no tendencies, like high-glove or five-hole. So I always did really good against Babs and I bet in all the years we played together he bought me at least 100 bottles. I made sure he paid his dues. He would actually supply my bar for Christmas parties all the time. Our whole team was competitive as hell. If you watch the practices today, they do all these crazy combat drills, but they end peacefully. If we had a practice where we did those combat drills, we would've never got through it without a major brawl. There would've been a dozen fights and practice would have never ended.

We got off to a fabulous start that year, winning 26 of our first 40 games, and were running neck-and-neck with the New York Islanders for the best record in the NHL. Needless to say, things were going great and Mr. Francis was excited as hell. There was not one player having a bad year. Babs was playing with Blake Dunlop and Jorgen Pettersson, and I was playing with Brian and Chappy. We were one of the best teams in the league, and we were getting recognized for it. The year before, it was the thrill of a lifetime when I went to the NHL All-Star Game in Detroit, and I truly believed I was a star in this league, but now I wasn't alone. That year, Babs and Lutey went with me, and when you get three players to the All-Star game from the same team, you're now a bona fide team.

The All-Star Game was on February 10 at the Forum and the fact that it was in L.A. was pretty spectacular. Bernadette was eight months pregnant with Jordy and she really wasn't supposed to be flying that close to her due date, but she went anyway to support me. We were in this together, and even though she didn't feel well, it wouldn't have been the same if she hadn't come. So I'm sure for her it was quite stressful, but for me, it was a wonderful feeling going to my second All-Star Game.

I was still only 24 years old, but instead of being in awe like last time, I felt like I belonged, so it was so different this time. Pat Quinn was the coach of our team and he said in the locker room in front of everybody, "Bernie, you're in charge of the pregame warmup. I don't know what you guys do in St. Louis for warmup, but you're in charge." In the past I might have gotten nervous, but I was much more relaxed this time and I think that showed in the game, too. Babs and I played on a line with Eddie Johnstone from the New York Rangers and Babs scored a goal and I had an assist. But the cool part was we that went head-to-head against L.A.'s "Triple Crown" line of Marcel Dionne, Charlie Simmer, and Dave Taylor and kept them off the board. We won 4–1 and Lutey made 42 saves and was the MVP, so he won the car from the All-Star Game.

That wasn't the only car Lutey ever won, which, in a funny way, is kind of a sore spot for me. There was a hockey booster club in St. Louis called "The Goaltenders Club" and they would always pick an MVP award for the Blues every year. I won it in 1979 and 1980, but when I won, I got a trophy and a handshake. Well, Lutey won it in 1981, and got a Rolex, and again in 1982, and got a white Corvette with Blues coloring. Nice luck, eh? I guess those two years Lutey won, they must have had a sponsor. It's all about timing.

Speaking of timing, about a week after the All-Star Game, we beat the New York Rangers 5–4 to take over first place in the NHL. *The Hockey News* did a story on us and I was privileged to be featured on the cover with the headline "Bernie Federko Silent Superstar for Surging St. Louis." You can imagine how excited my family was for me to make headlines in *The Hockey News*. We really were surging. We lost just once in an 18-game stretch and the timing couldn't have been better because the playoffs were right around the corner.

But if you remember, Bernadette was pregnant and about to deliver our first child. The team was leaving for Quebec on the morning of March 10 and I called Mr. Francis to tell him that I wasn't going because Bernadette was in labor. Mr. Francis was totally understanding, but Red was not.

Red was pissed. He said, "You know what, that's the way it is, you need to get on the plane." But I wouldn't budge. I told Red, "I'm not going," and I didn't get on the plane. I'm glad I didn't because we went to the hospital at about 11:00 PM and after 10 hours of labor, Bernadette gave birth to our first son, Jordy, on the morning of March 11. I obviously missed the game in Quebec that night and Red was all pissed off, but I wasn't going to leave my wife in labor. This was a new era that we were in and I was not going to miss the birth of my child. To be in the delivery room and experience that moment, I had tears of joy and even the doctor was crying. It was one of the most fulfilling experiences of my life. I didn't care about getting fined or suspended. Life is more important than any one hockey game.

In my absence, the Blues tied Quebec 5–5 that night. It was hard leaving Bernadette and Jordy, but I flew out early the next morning to meet up with the team for the game in Montreal. Looking back, I don't even know why I went because with Red's coaching strategy against Montreal, I knew I wouldn't play much. The Canadiens always played their scoring lines a lot and Red always played his checkers against them. So the Canadiens kept sending their scoring lines on, and our line sat on the bench and watched our checkers play. When we did get on the ice, we were playing against the top checking line in hockey with Bob Gainey and Doug Jarvis. Anyway, we lost 4–3 that night, and to be honest, I was thinking more about bringing Bernadette and our newborn son home when I got back in St. Louis the next morning.

We won four of our last 11 games of the regular season (with two ties), but one of the losses was an important head-to-head meeting March 24 against the New York Islanders. If we would have won that game, we would've had a four-point lead on the Islanders in the NHL standings (104–100), but despite holding a couple of leads, we lost 5–3. I think we were a little tired. When you've been playing at a high level for such a long time like we had, you get a little wary down the stretch and I think that's what happened. Red said we were a little full of ourselves, too, and I think he was probably right. All of a sudden, we had become one of the best teams in the league and no one really experienced this before, so it was a learning process. The Islanders finished with 110 points and we were second with 107 points, which was the most in franchise history at that point. Even though the Islanders beat us late in the regular season, some of them said that if they were going to lose to anybody that year, it was going to be us.

11

PLAYOFF DISAPPOINTMENT

OF COURSE, THE pressure of being a good team going into the playoffs was also going to be new to us. I only had seven postseason games in my career, and a lot of the guys had no experience at all. As I mentioned, the NHL that year seeded the teams from No. 1 to 16, based on the regular season standings, and since we were No. 2, we got No. 15 Pittsburgh in the first round. They gave us a scare, taking the best-of-five series to double overtime in Game 5 before Mike Crombeen scored one of the biggest goals in Blues history.

"Crommer" hadn't played hardly at all in that game, and Mike Zuke either, but Red shuffled them out in the second overtime, Zuky got the puck from behind the net, threw it in front, and Crommer scored. That moment was both elation and relief, thrilled that we won and thanking God that we survived, because just the thought of being upset by the No. 15 seed would have been devastating. But even though we won, we had just played five games in seven nights and needed double OT in Game 5, so that series took a lot out of us both physically and emotionally.

Fortunately, we still had home-ice advantage in the second round against the New York Rangers and we didn't have to travel for Game 1. But for some strange reason, after having one of the best home records in the league during the regular season, Red wanted to put us up in a hotel in St. Louis, an idea I was totally against. I can understand doing that in the Stanley Cup Final, when it's pandemonium everywhere you go, but this was St. Louis. Hockey was popular, but people weren't going crazy that we were in the second round. I bitched at Barc, saying, "Why are we changing what we're doing when we were so successful all year long?" I was pissed off. However, in the end, maybe because of my conversation with Barc, they didn't follow through, and we got to sleep at home.

There was no question in my mind that we were way better than the New York Rangers. We played them four times in the regular season and won all four of them, including two at the Garden, which was always a hard place to play. The Rangers had won their first-round series against L.A. three games to one by being physical. We beat them 6–3 in Game 1 of the best-of-seven series, but after that, they got really physical.

Unfortunately for us, Perry had been injured late in the year and his size and toughness was really missed. We still had a lot of grit on the team and plenty of guys who never backed down to anyone, like Bryan Maxwell, but they had a couple of guys named Ed Hospodar and Barry Beck. I think I got hit more times in that series than I've ever been hit, and I think Hospodar and Brian fought every game, or at least it seemed that way. Beck was a big factor, too. The Rangers did a good job of checking in Game 2 and won 6–4, so now we were going to New York for the next two games and our home-ice advantage was gone. We wound up losing both games, falling behind three games to one in the series. This was playoff hockey and we had lost the scoring touch that we had in the regular season. If you look at that series, Babs, Dunner, and Pettersson, a line that scored over 100 goals during the regular season, unfortuately hit a dry spell. You can't win without a balanced attack and that's what happened.

We came back to St. Louis for Game 5 and pulled out a 4–3 win to send it back to New York for Game 6. We were down early in that game, I scored a couple of quick goals to get us back in it, and we had a chance to tie. But then—how I can remember this to this day I don't know—Rick Lapointe and I had a two-on-one and I did the dumbest thing: I tried to pass him the puck. Everybody knew I was going to pass and after I did, I looked up and I had so much room to shoot. Doug Soetaert was the Rangers goalie and he was already across the crease on Lapointe, so he didn't score. That play still haunts me, and we ended up losing 7–4.

No excuses, but we had played a lot of hockey. After five games in seven nights against Pittsburgh, we played six games in nine nights against the Rangers, and I think we just ran out of gas. The playoffs are a totally different animal, and our inexperience hurt us. We had a lot of guys that did not have a good series against the Rangers and sadly, it cost us. It was devastating for all of us because we all believed that we were a really good team.

Brian and I were pissed. A couple of timely goals would have made a huge difference. And if Perry wasn't hurt, he would have fought anybody. I think he would have got Maxy going because as tough as Maxy was, he didn't fight anybody in the series. It's easy for me to say, but someone should have gone after Beck, but no one did. If we'd had Bob Gassoff, there's no question in my mind that he would have been the difference-maker and we could have won it all. That was, in my opinion, the Blues' second- or third-best team of all-time.

I think if the Blues could have kept Brett Hull and Adam Oates and Scott Stevens together, they could have won it, but like too many other Blues teams, that roster was blown up. Then there was Hull, Al MacInnis, and Chris Pronger, and there's no question those were great teams. But that 1980–81 team was the best team that I was on by far. That was the year, if we were going to win a Stanley Cup, that was it. I look back now and I wish we could have had another crack at that year.

We kind of realized it then, but now you look back and you really realize every team that won a Stanley Cup always got knocked off when they shouldn't have and got stronger the next year. Look at the Islanders. They had the best team in the league and got beat by the Rangers in 1979, then came right back and won four Stanley Cups in a row. You always have to take a step backward before you take a step forward. We had gone from barely making the playoffs in 1980 to now being the second-best team in the league in 1980–81. As disappointed as we were, we all felt, *Hey, this year is going to change things, and when we get back next year, we're going to be a team that can win in the playoffs, a team that could win it all.* We had so many good pieces to the puzzle and we were all excited about coming back.

Unfortunately, the problem was that so many guys had career years and they wanted more money. I guess you couldn't blame them. Joe Micheletti had a contract dispute and ended up getting traded to Colorado early the next season. But the move that affected us the most was a trade that sent Bryan Maxwell, Ed Staniowski, and Paul MacLean to Winnipeg for defenseman Scott Campbell. The Blues had drafted Campbell No. 9 overall in 1977, but he was also taken No. 1 overall by Houston in the World Hockey Association draft. He decided to sign with Houston, but a year later that organization folded and Campbell signed with the Winnipeg Jets of the WHA. Then when the NHL and WHA merged, the Blues made the deal with Winnipeg and we finally got him. Talking to Mr. Francis, Campbell was the franchise defenseman that every team needed, so we were real excited about that. He came to camp and looked great because he was big and strong and moved the puck well, but you could tell when you talked to him that something was wrong. It turned out he was dealing with post-concussion syndrome, and after only three regular season games, he just abruptly left the team one day and never played again. To lose a guy who was going to be the defensive nucleus of our club just killed us.

We had scored so many goals in 1980–81, we figured we'd be okay offensively, plus there was a prospect on our minor-league team in Salt Lake City named Joey Mullen that would provide even more offense. He had played at Boston College and went undrafted, probably because he was only 5'9" and 180 pounds. The Blues had signed him in 1979, and he had spent two and a half years in the minors. Blair Chapman, who had been my regular right winger, hurt his back in training camp and needed surgery, so we needed somebody in that spot who could score, and Joey could score. He had 120 goals in 182 games with Salt Lake City, and finally got a look with the Blues.

Joey was from New York and his dad drove the Zamboni at Madison Square Garden. That made Joey's call-up really special, because his first game was against the Rangers at MSG. We lost the game 8–5, but for him and his family and friends, that was a moot point. He had finally made it to the NHL, and what an accomplishment for a kid from Hell's Kitchen. That was reason to celebrate and there was no better place than the bar across the street from MSG. It was quite the party and we couldn't keep up, so by the end of the night, we left Joey with them. What time did he leave? Well, the next morning, we actually had to pick him up with the team bus at the bar. Joey still had his suit and tie on, and all of his buddies had autographed his white shirt, and he was just hammered. We were all laughing our asses off and Mr. Francis just had a little grin. He was so proud of Joey.

On the ice, it was obvious we weren't building on the previous year's success. The team was losing and I was slumping, and when things weren't going well for me, I would show it. One day we were practicing at Affton Ice Rink and I had a chance for an empty-net goal and missed the damn net. I was so pissed that I threw my stick over the glass and into the stands. Red immediately stopped practice to make a spectacle of me and told me to go get my stick. I couldn't believe it, but if I had to listen to him, I was going to do it my way. I could have skated to the Zamboni door and then walked up into the stands, but just to spite him, I crawled over the glass and dragged my skates on the concrete so that when I came back my skates would be too dull to stand up on the ice. It worked. I got my stick and came back, couldn't stand up, so I had to leave. I wasted about 15 minutes going back to get them sharpened and was happy that practice was almost over.

A lot of people labeled me a "whiner," but I would consider it more chirping than whining. To me when they made Brian captain, I felt that I was just as much the captain as he was, and for us to take over the leadership I had to alleviate some of the frustration and stress that was in the locker room. Because of who I was and my stature on the team, I could get away with saying things that no one else could. I knew that even if Brian wanted to say something, he wasn't going to. So if the practices were too long, or if we weren't getting the day off, someone had to say something and I just felt that it had to be me. I'm sure that there were lots of guys that would have loved to have said it, but weren't in a position to do so. I could say it, and even when Red didn't like it, I would say it.

It was never meant to be disrespectful unless I felt I was disrespected. If I didn't like something, I said it.

I was probably too chirpy at the beginning and that's why they shaved me. Looking back, I probably deserved it. But I didn't change the way I played, and I didn't change the way I acted. I was the same person as a teammate, no matter how successful I was, and I tried to help the guys around me. If the coach got pissed off, too bad. Sometimes I'd say something and then the coach would work us twice as hard. He'd take the pucks off the ice for practice and we'd just skate. Guys on the team would say, "We had to do that because of you." Are you kidding me? The coach was going to do that anyway. You know what? When he did that, I was the one that went as hard as anybody. The coach could have skated us all day and I wouldn't have cared. I'd just get a song in my head and keep skating back and forth. If you want to call it whining, that's fine, but I'll tell you what, there were a lot of times where the coaching staff gave the guys a day off because I said something.

It wasn't working with Red. After finishing second in the standings and Red being named coach of the year, we lost 8–1 in Minnesota in early March and it was his last game behind the bench. I remember Red had come out and named a bunch of players that were available for trade and that pissed off Mr. Francis. Mr. Francis, who already had one stint as the Blues coach in 1976, fired him and took over himself.

I don't want to put the whole blame on Red. We had guys that had had career years the year before that weren't having the same seasons. As a team, we scored 37 goals less and gave up 68 more goals than we did in the prior year. Babs went from scoring 54 goals to blowing out his shoulder in a fight in camp and he finished with 19 goals in 51 games. I had 104 points the year before and ended up with 92. But after Red became head coach and had some success, he was trying to do more than coach—he wanted to run the hockey club. Red was tinkering all the time and Mr. Francis got tired of Red getting too involved. He was very innovative, but he was asking us to do things that were kind of crazy. We would have off-ice sessions where we didn't skate and just worked out with weights. Teams are doing that now, but it was so different back then. We were getting away from just playing hockey. I think it was the best thing for Red because after he left us he became the head coach at the University of Michigan. There, he was teaching kids and he had a lot of information and experience that he could pass on, and because they were kids, he could intimidate them when he needed to. That's hard to do with pros. It was no surprise to me that Red was a successful coach and recruiter at Michigan. It was perfect for him.

Mr. Francis took over just before the trade deadline. He held a meeting after the firing where he announced he was taking over the coaching reigns and said, "You guys aren't in shape." He actually flew us to Springfield, Illinois, to a rink there, and we practiced twice a day for three days. We even came back to St. Louis for a goaltender's banquet one afternoon and then went back to Springfield to practice. I remember he had traded for Montreal defenseman Guy Lapointe, the future Hall of Famer, and Vancouver goalie Glen Hanlon. The Great Guy Lapointe was watching all of this craziness in disbelief. Glen Hanlon hadn't drank in two years and he started drinking again that night. I'm dead serious.

Mr. Francis really thought we were too soft a team, and that's when he came up with this idea of a bonus system, paying the team for reaching certain numbers and putting all the money into a pot that we could spend on the team party at the end of the year. Denis Ball, who was the assistant GM, made up a sheet and charted all kinds of different stats. We got $500 for shutouts, $400 for one goal, $300 for two goals, and $5 a hit. Denis, he was the nicest man in the world, so according to him we were getting like 60 hits a night—at least that's what he wrote down. We did make the playoffs and beat the Winnipeg Jets in the first round, but we got knocked out by Chicago in the second round. By the end of the postseason, we had $10,000 in the pot and Mr. Francis gave us the cash for our party at the Lake of the Ozarks. We rented condos for everybody, played golf and tennis, and even bought blenders to make cocktails—anything we wanted. We had the time of our lives, but in the big picture, we still couldn't get out of the second round.

That summer, it was contract time for me again. It had been a great three years for me since signing my last contract. The word that Barc used when he coached us in Kansas City was that he wanted us to be consistent and I was finally a consistent player. He said no one was ever going to have a perfect year; you were going to have bad days, but if you kept those to 10 percent of the 80-game schedule, you should only have eight bad nights or so. If they came all at once, well, you better be good the rest of the time. I never forgot that and I made sure that if I did slump it was for a very short term. Unlike the prior contract, this one went very smoothly with Mr. Francis. I had put together four great offensive seasons, leading the team in scoring every year and finishing among the Top 10 NHL scoring leaders three times. Mr. Francis rewarded me with a new four-year deal that paid equal to all the other top scorers in the league, which was such a feeling of accomplishment. Also that summer, Mr. Francis made a big trade, acquiring defenseman Rob Ramage, who had been the No. 1 overall pick in 1979, in exchange for a first-round pick. After losing who we thought would be our star defenseman, Scott Campbell, due to post-concussion syndrome, we finally had a bona fide defenseman.

Rammer helped a lot, but we were still mediocre at the beginning of the 1982–83 season, and by mid-December, rumors of Ralston Purina selling the team and moving to Saskatoon started to circulate. Mr. Francis had his hands full dealing with all the speculation, so he handed the coaching reins back to Barc. Barc was doing a good job, but all everyone talked was, 'Where are we going?' My understanding of what happened was that R. Hal Dean, the CEO at Ralston Purina, was turning 65 years old and that was the company's mandatory retirement age. They were looking for someone to replace him and the board was adamant that the company was going to get rid of the hockey team. That's when a guy named Bill Hunter came into play and offered to buy the team and move it to Saskatoon. Ralston officially put the Blues up for sale on January 24, saying that they had lost $8 million in the last five years. Hunter offered $11.5 million and Saskatoon became the front-runner, and Hunter had plans to move the team into a new 18,000-seat, $45-million arena.

If that wasn't enough to be dealing with, Eddie Kea, who was 35 years old and in his fourth season with the Blues, fractured his skull during a game. Eddie, who had been playing with us, got sent down to Salt Lake City for a conditioning assignment. He was playing the last game of his conditioning assignment in the minors and was checked into the glass. Like a lot of the old pros, Eddie wasn't wearing a helmet and he hit his head on the glass and then on the ledge of the boards. I'll tell you what, it was a sad day when that happened and Eddie never really recovered from that. What blows me away is the NHL didn't want to pay any insurance money because he was in the minors and not under the league's insurance, but that was bullshit because he was on a conditioning assignment. Mr. Francis fought that hard and the league finally did give Eddie some money. I always said that Mr. Francis was one of the most honorable men of all time and he proved me right again.

So it was no wonder why we weren't playing well. It was like there was a dark cloud over us. The fans even stopped supporting us because they didn't think we were going to be around. Ralston continued to try to find local buyers, but when they exhausted all their contacts, it looked like the team would have to relocate. The constant rumors really affected my play, as I finished with less than

30 goals and 90 points for the first time in five years. We finished the regular season with just 65 points, falling 42 points in the standings in just two years. We made the playoffs, but got knocked out by Chicago in the first round.

Ten days after the loss to the Blackhawks, Ralston still didn't have any bids from anyone in St. Louis, and on April 20, they agreed to sell the team to Saskatoon. We didn't know what was going to happen, and even Mr. Francis didn't know if there was going to be a team here. It was really bad. On May 15, all the employees in the Blues' office were let go. In late May, the Saskatoon group went to New York for a special meeting with the NHL, and the relocation was denied by a vote of 15–3. The league maintained that Ralston still owned the Blues, and until Ralston approved an alternative option to Saskatoon, they were going to continue to operate the organization. Ralston disagreed and refused to spend another dime on our club.

The whole situation was so messed up that when the NHL held its annual amateur draft on June 8, 1983, the Blues were not represented at the draft table. There were 12 rounds and 242 picks made and not one selection by the Blues. The league assumed control of the team, but said they would not operate it. We were all flabbergasted because even though there were serious issues, we thought someone would surely carry out the draft—unless they thought the franchise was going to fold. As players, we thought we might all be part of a dispersal draft and end up on different teams, but everything remained in limbo and it just dragged on and on. When Mr. Francis' contract expired on June 30, he accepted the job as the new general manager of the Hartford Whalers, and now we really had problems.

Being from Saskatoon, I was in a precarious position because there were all these rumblings about moving and I had to be careful about what I said. This was my hometown. I played junior hockey there with the Blades and I love the city. It wasn't that I didn't want to go back to Saskatoon, but I wasn't going to say that because I also loved it in St. Louis, so it was really a Catch-22. I was getting all kinds of press in Saskatoon: What are you thinking? Like I said, I had to be very careful with my comments and I had to keep my answer the same because whatever quote I gave to the Saskatoon newspaper was going to show up in the *St. Louis Post-Dispatch* or the *Globe-Democrat*, and vice-versa, so I stayed very neutral through the whole thing.

My folks, my in-laws, everybody in Saskatoon, was excited about the chances of the Blues coming. The Oilers were in Edmonton, the Flames were in Calgary, Vancouver had a team, and Winnipeg had a team, so Saskatchewan was the only province in Western Canada that didn't have a hockey team. Bernadette and I were at the lake, so we saw firsthand what people were thinking in Canada. Everybody up there thought, *Oh God, Saskatoon is going to get a team*, but I always thought, *There's not a chance with only 150,000 people. There's no way they can support an NHL team.*

But you know what, Ralston was really adamant about selling it and they were the only buyer. We just said to ourselves, if it happens, it happens. While in Canada, we didn't know what was going on in St. Louis. We could get the St. Louis radio station, KMOX, to come in at night, so we'd hear a little bit. But being at the lake with no cell phones back then, we didn't know unless we called our friends in St. Louis. We were waiting and waiting to hear what was going to happen, and then all of a sudden the report was that a California businessman was getting involved. On July 21, Harry Ornest bought the Blues for $12 million, and for the first time in months, we knew we were staying put in St. Louis.

We were all relieved because we all had our lives in St. Louis. As much as it would not have been a bad deal for me, I was very relieved to stay here. St. Louis was a great hockey town and I just couldn't believe a town like this, with a building like we had, and the following that we had, would be allowed to move. But little did we know what we were getting into with Harry Ornest. We had heard the rumors about how cheap he was, and that he was only here to make money, but we were all clueless at the time.

Harry hired Jack Quinn as president and Jack hired Ron Caron as general manager and Ron hired Jacques Demers as head coach. Jacques had been the WHA's coach of the year in 1973 when he coached the Indianapolis Racers. He had also coached in the WHA for Chicago and Cincinnati and then was the head coach in Quebec City when the WHA merged with the NHL. So you come to training camp and now you've got a new owner, a new GM, and a new coach. The head candidates for GM had been Bud Poile and Pat Quinn, but Harry Ornest ended up hiring Caron, most likely because Mr. Caron was willing to be paid less to get the opportunity to be a general manager for the first time in the NHL.

Mr. Caron was so animated, you never knew what he was thinking. Just having a conversation with him, I didn't know if he liked me, hated me, or what. But as far as the coaching choice,

Jacques was great and I really got along with him. We didn't know what to expect when he came in, but he had the best attitude. He was a bubbly guy all the time, had the utmost respect for all of us, and was a great communicator. And most importantly, Jacques embraced Barc, and Barc stayed on the staff. It was very important that Barc was still going to be respected and Jacques did that right off the bat. We were so happy that we had some stability again.

We were playing for each other early in the 1983–84 season, and I think we were also playing for Barc. He was still sick and we never really knew when it could be the end for Barc, so that was a rallying point for us. The other big thing for us that year was we had Dougie Gilmour coming up. Because the Blues didn't participate in the draft that summer, we had no prospects coming to reinforce our team. But fortunately, Mr. Francis had drafted Dougie the year before, and with a great season in junior hockey in 1982–83, he was ready for the NHL. He acted like an old pro right from the start, understanding what the pecking order was. He was a big scorer in junior, but when he came to St. Louis, he knew he had to bide his time and learn the defensive side of the game. He didn't say anything, he listened and he watched.

We were somewhat of a blue-collar team, but on paper we were a pretty good team. Brian was coming off a year where he scored a career-high 46 goals. We still had Babs and Perry and Jorgen, and Joey coming into his own, and Rammer was our star defenseman. We felt pretty good about ourselves after winning six of our first eight games, but right away, we saw some of Harry's penny-pinching that we had been hearing about.

12

HARRY THE CHEAPSKATE

WHEN HARRY TOOK over, we had 50 players under contract and Ron Caron terminated 11 of them, leaving us with 39 players in the organization. It was quickly obvious that Harry was only worried about payroll. The front-office staff went from 25 to 15, and even though we were down to 5,000 season-tickets holders because of all the turmoil surrounding the possible move to Saskatoon, Harry raised ticket prices 10 percent. The team went from having team-paid pregame meals to players being on our own to find a restaurant, and we knew that was all Harry. There's no way that was Ron's idea. He had been in Montreal and they were the epitome of a franchise that did things right and took care of their players. It wouldn't have cost the organization that much money to pay for a pregame meal, and all it did was create stress for us.

Susie Mathieu, who was more valuable and loyal than anyone in the Blues' organization in all the years I played, would call ahead and find a restaurant for us, so that we didn't have to waste a bunch of time going around looking for one. When we'd go to Chicago or any of the divisional cities where we went four times a season, we would stay in a different hotel every time so that we could get the introductory rate. So we'd stay in a different hotel every trip so that we were a first-time customer at each one. The only good hotel we had was The Drake in Chicago, but we only stayed there because the brother-in-law of our team president, Jack Quinn, ran the hotel.

Of course back then, it was very rare for us to take charter flights —they were almost all commercial—but the routes we took to get to places were ridiculous. They would book the earliest flight at 6:00 AM and take three connectors with a five-hour layover somewhere just because it was the cheapest option. I remember going to Montreal one time, we went from St. Louis to Pittsburgh to Cleveland to New York to Montreal. We had no minor-league system. Everybody who was in St. Louis was who we had. Guys in the minors who weren't good enough to play in the NHL just got loaned out to other clubs. We did all kinds of stuff like that and it was just awful. It didn't matter to Harry because his motto was, "Get it as cheap as you can get it."

Probably the most famous Harry story of all time was when we were taking the annual team picture, and he wanted us to wear tuxedos. He had obviously cut a deal with the tux company because he promised all of us that if we wore them for the picture, we could take them home after practice and keep them. So all of us were in tuxes and Brian and I were sitting behind two baby grand pianos with top hats on. We took the picture before practice, changed into our hockey gear and guess what? By the time we got off the ice, all the tuxes were gone. I still don't know to this day what happened with those tuxes—Harry either kept them or he sold them—but none of us ever saw them again. Every corner that could be cut, was. It was pathetic.

Ron Caron did the best he could with what he had. In December, he made his first big trade, sending Perry to the Montreal Canadiens for Doug Wickenheiser, Gilbert Delorme, and Greg Paslawski. Ron had been the director of player personnel with the Canadiens before joining the Blues, and in 1980 he voted for the club taking Wickenheiser over French-Canadian Denis Savard. Well, Wick didn't pan out in Montreal and that was part of the reason Ron was let go and later came to St. Louis. Ron still loved Wick and felt that giving him a new team would resurrect his career. Pazzer, who was fast and had a good shot, was a great prospect and Gilbert was an up-and-coming defenseman.

I remember press clippings calling us a team of "rejects," but it was a good group. We weren't fancy, but we believed that we could always hang in there. I think everybody hated playing against us because we were just a real blue-collar team and we had some guys who could score. There were rumors that I was probably going to be the next player on the move. Harry Ornest was all about payroll and, even though I was in the Top 10 in scoring in the league, I was the highest-paid player on the team, so I thought there was a good chance that I could be moved. But I had been in St. Louis now for eight years, and with every point I was putting up, I was getting closer to the franchise record held by Gary Unger (aka Ungie). I tied the record of 575 points in early December, and the day I broke it is a day that I'll never forget.

On December 13, Bernadette went into labor with our second son, Dusty, and had him at about 9:00 in the morning. I had been up all night with Bernadette, trying as best as I could to ease the process. The thrill of seeing Dusty born was every bit as exciting as I had remembered when Jordy was born, just so unbelievable. It was late morning before I left the hospital and went home to grab a nap and then swing back by the hospital before I went to the game.

We were playing Chicago and what a perfect opponent when you are riding a high like the birth of a son.

It was different this time because when Jordy was born, I had a bunch of adrenaline, but there was no way to use it because I didn't play that game in Quebec. But when Dusty was born, I could go play. I probably wasn't aware that I was tied with Ungie in points, so I wasn't thinking about breaking a record. I just wanted so badly to score a goal for Bernadette and the baby, and it happened. I had a goal and an assist and set the record with 577 points, which is a neat thing to look back on because I became the Blues' all-time leading scorer the same day Dusty was born. I am surprised that, 34 years later, I still hold the record, so it's kind of an extra-special day every year on his birthday.

We hovered around .500 for most of the year, but by February we were falling in the standings, and even though I was in the top 10 scorers, I was in a slump. I remember we were going on a short two-game road trip to Detroit and Philadelphia, and Harry was going to come along with us. The first game was in Detroit and I wasn't very good again, but the team played well and we won 4–3. You could never really sleep after a game with all the adrenaline, so we usually just went somewhere and relaxed for a little while. That night, Joey, Dougie, Wick, and me went down the street from the hotel to have a burger and a beer or two.

There weren't many places to eat, so you could either take a pizza back to your hotel room or do what we did. Plus, my cousin who lived in Detroit had come to the game with a friend who was dying of cancer and wanted me to meet him. I couldn't make up a story like that. Well, we got back at about 12:30 AM, which to me was not a big deal when you consider we didn't leave the rink after the game until about 10:30. We were playing the next night in Philadelphia and, yes, the fact of the matter is there was a midnight curfew the night before a game. But I couldn't believe it when we walked into the hotel and saw Barc waiting up for us, accusing us of breaking curfew.

We're a half-hour late and he's flipping out. I said, "Barc, calm down." He told me not to tell him to calm down and I told Joey, Wick, and Dougie to go to bed and Barc and I would handle this. I said, "Barc, it's all a true story, we were getting a bite to eat and we didn't do anything wrong. We were just having a couple of beers to unwind." I have no idea how he even knew we were out. He was really pissed that this happened, but of course with the relationship that Barc and I had, he eventually calmed down.

I thought it had all died down when we flew to Philadelphia the next day, but it hadn't. We lost 5–2 to the Flyers, which shouldn't have been a shock because the Blues hadn't won there in maybe 10 years, and it was my fourth straight game without a point. On the flight home from Philly, Jacques called me up to business class where he was sitting and told me, "You're struggling and Harry was on the road trip and you guys shouldn't haven't been out in Detroit. What do you think I should do? Harry was with us. I have to do something."

I had no idea how to answer that. I felt I had done nothing wrong other than not playing well, but it had nothing to do with the night in Detroit. Again I thought it was over with, but the next day we were playing the Washington Capitals at home. As usual, I went on the ice for the morning skate and when I finished and started to head to the locker room, Jacques came over to me and said, "You're not playing tonight. I want you to stay out and do a little extra skating."

I had never been so shocked in all my life. I was flabbergasted. I was like, "You have got to be shitting me. I'm going to be a healthy scratch?" Jacques left the ice. Barc was left trying to calm me down.

He was on my side, but said, "You know, he's the coach, you've got to do what he says."

Then I'll never forget this, when I finally got ready to leave the rink, Jacques said, "Don't even come to the game tonight. I want you to relax and take your wife out for dinner and we'll meet you on the charter tonight after the game to fly to Chicago. Have a good night." You've got to be kidding me! Have a good night? Fuck me!

Well, what choice did I have? So, I took Bernadette out and it was the first time we ever had Mexican food. I had never even had a margarita in my life, but trust me, I had a lot of them that night and, boy, I liked them a lot. While I was out on the town, the guys lost to the Capitals and then I met them at the plane. The coaches always sat in the front of the plane, so there was no way of avoiding them, but it was funny. I had plenty of tequila in me, so I just grabbed a six-pack from the flight attendant and marched right to the back of the plane without talking to any of them. We played in Chicago the next afternoon, and I was still bitter. We lost a tough one, 6–5, but my point slump ended. I got two assists in the game, and Jacques was like, "See, you're back." That was a bunch of bullshit, but I guess it took the pressure off of him from Harry.

Despite all the BS and a regular season record that was below .500, we still finished in second place in the Norris Division, and statistically it was my best season. In the fourth to last game of the year, I had a hat trick against the Edmonton Oilers in Edmonton in front of all my family, reaching the 40-goal plateau for the only time in my career. I wound up in ninth place in the NHL scoring race with a career-best 107 points. Joey scored 41 goals, which was the most ever scored by an American-born player, and Dougie had a great start to his NHL career, scoring 25 goals.

We were feeling pretty good about ourselves going into the play-offs because, in addition to the balanced scoring, Lutey was slowly finding the form that he'd showed in his great year in 1980–81. We played Detroit in the first round, and after splitting the first two games in St. Louis, we won both games in Detroit, one in over-time and the other in double OT. Jorgen Pettersson was the hero, scoring five goals in that first-round series, which we won three games to one.

It was off to Minnesota for the second round, which was a great series and went all the way to Game 7. We led the game late in the third period until Lutey couldn't pick up the sight of a puck that Willi Plett shot from just over center ice. That tied the game 3–3, and sent it overtime. Unfortunately for us, Steve Payne scored the game-winner for the North Stars early in OT to send us home for the summer. It was such a disappointment to be that close to moving on to the semifinals, but for all the shit we had gone through, it was a pretty good year.

As I got older, it seemed like the hockey seasons just blended together and the summers didn't even exist. We came back to training camp that fall not really knowing what was in store for us. Camp was in Peoria, Illinois, where the Blues' minor-league affili-ate now was, and we knew that it was going to be a long camp. We started in Peoria, then went to Western Canada for the end of the preseason, and then opened the regular season with four straight road games on the West Coast, so we were gone for 28 consecutive days. It's funny, but Mr. Caron tried to make us believe that we were going to have a little vacation during this miserable stretch on the road, promising us a day or two on the golf course, but we never got to play once. So during a bus ride in an early autumn snowfall to one of the preseason games in Alberta, I took some golf balls and rolled a few up to the front of the bus to send him a message.

The early part of the season seemed to be hard on Barclay, but of course he never complained. In December, he started chemo and radiation, so once again it was hard not having him around. We won our share of games, perhaps more than people expected, but Harry's tight purse strings always seemed to catch up with us. Ron Caron had now put a pretty good team together, but was Harry going to let it ride? The answer was no. In February 1985, Lutey was in the fourth year of a five-year contract, making around $400,000, and Harry knew he was going to cost too much to re-sign, so he traded him to Hartford. Mr. Francis was the GM in Hartford, and of course he wanted Lutey, so Mr. Caron traded Lutey for Greg Millen and Mark Johnson. Millsy and Mark were good players, but it was all about the money. Then at the end of the year, Mr. Caron sent Jorgen to Hartford to complete the deal. That was a big blow to all of us, losing Lutey, because he was there from the beginning. There was no question he was one of the best goalies in the NHL and we were going to miss him.

Three weeks later, we lost Wick for the year in the infamous "snipe hunt" accident, and it was such a shame because he was really re-establishing himself in St. Louis and seemed to be hitting his stride, with 23 goals and 43 points in 68 games.

If you've never heard of the snipe hunt, it was an annual prank that started with the original Blues in the late 1960s and was intended to scare the daylights out of unsuspecting teammates. It was one of the most unbelievably planned events you could ever imagine, and it basically took everyone's cooperation in the entire town of Eureka to execute. Everyone would meet at Joe Boccardi's restaurant for some dinner and cocktails and then when it got dark, we would go out and "snipe" hunt. There really is such a bird and they do exist in Missouri, but this ordeal had nothing to do with them. They would pair the rookies together and give them a flashlight and a fishing net and they would make them go to the end of a corn field and wait for everybody else to chase the "birds" down between the rows of corn. The veterans are telling you how to take them out of the net and put them in the sack.

They end up arresting the rookies for poaching, and it's a real conservation officer that arrests you. The year Brian and I were rookies, we got arrested, handcuffed, put in a police car, went to jail, and they actually had a trial at the courthouse. They had all the farmers and their families in the courthouse jeering you. They had the guy saying, "These are our birds, you can't do this at night." They even fired fake gun shots and broke us out of jail. Well, of course it's all a ruse, but you have to find that out for yourself. If you were there, you'd swear it was real.

It must have taken so much coordination between the head of NHL security for the Blues and all the farmers in Eureka because every step was in place. This was like a Broadway play, really quite the production, and it was one of the great traditions that we tried to continue from team to team. Every year you'd have a couple of rookies come in and guys would build it up in the locker room, saying "We're going snipe hunting next week, how great is that going to be?" We did it to Bill Stewart and he was so mad, he was ready to kill somebody. Jorgen Pettersson was stressed out so badly because they found him guilty and said they were going to deport him back to Sweden. That's how well it's done, and when you're part of it, you're drunk and sitting in the courthouse trying not to laugh. Then at the end of the night, you'd go back to Boccardi's and party.

But on March 13, 1985, the snipe hunt was no laughing matter. Wick had a few buddies in town from Regina, Saskatchewan, and we were having such a good time, but you want to talk about a downer from an upper. As we were leaving Joe Boccardi's for the snipe hunt, Wick was running and tried to jump into the back of a moving truck and he fell back out and landed awkwardly on the street. We had to take him to the hospital, but we knew that things were not going to be good. He needed knee surgery and—bingo!— done for the year. It was a freak accident, just jumping in the back of a truck, and for that to happen to him, it was tough. Needless to say, there was never another Blues' snipe hunt.

We could have used Wick that year. Brian, Joey, and I combined for 107 goals, with Joey scoring 40, Brian 37, and me 30. I finished with 103 points, my second straight 100-plus season and my third overall. We narrowly won the Norris Division tight, but for the second straight year, we ran into Minnesota in the playoffs, a well-oiled machine, and got swept in three games by the North Stars.

In the past, we'd always tried to build on our success from year to year, but it was difficult to do under Harry because he was always scheming and the roster was turning over like a revolving door. When we got to training camp at the start of the 1985–86 season, the St. Louis City collector had shut down the Arena because Harry owed $300,000 in amusement taxes. He didn't think he owed it, but he had to get a court injunction so we could play there. Then we were missing Joey Mullen, who was having a bitch of a time in his negotiations for a new contract. He was coming off consecutive 40-goal seasons, so he should have had good leverage, but he was dealing with Harry and Jack, so that didn't get resolved until three days into camp.

There were also some trades, so we had seven new players, including Mark Hunter, Ron Flockhart, and Ric Nattress from Montreal; Rick Meagher from New Jersey; and Bruce Bell from Quebec. We had a great bunch of guys that always hung together and we just made the best of the situation. Jacques was not over-bearing and Barc, although he probably wasn't feeling his best after going through treatments, was back on the bench. But every-thing was being done on the cheap and the bottom line was we were a .500 team that wasn't drawing very well at the gate, and by December, Harry began complaining publicly that the Blues couldn't survive in St. Louis with such poor attendance.

I remember his exact quote: "I am committed to St. Louis but also committed to not go broke." All you could think was, *Here we go again.* There was an offer to buy the team and move it to Hamilton, Ontario, and then trade rumors began to circulate and my name started making the rounds again. Just when we thought it couldn't get any worse, Brian was checked hard into the end boards in Minnesota in mid-January and broke the scapula bone in his shoulder. He was most likely out for the rest of the season, and for a team with no depth, this was a major blow.

I guess fortunately for us, we were on our way to California. We always looked forward to going there, especially when the weather was cold in St. Louis, but this time it was even better because we had back-to-back games in L.A. That was very unusual to have two games in one city, but if it was going to happen, this was the right city.

It was no picnic getting out to L.A. if you remember how cheap Harry was with the flights. Remember, St. Louis was the main hub for TWA and there were numerous direct flights to LAX. Instead, we took a new airline, Jet America, because of course we got the inexpensive introductory rate. But they didn't even fly into L.A., so we had to connect through Dallas and then fly into Long Beach and then bus from the Long Beach airport to LAX, where we stayed at the airport Marriott. We left early in the morning and it was dark by the time we got to the hotel. We were tired, but were going into L.A. two days early, so with no game the next day, a few of the guys.

Even though we didn't have a game the next day, for whatever reason Jacques decided that there was going to be a curfew that night. Some of the guys came and asked what I thought they should do. I knew Jacques pretty well and knew there was no way that he was going to check, so I told them to go ahead, but don't be too late. So off they went, while the rest of us stayed back and sat around drinking beer at the hotel. Well, I'm not going to mention any names, but one of our better scorers got so drunk at the bar that he fell off the barstool and busted his nose. When the guys brought him back, there was a trail of blood all the way up the elevator, down the hall right to their room.

Now it's 1:00 in the morning and out of the blue, again not mentioning any names, one of our defensemen throws a chair off the balcony that lands on a car, and of course now shit is going to hit the fan. Security came to the room, and they called the man listed in charge, Jacques Demers. He was already asleep, so when he came down the hall he was extremely pissed off. He couldn't be ticked about curfew because we were all in the hotel, but he walked in and saw the blood and he knew something was all fucked up. He didn't know that anyone went out, but that obviously didn't matter.

We practiced the next day and everything seemed fine, but things took a big turn after we lost the first game the following night to L.A., 6–3. On the Marriott shuttle back to the hotel after the game, Jacques had the bus driver pull over about halfway back, where he got out and puked. I don't know if he was sick or what, but he was in a real sour mood and we knew he was going to find a way to let us know about it. We expected our practice the next day to be a real tough one, but surprisingly enough, it was as normal as could be.

Then the next day at the morning skate, before the second game against the Kings, he made the announcement that there had to be punishment for what transpired from the previous three days. He said some guys weren't going to suit up and instead of the usual 20-man lineup, he was only going to dress 17. I'm thinking, *Who's getting punished here?* Now Jacques didn't know if any of the guys had missed curfew, but if he were guessing, he had to guess the guy with the broken nose. Hell, there had been that trail of blood all the way down the hall to his room. But that wasn't the case, he played and even scored a goal. Jacques didn't really know who had thrown the chair off the balcony, but I suppose he guessed right because the guilty defenseman didn't play.

It's really not a big deal having three less guys dress, but when Jacques went to just playing seven of us in the third period, that was a big deal. You would come to the bench, sit down for just a minute or so and then go right back out, and it didn't matter if you were a forward or a defenseman, you played both. I had never been a part of anything like that in my career, but amazingly we ended up winning 4–3, and once again Jacques looked like a genius.

But once again we could never get too excited about any success because with Harry always bitching about the payroll being too high, you knew something was going to give, and it did.

On February 1, Joey Mullen scored the game-winning goal against Detroit at the Arena and they traded him right after the game. The goal that night was his 28th of the season, in just 48 games, and it was No. 126 in 256 games. Why would you even think of trading a guy like that?

Jacques sent Joey upstairs to see Harry and Jack Quinn, and then he summoned us all back into the locker room to break the news to us. We were all pissed off because Joey had become a special friend in those three years, and I was really close to him. Joey was like a little brother to Bernadette and me. He would always stay with us before training camp started and even after camp until his wife came in from Boston. I knew the night he got traded was going to be a long night, so I told all the guys to come back to my house.

I don't know if I can blame it on the trade or what, but that night I drove my Jaguar through the front of my garage. We had a side-entry garage and when I pulled my car in, and got out of the car, I realized it wasn't quite far enough into the garage to close the door. Instead of just sitting back into the car and driving it forward a little bit, I just stuck my foot in and stepped on the gas. But unfortuately I fell back and accidentally floored it, slamming into the back wall and knocking all the bricks out on the back side. Once again, Harry's antics had gotten to me.

The next day they had a press conference to officially announce the trade and, not surprisingly, Ron Caron was out of town, so Harry announced it. I'm sure Mr. Caron didn't want to be there. Brian and I hated what was going on, but we both felt very fortunate that we were the two guys that were the mainstays. I guess we were the franchise, but was that good or bad? It was very flattering at the time, but looking back, we suffered through an awful lot because all of these good players were being moved.

In the trade for Joey, we got Gino Cavallini, Charlie Bourgeois, and Eddy Beers from Calgary. We always welcomed the new players, but we were just trying to keep it together. With Joey gone, Hunts took that spot on my right side and he ended up scoring 44 goals that year, and for the third straight year, I topped the 100-point mark, with 102 points. It wasn't the most points I'd ever had but I felt it was my most complete year. I wasn't in the Top 10 scorers that year, but I was close at No. 13. But what amazed me once again was that for the third straight year I was overlooked for the All-Star Game. I had 312 points in a three-year stretch from 1983 to '86, but no All-Star Games.

We finished the regular season just over .500, which got us third-place in the Norris Division, but little did we know at the time, we were about to be part of one of the most memorable playoff runs, and magical moments, in Blues history.

13

MONDAY NIGHT MIRACLE

WE WENT THE distance in each of the first two rounds, beating Minnesota in Game 5 of the Norris Division Semifinals and then Toronto in Game 7 of the Division Finals to advance to the Clarence Campbell Conference Finals against Calgary. When you looked at us, we certainly didn't have the best team in the NHL, or even a top-four team, but we had more heart than anybody else. And that was never more evident that season than on May 12, 1986, which was Game 6 against the Flames, or as it would become better known, the "Monday Night Miracle."

It was my 30th birthday and it was a do-or-die game for us, trailing 3–2 in the best-of-seven series. The morning skate was business-as-usual, same attitude, just saying let's give it all we've got, that's all we can do. You always play the hardest when your back's against the wall, but for whatever reason, when the game started, it was just one of those nights when things didn't go well and we fell behind early.

I remember going into the second intermission, we were down 4–1 and everybody in the locker room was pretty quiet. You could just see by looking at the faces that being down three goals was probably too big of a hole. But then Jacques came in and gave us the best speech that he ever could. He said, "Guys, I'm so proud of you, this has been an unbelievable year. You have gone further than anybody expected, you stuck together through an awful lot

189

of shit, and you know what? Maybe we've only got one period left, but let's give it all we've got and you never know what can happen." Basically he was resigned to the fact that it was over, but he was saying we've still got a period left. And with Barclay standing right next to him, motivation was not going to be an issue.

We scored early in the third period to make it 4–2, but Joey Mullen, who we had been traded to Calgary, made it 5–2 with about 13 minutes left in regulation. We got down inside the last 10 minutes and everybody was trying to stay positive, saying, "C'mon, one goal every three or four minutes."

We still believed, but we needed some crazy things to happen— and then they did. Brian, who probably shouldn't have even been playing because of his bad shoulder, scored his first goal of the playoffs to make it 5–3 with 11:54 left, and then Greg Paslawski cut the deficit to 5–4 with 4:11 to play. We went from being totally out of the game to being in a position to tie it, and now the Flames were on their heels. The roof was starting to come off the Arena, and when Pazzer scored his second goal of the game to tie it 5–5 with 1:08 left, it blew off.

We were playing well, but if you watch the replays, Calgary made so many stupid plays. For example, on that goal that Brian scored, the Flames' goalie, Mike Vernon, kicked the puck right to him. On Pazzer's game-tying goal, Vernon stopped the puck from going around the back of the net and then left it for Jamie Macoun, and then Pazzer lifted Macoun's stick and scored. I think when Pazzer scored his second one, Calgary knew they had no chance, it was over. We went into the locker room for the overtime and Jacques, instead of saying, "Great job," he said, "We're winning this game." He and Barc, they had the biggest smiles on their faces. After what we just did, chances were that we were going to score in overtime.

So we start OT and what happens? Joey Mullen hits the post. Could you imagine how that would have felt if Joey would've won the game for Calgary? But he hit the post and usually that's the kiss of death. If you hit a post, it seems like more often than not that the other team is going to come right down and score, and that's exactly what happened.

Calgary's Paul Reinhart had the puck at center ice along the boards, but it hopped on him. I was able to track it down, get by him, and create a two-on-one. All five Flames were chasing back into the zone to pick up a man, but no one was worried about the puck. I passed it to Hunts and his shot was blocked and fell right to Wick. With Vernon way out of position, Wick put it in the back of the net and it was pandemonium! The Arena was rocking, every person in the building was standing and screaming, and no one wanted to leave.

An hour later, people were still chanting and banging on the seats. We were in the locker room and it felt like the walls were going to cave in. I had never, ever heard something like that before, and 30 years later, I still don't think I have. I laugh now because when you talk to people, they all say they were there that night, so evidently there were 100,000 people in the building. What a wonderful birthday present for me! That's how you turn 30 in style!

Two nights later, we were in Calgary for Game 7, one game away from the franchise going to the Stanley Cup Final for the first time since 1970.

It was such a tight game throughout the night. We were losing 2–0, but scored with one minute left in the third period to cut the lead in half, and all of a sudden the Flames' asses started puckering up because of what had happened in Game 6. We honestly thought we were going to do it again, but no such luck this time as we fell 2–1 and dropped the series in seven games.

I'd like to see the replay of the last minute of that game again. There was a puck coming around the boards to me in the corner and I swear to God the referee got in the way. Dougie Gilmour was all alone in front of the net. I know if I would have got that puck, I could have passed it to Dougie. Who knows what would have happened if he scored? I guess it just wasn't meant to be. The loss really hurt, but being the underdogs and finishing one goal away from the Stanley Cup Final, that was pretty amazing. That's the only bad part about the Monday Night Miracle, that it didn't lead to anything. If we got to the Final, then it's really something, but when you lose Game 7, it didn't really mean as much.

All we wanted to do was get back to St. Louis, but thanks to Harry, we couldn't even do that right away. By the time we left the rink, we found out that he had canceled the team's charter flight home. I know we're talking about Harry, but can you believe that? We were in Game 7 to go to the Stanley Cup Final and we don't win, so he cancels the charter! If we had won, the flight would have been taking us to Montreal to play the Canadiens, but once we lost, I guess he didn't want to spend the money. It was sad, really.

Susie Mathieu was now stuck with the problem of getting us all home from Calgary. She tried to book all our flights on her credit card, but that would have put her over her limit, so she asked if she could use my card, too. Of course, I gave her my card and she charged some of the flights to me. Not surprisingly, because they were last-minute bookings, she couldn't get us all on the same flight. So some of the guys went on one flight through Denver, some went through Minneapolis, and I think some even went through Chicago.

Harry must have been sure that he was going to sell the Blues. It was obvious that he didn't give a shit about us; nothing else made sense. The season was over and he knew that he wasn't going to be dealing with us anymore, so I guess he wanted to take as much money as he could and run. I guess we had to give him credit for saving hockey in St. Louis, but at least get us home. Again, though, that was just one of many crazy things that happened in Harry's three years. From the time he bought the team until the Monday Night Miracle series against Calgary, only four players were left: Mark Reeds, Rob Ramage, Brian, and me. Hopefully, this mess was going to end.

I had signed a contract extension in the spring just before the start of the Calgary series, and if only I had known that Harry was selling the team, I would have never done that. In hindsight, I should have waited until the season was over, but Jacques and Barc were pushing so hard for me to sign a new deal. When we started negotiations in the spring, I was on the verge of having my third straight 100-point year, and Harry was trying to lowball me with a contract. He felt that I should be giving the Blues the "hometown" discount.

Jack Quinn and Harry must have been from the same peapod because they were both the cheapest SOBs you would ever know.

They didn't want to give me the money. They wanted to barter everything. In other words, you sign for this and we'll throw in some other stuff. It was crazy, but after several negotiating sessions, I realized that this was the only way we were going to get this done. I didn't want to go anywhere else to play—I loved St. Louis—so in the end I was willing to give that hometown discount. I took a base salary that was less than I should have, and Bernadette came up with all kinds of perks, things that Quinn could barter for with other people. So we got plane tickets, a new dealer car for Bernadette every two or three months, and they even agreed to make the payments on my Jaguar. It was embarrassing, but basically because we didn't want to go anywhere else, we were content, so we gave in.

Harry had given me three years and an option. After I had agreed to the terms, they asked if they could wait for the right time to make the official announcement. They wanted to do it during the playoffs because they wanted the press. So we got to that point and I was leading the league in playoff scoring and we were going to the Semifinals against Calgary, so they announced it and we did get a lot of press. But if I would have only known that by the start of the next season Michael Shanahan's local group was buying the team, I would have waited. There is no doubt in my mind that I could have negotiated a much better long-term contract with maybe even a no-trade clause. It would have been nice to deal with a reasonable man.

All of us knew that Jacques was at the end of his coaching contract, too. He had been talking to Harry, trying to get a new deal in place, but like me, Harry wasn't offering him shit. So one night, just a week or two after the playoffs ended, Jacques called me and said he had something to run by me, so Bernadette and I met him and his wife, Debbie, at TGI Friday's on Olive Boulevard. He talked about his frustration with Harry and his inability to get a new contract done, and that he had an offer to coach the Detroit Red Wings. As much as I liked playing for Jacques, I understood his frustration and he was a good friend, so I told him he would be crazy if he didn't go to Detroit. Jacques did take the job, but it eventually came out that he had a handshake deal with the Blues, so the Blues got some compensation back when he signed with the Red Wings. You will never guess what the compensation allegedly was: Three exhibition games against Detroit where the Blues got all the gate money. There's Jack Quinn collecting that cash again.

I really missed Jacques. As I said, he was a great motivator and he just let us play. He knew personalities and he got the best out of all of us. When it came to being a tactician, he was not the best. I remember when he would go over something on the chalkboard and none of us had any idea what he was talking about. If we had a new kid on the team, we would say, "Don't even watch this." Jacques would have 25 Xs and 15 Os on the board and they were all over the place. Jacques was not an Xs and Os coach by any means. He was a motivator and that's why he was so good.

Even though he wasn't good tactically, I was quite shocked when his biography, *All Spelled Out*, came out in 2005 and he revealed that he was illiterate. I mean, looking back, there were maybe little things that happened that made us stop and think. For example, it was Barc who wrote the lineup on the board. Jacques never did, so thinking back, why did Barc always do that? Did Barc want to, or was it because Jacques couldn't do it? The other thing I started wondering about, when we would go on the road, the first thing Jacques did when we got to a new city was buy a newspaper. Was he trying to cover up the fact that he couldn't read? The way it was played up in the book was that he couldn't read or write, but I have a hard time believing that. I've never had that conversation with Jacques, though, and I guess there's no reason to lie about something like that. Whether or not he really was totally illiterate, he sure as hell did a great job coaching.

So now after nearly going to the Stanley Cup Finals, Ron Caron spent the summer of 1986 trying to replace Jacques Demers. I am sure there were lots of experienced NHL coaches that would have wanted to take the job, and I am sure there were lots of former players that had aspirations of coaching in the NHL, but for whatever reason, Ron chose Jacques Martin. He had been coaching junior hockey in Guelph, Ontario, of the Ontario Hockey League. This was a big break and a big step for him.

Taking the job early in the summer, Jacques Martin wanted to get familiar with the players, so he planned trips to visit them wherever they were. That's nice, but you would think that you'd start with your top players. Well, he flew to Alberta to see Brian, which made sense. Brian had been captain of our team for a long time. So you'd think I would be next, right?

Nope. He didn't come see me at all. When I got back to St. Louis before training camp, I found out that he had traveled around most of North America, and I was one of the only guys he didn't visit. I met Jacques Martin for the first time just before training camp at the Arena. It wasn't really a meeting, it was him telling me that he was the boss. He told me I was 30 years old and I couldn't play anymore. He told me, "You're going to have to take a step back."

What? I just came off three straight 100-point seasons and he's telling me that I can't play anymore? I had 102 points the year before, and even though it wasn't my highest point total, I felt like it was my best season ever because I wasn't just an offensive guy. I played in defensive situations and I was a complete player. Plus, with Brian out injured, Jacques Demers had me playing on two lines so I had tons of ice time. But my numbers spoke for themselves and for Jacques Martin to say to me, "You're 30 years old..." was insulting.

Doug Gilmour and I had just led the league in scoring in the playoffs and he had the gall to tell me I wasn't capable of playing as much as I had in the past. And if Jacques Martin needed another reason to let me be, I had just signed a new four-year contract that paid me with the best of them. So I don't know where he was coming from. If he heard something about me that he didn't like, why didn't he just confront me? What was the problem? If he would have talked to Jacques Demers, he would have told him that I was the easiest guy in the world to get along with. Why didn't he talk to Barclay?

And please, Jacques was 34 years old, four years older than me, with zero NHL experience, and he's going to tell me that he knows more than me? They even hired a Canadian university coach named Doug MacLean to be Martin's assistant coach. Wow. Not to say this wasn't a great opportunity for two young coaches who later went on to have successful careers, but at that time... really? Jacques and Doug, two guys that have never played or coached one

game in the NHL, and now they're coming in to run the operation. Maybe the rumors about Harry selling to the Mike Shanahan
group weren't true. This obviously was the cheapest hire you could
get, and it looked like Ornest and Quinn were still in charge.

As it turned out, some good news did come out at the start of the
1986–87 season, and that was that Harry was for sure selling the
team to Mike Shanahan and his local group. That was a breath of
fresh air on the home front, but still the atmosphere was not great.
We had gone to the conference finals the year before and we didn't
feel like that was a fluke, but we had finished the regular season
below .500 and didn't add anybody to the lineup. And Jacques
Demers and Barc were such a big part of it, and now we've got this
new coaching staff. It was a totally different training camp because
we were trying to figure out what Jacques Martin was putting in
place, and it was so different for me because instead of a highly
vocal, very confident, fun, happy guy in Jacques Demers, we had
this quiet, stone-faced guy who had very little personality.

I scored in the first couple of games that season, but then I
went in the tank. I didn't score for seven in row, but when I finally
did, on November 1 in a 3–3 tie against Pittsburgh, it was special.
Ungie was the Blues' all-time leading scorer, with 292 goals and I
passed him with that goal. He was such a renowned goal-scorer, so
it was quite flattering. As I have said many times, I never thought
of myself as a goal-scorer, so to be the all-time leader of an NHL
franchise at that time felt amazing. And now I was just seven goals
away from 300, and obviously no player in Blues history had ever
reached that milestone. Brian probably would have if he had not
been hurt so much along the way. Remember, I was the passer and

he was the shooter, but because of all the time he'd missed, I was closing in on it first.

It took longer than expected, but on January 7, 1987, I scored No. 300 against Lutey and the Hartford Whalers at the Arena. It was a wrister, high over the glove, from just outside the top of the left faceoff circle, and it was probably the best shot I ever took in my life. I think when anybody scores 300 goals, that's a big deal. But I had been in the NHL for just 10 years at that point, and that's 30 goals a year, which was pretty damn good. And the fact that I beat Lutey made it more special because he was a good friend and such a great goalie.

The goal felt good, too, because I hadn't been scoring much; it was already January and that was only my 10th goal of the season. I was struggling to score and that was really playing with me mentally. I don't know who I was blaming—myself or Jacques Martin—but Jacques was using me in a different role. He told me that I couldn't play as much, and I wasn't. Plus, because of the way he treated me, I didn't have a lot of confidence in what I was supposed to be doing. He didn't really give me that drive that Jacques Demers did. I don't know, maybe it could have been fatigue after playing until the middle of May the year before. Maybe there was some truth to the fact that I wasn't going to start quick because of my age, but to me, 30 meant nothing.

Two days after scoring my 300th goal, however, I got all the rest I needed. The first shift of the game on January 9 in Edmonton, I went out to block a shot and so did Mark Hunter. Hunts got spun around and he windmilled his stick and caught me in the corner of the jaw. My jaw collapsed inside my mouth and the searing pain caused me to drop to the ice. I never stayed down on the ice when I got hit, so the trainers quickly came to my aid. They helped me off the ice and immediately into the back of an ambulance and took me to University Hospital in Edmonton. I had my skates taken off in the ambulance, but I remember sitting in the waiting room with all my equipment on, waiting for an X-ray.

I was actually third in line if you can believe that. After several minutes, they finally did the X-ray and it was no surprise that my jaw was broken in three places—on both sides and in the middle of my chin. I clearly needed surgery to wire my jaw together, but that was going to have to happen back in St. Louis because the hospital concluded that because I was playing for a non-Canadian team and because it was non-life threatening, they were not going to do anything. They just gave me some Tylenol 3 and sent me back to the rink. My jaw was a mess, but at least I was finally able to get out of my equipment, take a shower, and get dressed.

That game was the first of a three-game trip through Western Canada and Minnesota, so for me to get back to St. Louis wasn't going to be easy. It was about 10:30 PM when I took off from Edmonton to fly to Vancouver. Then I had a midnight, red-eye flight from Vancouver to Toronto, and with the time change, it was 7:00 AM when I arrived in Toronto. Thankfully, I was able to upgrade my ticket to Toronto to first class, but as I said, all I had for the pain was Tylenol 3, so it was not an easy night. Luckily, I was able to sip some whiskey to make things easier. The final two legs were Toronto to Detroit, and then Detroit to St. Louis, but when we took off from Detroit they re-routed us while we were in the air to Memphis because of bad weather in St. Louis. By the time I landed in St. Louis at 5:00 PM Saturday, I was a basket case. My face was swollen like a balloon and I was bleeding out of the middle of my two teeth and all my Tylenol 3 was gone.

Susie Mathieu had a police escort waiting at Lambert Airport to take me to the hospital, but I wanted to stop by my house, so that I could change clothes and see Bernadette and the boys. Bernadette, who was six months pregnant with our third child, didn't even recognize me. What an ordeal! It was 1987, but this was still the National Hockey League. I mean, are you kidding me?

If that happened today, there would be a lawsuit. I finally had surgery the next morning about 36 hours after breaking my jaw, and I'll never forget the moment when I came out of the anesthetic. I was fighting like a bastard because having my mouth wired shut was the most uncomfortable feeling that I've ever had in my life. You're clenching your jaw muscles as hard as you can and there's no relief. They told me I was going to be like this for the next eight weeks and I was thinking, *Oh my God, this is the worst injury that I've ever had.* I had never missed an extended period of time due to injury ever in my career—junior or pro—so I knew that was going to be painful, too.

The injury meant that I wasn't going to be able to play January 31, a night the Blues had arranged to honor me for scoring my 300th goal. I went to center ice with Bernadette, and we had Jordy and Dusty by our side, and I was just there to wave to the crowd. I wasn't expecting anything, but they gave us 300 commemorative pucks to throw out to the crowd, and then Mr. Shanahan surprised me with a new set of golf clubs with a personalized Blues golf bag with my name and No. 24 and the players gave me a membership to Norwood Hills Country Club. I was handed the microphone, and even though my jaw was wired shut, I was thankful that everyone could still understand what I had to say in appreciation. That was so special. What a difference having Mike Shanahan and his new ownership in place! Harry would have never done anything like that.

As disappointed as I was to be out of the lineup, it had been 10 years since I'd last been home during the winter, so this was an opportunity that we needed to take advantage of. I still had a couple of weeks before they were going to cut the wires, so we flew to Saskatoon at the beginning of February with Jordy and Dusty. It was going to be great to see the family in the winter for a change and the boys were really excited about it. We were able to spend a week there and it was great, but six weeks into a wired jaw can't make for much good.

I had a tooth out on the top-left side of my mouth, so I had a way to get the food into my mouth. But I couldn't chew, so I had to put all of my solid foods through a blender and suck everything through a straw. I would blend the meat and potatoes and gravy together and it would taste delicious, but it went so slow through the straw that everything was cold before you got a quarter of the way through. Having to constantly reheat everything in the microwave became such a chore that it was easier to just not eat at all. I even tried blending my favorite Chinese food in Saskatoon, but that didn't go well either. Being home in Saskatchewan with the best two cooks in the land, my mom and Bernadette's mom, all of the great smells were killing me.

Needless to say, when my doctor, Ken Cramm, removed my braces on February 16, I had lost 21 pounds. What a relief, but I was starving. When I left the doctor's office my first stop was McDonald's. Every time I'd driven by there I almost had tears in my eyes, so I had to have some french fries. It hurt so bad to even chew the french fries, but it seemed like one of the great meals of my life.

The very next day, February 17, we played the Vancouver Canucks and whether Jacques Martin thought I was ready or not, I was playing. I stayed in shape as best I could, not skating but riding the stationary bike. I knew I'd be a little short on energy, but I also knew the adrenaline from being back would kick in. I donned a helmet with a full protective face shield, got my timing at the morning skate, and I was ready to go. To everyone's amazement, I had a goal and an assist that night. It was the first time in my life that I felt fast, because I was 20 pounds lighter. Maybe I should have always played that light.

That was the first time since my first full year in the NHL that hit a rough patch. The coaching change really hurt me and I think it was more the lack of respect that I got from Jacques. I think I had the worst plus-minus in the league the first third of the year. In a weird way, I think the jaw injury actually helped me because it gave me a newfound passion. I had really missed the game and got some great words of encouragement from Barc.

I scored 10 goals in the last 24 games of the regular season and finished with 20. I finished second on the team with 72 points behind Dougie, who had a great season. When I got hurt, he exploded. He ended up with 105 points that year, his fifth in the league, and joined me as the only other player in Blues' history to hit 100 points. I was delighted for him. He was the guy that was probably going to take my job at some point and I couldn't have been more happy because we were a better hockey team now. This would be the first time in nine seasons that I did not lead the team in scoring. But I had found my legs again, and I think a lot of it had to do with desire.

Jacques Martin was a downer for me, he really was. I'll never forget in that first meeting we had, Jacques said, "We practice every day, travel is not a factor."

I think I just told him that I disagreed, that travel was a factor. But I should have said, "How would you know? Because you rode the bus in junior hockey?"

Three-quarters of the way through that year he came and said, "You were right, we need to have some days off, the travel is too hard."

I said, "Really!" But he hadn't asked—he just commanded. It was terrible. Although, I think he finally started to give me some respect.

Despite all the chaos of the new coaching staff, we ended up winning the Norris Division and played Toronto in the first round of the playoffs. I was lucky because Bernadette was going to deliver our third child, Drew, at any moment and we were opening the series at home. The night before Game 1, Bernadette started going through her labor pains. With the first two deliveries, we had rushed to the hospital and then ended up waiting eight hours before she had Jordy and Dusty. So this time she told me that she was going to walk around the house until she was ready to go. Then at 2:30 AM, she came upstairs and said, "I'm ready!"

We already had the bag packed and we got ahold of the babysitter, who was waiting for us to call. As soon as the babysitter arrived, we jumped in the car and started driving to St. John's hospital. The first two times I drove 100 mph to get there and then we waited, like I said, for hours. So this time, I was stopping at every light and taking my time, and she said, "C'mon, we've got to go!" So I stepped on it.

We arrived at St. John's and I dropped her off at the emergency entrance, still thinking I had plenty of time. Well, by the time I parked the car and got to the maternity ward, they told me that I didn't have enough time to put a gown on, just to throw on a mask and get in there. It happened so quickly that her doctor didn't even get there in time.

Drew was born on April 8, and "8" was really fitting. That's why Drew's middle name is "Barclay." Not only was Barc our favorite person, but Barc was the great No. 8, which hangs from the rafters at Scottrade Center. It was so wonderful, another healthy, beautiful baby, and the hat trick: three boys. Bernadette was beat. I stayed with her at the hospital until it was time to go to the morning skate. We opened the first round against the Maple Leafs that night with a 3–1 victory in Game 1 and I had two assists. Looking back, I guess I should have had more kids because I seemed to play well when they were born. We won the first and third games of the series, but seemed to fall apart after that and unfortunately lost the series in six.

When we came back to start the 1987–88 season, Barclay was no longer on the bench. When they originally diagnosed him with cancer years before, he had two tumors, but now they found another one. He'd had a tough summer and his health was quickly declining. He was taking chemo and radiation and he lost all his hair. When we saw him, he had a baseball hat on and he was so drawn and skinny and weak, but still he never changed his disposition. Barc was always more worried about everybody else than himself. He had his group of guys and he loved us all, but now he wasn't around. The Blues hired Joe Micheletti as an assistant coach to take over his duties with the defensemen.

Brian was back that year, finally healthy after playing just 58 games combined in 1985–86 and 1986–87 because of that shoulder injury. With the constant changes to our roster every year, leading to the slow starts, getting Brian back was great, but then in early December we suffered a big blow. Dougie Gilmour suffered a concussion and was out for a month. Thankfully, we were able to keep our heads above water during his absence, and when we got him back, we went on a roll, winning seven in a row.

The first game of that streak was a 4–1 victory in Montreal. We had a day off before our next game in Quebec, and surprisingly Jacques Martin gave Greg Millen, Brian, and me the day off. We got to sleep in while the rest of the team went to practice, and when we woke up, we rented a car and went up the mountain to Mont Sainte-Anne in Quebec. What better way to enjoy a day off than at a ski resort? We didn't go skiing during the day, just did a lot of people watching and beer drinking. That night we had a good dinner and drank plenty of wine, and then afterward decided on a whim that we should go skiing under the lights.

We'd never skied, so, yes, it was crazy, but who cared at that point? We certainly weren't dressed for the slopes and must have looked pretty foolish out there, wearing suits and long cashmere coats. We didn't want to buy ski gloves or toques, so we went to Lost and Found and picked through the stuff until we found ones that fit. They didn't even match. We didn't break curfew, and better yet we didn't break any bones, but—oh my God—that was a drunken stupor.

We played the next day against the Nordiques and Millsy stood on his head, making 37 saves in a 5–3 win. I don't know how he did it because we were whipped from the day before. I didn't do shit in the game until I scored the game-winner. We got on the bus after that game and we were just laughing our asses off. Nobody else knew and we certainly weren't going to tell anyone.

14

PLAGER, KELLY PASS AWAY

A COUPLE OF weeks later, the NHL All-Star Game was held in St. Louis and Rammer was our lone representative. Barc and Bobby were supposed to be "honorary captains," but Barc wasn't going to make it. We all went up to St. Luke's Hospital and said good-byes, each one of us going into his room individually. It was short but really amazing. I was crying and it didn't faze him at all. He was dying and he was like, "I'm going to be alright, I want to make sure you guys are going to be alright." He talked about hockey, he talked about me continuing to do my job. It was so emotional for me. We just talked and I was lucky that I was able to get those few moments with him. I thanked him for everything because I knew that this was the end. He just smiled and said, "You don't have to thank me for anything." Here he was, so frail and in pain, but right until the end I've never seen a guy who was so honest and unafraid. I've never met another person like that, who was totally consumed by the people that he really loved instead of what was going on with himself.

On February 6, 1988, two days after we visited him in the hospital, Barc died. That was very heartbreaking and traumatic for all of us and that was the first time in my life that I had somebody real close to me pass on. Barc was only 46 years old and I was 31, so it made me realize how short life really was. I will never forget his funeral, which was lined up with people wall-to-wall. Because the

All-Star Game was in town, every team in the NHL was represented. It was so hard to watch the pain on his wife, Helen, and all
of his kids. It was so tough on his brothers, Bobby and Billy. The
Plager brothers were the St. Louis Blues.

It didn't make sense, but it put your life in perspective. One
of the worst things that happened to me, I thought, was getting
sent down to the minor leagues. I was the team's first pick and
I was MVP of the Western Hockey League. I'm coming here
to be Rookie of the Year in the NHL, not the CHL. But "Barc
the Spark" took me under his wing and I was fortunate because
if I wouldn't have been sent down, I may never have started that
special bond with him. I know it was his guidance in Kansas City
that got me through those early disappointments.

He was my mentor all those years. He showed me a lot on the
ice, but it was those conversations I had with him off the ice that
helped mold me as a player and a person. He taught me how to be a
professional, and that was the greatest thing that ever happened to
me. He knew my game better than anyone. He also used to laugh
at me, saying, "All of you Ukrainians are all so moody and emotional." I don't know if we all are, but I was, and he recognized
that. But no matter how many arguments or fights we had, it was
all constructive. We got mad at each other, but it was all in the
right context. I loved him to death. Even with him giving us the
down payment for the house, I remember trying to give him the
money back and he wouldn't take any interest, so we bought him a
big-screen TV. We had to force him to keep it. He was just a very
special person and for him to pass away, it was incredibly tough,
the saddest time that I had ever experienced.

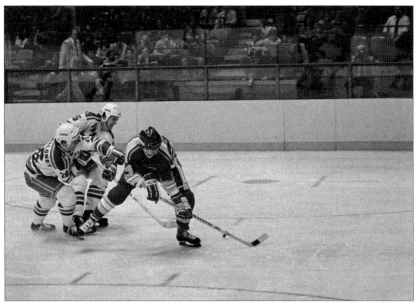

Fighting off two Rangers at Madison Square Garden in October of 1980.
(AP Photo/Ron Frehm)

The 1981 All-Star Game in Los Angeles, with (from left) Mike Liut, Wayne Babych, and trainer Tom Woodcock.

Waving to the fans while being honored for scoring my 1,000th career point. This was prior to the start of the Blues–Devils game on March 24, 1988.
(AP Photo/Jeff Roberson)

HARTFORD WHALERS
Hockey Club

One Civic Center Plaza
Hartford, Connecticut 06103
(203) 728-3366

March 22, 1988

Mr. Bernie Federko
ST. LOUIS BLUES HOCKEY CLUB
5700 Oakland Avenue
St. Louis, MO 63110

Dear Bernie:

Let me take this opportunity to sincerely congratulate you on your fine
achievement of reaching 1,000 points on Saturday, March 19, 1988. I would
have liked to have personally congratulated you after the game, however, I
didn't think it was the proper time since I knew how important the game was to
your team as well as the Whalers.

I am sure you will continue to pick up many more points as you move along, but
you can be very proud not only on what you have done, but being so consistent
in doing it.

The very best to you and your family. I will continue to pull for you, keep
it going.

Kind Regards,
HARTFORD WHALERS HOCKEY CLUB

Emile Francis
President and General Manager

acd

1986–87 ADAMS DIVISION CHAMPIONS

Always classy, Emile Francis sent me this letter after I scored my 1,000th career point.

Being on the ice at the Hockey Hall of Fame game was a blast, and a lot less stressful than…

Getting etched in glass at the Hockey Hall of Fame in 2002 was an indescribable honor.

But the absolute best part of all of it was getting to share it with my family—especially Mom and Dad.

Giving my acceptance speech.

Foam Lake's Hockey Heroes, Ted Hargreaves, Dennis Polonich, Bernie Federko and Pat Elynuik stand in front of the center panel of the Hockey Heroes sign. The sign is located along Highway 16 and also features photo panels of the four players. The dedication and unveiling ceremony was attended by nearly four hundred people.

Hockey Heroes Day in Foam Lake in July 2002.

Here I am doing television play-by-play with my old partner, Ken Wilson, between periods in an October 2002 game against the Predators in St. Louis.

(Bill Greenblatt UPI Photo Service/Newscom)

It was an honor to unveil my statue on November 1, 2003.
(UPI/Bill Greenblatt/Newscom)

Here is my family with Emile Francis after my Hall of Fame induction ceremony. From left: Bernadette, me, Emile, Jordy, Drew, and Dusty.

Me and Bernadette enjoying a Cardinals game at Busch Stadium in 2014.
(UPI/Bill Greenblatt/Newscom)

In 2017, I had the unbelievable honor of playing in the Winter Classic alumni game in front of a sold-out Busch Stadium. I can honestly say that even with all the hype it got, it was much more than I could've ever anticipated.

(Photo by Jimmy Simmons/Icon Sportwire via AP Images)

The All-Star Game on February 9, 1988, was very solemn without Barc, but it was a special time for the great hockey fans in St. Louis. We got to enjoy the festivities leading up to the game with our son Jordy, who was only six at the time. They had a little pregame ceremony and Jordy and Brian's son, Shawn, got to spend some time on the ice playing a little hockey with Gordie Howe. It was a thrill for Jordy, but it might have been a bigger thill for Brian and me to have our kids out there with Mr. Hockey. I wish that I had been playing in it, but honestly I wasn't deserving. That would have been some game to play in, too. Mario Lemieux put on the show of shows—three goals and three assists—and he scored the game-winner in overtime for a 6–5 win for the Wales Conference.

Lemieux was one of the biggest stars in NHL history and it wasn't long afterward that the Blues would have one of their own.

On March 7, 1988, Ron Caron pulled off the blockbuster trade, sending Rob Ramage and Rick Wamsley to Calgary for Brett Hull. When we first heard about it, we were thinking, *Here we go again!* Ron had already traded our best right winger, Joey Mullen, to Calgary and now we're dealing our best defenseman, Ramage, to the Flames. Rammer played over half the game every night, and when Brian was hurt, Rammer wore the "C." He was a huge part of our team.

Trades are part of the business and we understood that we had no control over it, but we had heard what others were hearing. We were getting Bobby Hull's son, but we had heard a lot of bad things about Brett, too, that's he's lazy and everything else. But as always, it was out of our hands, so like everyone else we gave Brett the benefit of the doubt. It didn't take long for him to win us over.

I remember the first game he played was in Toronto. I played with him a little bit and watching him shoot the puck, you knew he could score and that he did. He scored five goals in his first five games. He was a wonderful kid and had that dashing smile. He was respectful of all of us and very respectful of our great game. Yes, he was Bobby Hull's son, but he didn't stick that in anyone's face. He was going to make it on his own and you could see he had the skill to do it. We didn't know what to expect, but Ron Caron had made this deal thinking that Brett Hull was going to be the future of the Blues, and as it turned out, he was damn right!

In the last two months of that season, Brett's career with the Blues was just taking off and Brian Sutter's was coming to an end. Brian had a different role after the injury and Jacques Martin wasn't playing him as much as he'd been used to. He put Brian on the checking line and Brian hated that. He only scored 15 goals that season, but I was so glad he was able to score No. 300 in his career. We had spent a lot of time together both on and off the ice. I'd played a big part in his career and he had played a big part in mine. I knew that meant a lot to him and I was extremely happy for him.

A couple of days after Brian got to 300 goals, I picked up my 1,000th career point, on March 19, and strangely enough, it was against Hartford again. Both my 300th goal and my 1,000th point were against Lutey and Mr. Francis. I became only the 22nd player in NHL history to reach 1,000 points (though I certainly received much less notoriety than the 21 before me). Mr. Francis, who I've said countless times is the classiest man of all time, sent me the nicest letter of congratulations. Meanwhile, I wanted to do something special with the puck, so I decided to give it to Dan Kelly, whose great voice had been such a big part of my career. Mom and Dad had even heard him call my goals listening to KMOX back in Saskatchewan, so Bernadette and I decided to give the puck to Dan Kelly with the inscription, "Thanks, Dan, you've called them all. Hopefully many more!"

I finished the season with 20 goals and 89 points and ended up leading the Blues in scoring again. How's that for not being able to play anymore? It was the ninth time in 10 years that I led the team in scoring, and of the 12 years I played in St. Louis, excluding the year that I got called up, I was either first or second on the team in scoring. I was doing what I was supposed to do, being consistent, which is what Mr. Francis and Barclay had always wanted.

We finished second in the Norris Division, and after losing to Toronto in the first round of the playoffs the year before, Ron Caron was threatening in the newspapers that he would blow up the team if we lost in the first round again. I laughed. Blow things up? Hell, he did that every year. Both Brian and I blew it off. He could say what he wanted, but we weren't going to worry about that. We got paid to win and that's what we wanted to do. We were playing Chicago in the first round and we had never beaten the Blackhawks in a playoff series before, losing all four times we had met them in our history. We were confident, but we were so inconsistent on defense without Rammer that we didn't know how it would go. The Hawks could score, so everything had to be tight-checking in order to shut them down. We played the series perfectly. We got good goaltending, Tony Hrkac had a four-goal game in Game 4, and we beat the Hawks in five games.

There is nothing like beating Chicago in any sport when you are from St. Louis, so everyone cherished that moment. But that win created some drama because it set up a second-round series against Detroit and Jacques Demers. The drama didn't last long, though. It was as anti-climatic as it could have been, as the Wings outplayed us terribly and we lost the series 4–1. I did not play well in the playoffs, finishing with two goals in 10 games that year. I was the guy that the other team checked, and Detroit checked well. But as always, I had a job to do and I didn't do it, so I blamed myself. I had always found a way to come through, but not this time. I felt, though, that the Red Wings were the better team and we got beat by the better team. Losing to Jacques Demers may have been a nasty thing for Ron Caron, but it really didn't matter to me. Jacques was a good friend and I respected him as a coach. He was good for the team in Detroit and that's why they were winning.

The loss put Jacques Martin on the hot seat after just two seasons. Ron Caron was adamant that he was going to blow up the team if we lost in the first round, but we didn't lose. However, after losing in the second round, he fired Jacques and none of us were that surprised. After the turmoil the franchise went through with Harry Ornest, we were trying to sell hockey in St. Louis. And Jacques didn't help; he just had no charisma. And even though we won that series against Chicago, when you're trying to sell the game, it wasn't going to work with Jacques.

Brian might have been the happiest guy to see Jacques fired. He was definitely not a fan of Jacques. He had always been the go-to guy, but under Jacques he wasn't even on the power play. Brian had lost a step, yeah, and he was getting older, but he was pissed off because he wasn't playing as much as he thought he should have been playing. Brian had pride in himself, so I would have never blamed him, because Jacques had done the same with me.

Ron also came out and said that Jacques didn't do enough with the young talent that we had. I guess if there is any defense for Jacques, it's that I don't know who this young talent was that Ron was talking about. Keith Osborne was our first-round pick in 1987. Did anybody ever hear of him? We didn't really have the slew of young talent that Ron thought we had. Ron always thought we were a much better team than we were. Even in 1986, when we went to the Conference Semifinals, if you look at our roster, we weren't as good as Calgary. Either way, that was Ron's reasoning for firing Jacques. Jacques felt the reason they fired him was because he was a quiet guy and not many successful coaches in the NHL are quiet guys. But he was gone, we were glad, and now the Blues were in search of a new coach.

I remember going in for my end-of-the-year meeting and I got called into an office by Jack Quinn and Mr. Caron. They looked at me and asked, "Do you think Brian would like to coach?" I really couldn't answer that question. Brian and I had many conversations in our time together, but we were players and never discussed whether either of us ever wanted to be a coach at some point in time. He had the personality of a coach—Brian liked to be in control of things all the time. In the last two or three years of his career, it became apparent that his desire was to be in management. He wouldn't admit it, but he would always stay after practice to talk to the coaches, so he wasn't fooling any of us, he was posturing for that. But I didn't know if he would take it.

It was pretty evident to me during the conversation that the Blues felt Brian was not capable of playing anymore because of his injuries. They told me that they had run the idea past Brian, but they wanted me to convince him that this was the right thing to do. Brian was my best friend, so I didn't mind talking to him about it.

When I got home, I went over to his house and sat down with him. He didn't like the idea, and in fact he was dead set against it. Brian thought he could still play. He played the game hard-nosed all the time and his body took a lot of abuse and it was breaking down. He was hurt and he had missed a lot of games. But it's very frustrating as a player, for all of us, when you start losing your step or your skill. I couldn't tell him that he couldn't play anymore, and I didn't do that, but I did tell him that he had a bad shoulder and his knee was bothering him. I said, "Brian, for 12 years now you've always played the game like you're 250 pounds. Guys are bigger and stronger and you haven't changed your mentality. You want to fight everybody and you can't do that. Unless you can change your game, why would you want to continue to play?"

This was also an opportunity of a lifetime to coach the Blues. My whole thing to him was, "Brian, at 31 years old, you are being offered a head coaching job in the National Hockey League. I mean that's unheard of. Once they hire somebody else, this may never come up again." I said, "Who in the NHL is ever going to get offered the head coaching job on the team they're playing for without going to the minor leagues to coach first, without any coaching experience at all?" Plus, they were offering him the same amount of money that he was going to make if he kept playing. He was making at least $250,000, so he was probably going to be one of the highest-paid coaches in the league. To me, it was a no-brainer. I don't know if I persuaded him, or what exactly drove him to the decision, but he finally accepted the job, and when he took the job he was very happy. I didn't know it at the time, but everything was about to change between us. Our days of being best friends were coming to an end.

Bernadette and I came back from our lake house in Saskatchewan in mid-August. Out oldest son, Jordy, was now in school, so we came back earlier than usual. Now remember, we still lived across the street from the Sutters, so we assumed that everything was going to be like it always was. But right from the start of training camp, Brian was so different. He was management and I was a player. To him that couldn't mix. There would be no friendly relationship anymore. All of these years we had always ridden to the rink in the same car together, but not anymore. I understand as a coach you have to get there before the players, so that wasn't unusual, but he told his wife that she couldn't ride with my wife anymore to the games. When Judy told Bernadette that Brian wouldn't allow it, Bernadette was dumbfounded. They were best friends and our kids were best friends. What a change! Brian was the boss and he had to be the guy in control. I couldn't believe how quickly he forgot about being a player. He had played with all of us, but that didn't matter because it became all business.

It was even clearer that it was all business with Brian when the story surfaced that Dougie Gilmour was facing sexual allegations. We didn't know anything about it until it came out, so it was a shock to all of us. This was such a sensitive issue and we understood that the Blues management wasn't going to give us any details—they just told us that there were some issues going on. We had to ask questions behind the scenes like anybody else. I remember at the March of Dimes golf tournament, Jack Quinn approached me and made it clear that they needed our support. Dougie denied it, so of course we were going to be supportive of him. There was no proof of this and we didn't believe it for a second. He was a great guy and a true friend of all of ours.

But these were serious allegations. Whatever was going on behind the scenes we weren't privy to, but it sure looked like he was going to get traded. I don't know how long they had known about the accusations, but the decision came quickly that indeed they were going to move him. The story broke at the start of training camp and by the end of camp, the deal for Dougie was done. A week after the lawsuit was filed, they sent him to Calgary in a seven-player trade. We gave the Flames Dougie, Mark Hunter, Steve Bozek, and Michael Dark and we got Mike Bullard, Craig Coxe, and a prospect named Tim Corkey, who remained just that—a prospect.

I remember when they announced the trade, Dougie and his wife, Robyn, lived right off Clarkson Road in Chesterfield, not far from our house. The evening after the trade was announced, Brian and I rode over there to say goodbye to him. We had a beer with Dougie and when we left their house, I'll never forget getting in the car and driving back home. We were both real quiet. It was an extremely challenging time for the entire organization.

As it turned out, all charges were dropped, but we really took a step backward. When you deal a guy like Doug Gilmour, who ended up becoming a Hall of Fame hockey player, our team was not nearly as good. But how many times had I seen this done in the past?

From that moment on, I didn't talk to Brian much. He called me into his office about three days before the start of the season and asked me to be the captain. He said, "You're the best guy for the job. You've been here forever and the guys respect you. The fact that you and I are close, we can still carry on a relationship as a coach and a player. Being the captain, we can still talk." I very much appreciated what he had to say, but before accepting the great honor, I wanted to talk to Bernadette about it and to sleep on it. I went home and of course Bernadette said that this was a no-brainer. I agreed, but I thought about it all night. I had always thought of myself as a leader on the team, so of course I should accept the honor. The next morning, October 4, 1988, I proudly became the 10th captain in Blues history. I wanted no fanfare with it. Just have the "C" on my sweater for the first game.

Two days later, the season started, the "C" was on my sweater, and Brian never really spoke to me again. He told me that we were going to talk and discuss situations, but that never happened. All of a sudden I couldn't question anything he had to say or do, and to make it worse, he made me a left winger. Losing Dougie in the trade had already hurt us up the middle and now he took me out of the middle because he said he needed a left winger. That made no sense to me. I was having another slow start, but that wasn't surprising. The older I got, the harder the beginning of the season was. But four games into the season you're going to play me at left wing on the checking line?

Our fourth and fifth games of the season were back-to-back in Detroit and Pittsburgh. The checking assignment the first night was Steve Yzerman's line and then it was Mario Lemieux's line the next night. I'm not pointing fingers at any one of us on the checking line, but our plus-minus was −10 in those two games: −5 in Detroit and −4 in Pittsburgh. It was like, *What the fuck? I'm a checker now? Evidently, not a very good one.*

It was a tough first month. I didn't score my first goal until the 10th game of the season, and I can honestly say at that point, I still hadn't had even a casual conversation with Brian. That finally happened on November 17 and there was a reason for it. The Blues had gone 16 years without winning a game at the Spectrum in Philadelphia and both Brian and I had been part of that dubious stat for 12 of those years. Obviously, the Flyers had some real good teams during those years, but it seemed that no matter how good or bad we played, we just couldn't win at the Spectrum. It was the only building that Brian and I had never won a game in. Well, that day, for whatever reason, maybe it was the law of averages, we beat the Flyers 3–1. I scored two of the goals and was even the first star, so it was a momentous day. After the game, Brian came in and punched me, like he always punched everybody. Then he hugged me and he said, "We did it! We beat the Flyers in Philly!" It was extremely weird.

After the win in Philadelphia, we traded Mike Bullard for Peter Zezel. Bullard, who had just come in the trade for Gilmour, was coming off a great year in Calgary the year before, with 48 goals and 103 points in 79 games. But with us, he had just four goals and 16 points through 20 games and it just seemed that he and Brian didn't see eye-to-eye. Brian was trying to play Hullie and Bullie together and it wasn't clicking either, so they made the trade to try and find a compatible centerman for Hullie.

So now we had Cliff Ronning, Ricky Meagher, Tony Hrkac, Peter Zezel, and me, but Brian still had me playing on left wing for the benefit of the team. Every game that went by, though, it became clearer that I wasn't a winger. It's hard to make a left winger out of somebody that has played center his whole life. As captain of the team, I had to keep a positive approach, but I tried to tell him that the experiment should be over. He just ignored it, which made me start to think that he was enjoying my troubles.

It finally got to a boiling point. We lost 5–2 to Chicago on December 11 and 4–3 in New Jersey two nights later, dropping us one game below .500, and that was the last straw for me. I was so distraught that I bought a case of beer, stormed up to his room and said, "Done. I'm not fucking playing left wing anymore."

I think I did most of the talking and he just listened, but I know we drank a lot of beer. I don't even recall what exactly I said, but he must have finally got the message, because he did start me at center two nights later when we came home to play Hartford. I was excited to be back in the middle and I always liked the challenge of playing against Lutey. But that night, something went dangerously wrong. I was in front of the Hartford net looking for a rebound, and as I went by the crease, Lutey kicked out his leg. I felt this sharp pain in my ankle, and all of a sudden lost control of my foot.

I got to the bench, and when I pulled back the tongue of my skate, it was covered in blood, and by the time I got into the locker room, my boot was full of blood. I had cut a tendon in my ankle.

As bad as it seemed, though, I was extremely lucky because it was only the tendon sheath that had been cut. If it had been cut all the way through, it could have been career-ending. Thankfully, I only missed 10 games.

My first game back was January 7, the same night that Dan Kelly was honored for receiving the Lester Patrick Award for his contributions to U.S. Hockey. Unfortunately, Dan was in the hospital battling lung cancer and he couldn't be there. The last game he called had been at the Arena on November 19, two nights after that big win in Philadelphia. Dan was different than Barc because when Barc was sick, he still came around when he felt good enough. But Dan didn't want to be seen the way he was, so after that game on November 19, we never saw him at the rink again. So the night before they were honoring Dan, NHL president John Ziegler Jr. went to the hospital to present him the award. That night, Dan also received notice that he had been selected for induction into the Hockey Hall of Fame, which was very deserving.

Dan was arguably the greatest hockey announcer of all time. It's interesting, coming to St. Louis, I never knew who Dan Kelly was. We had *Hockey Night in Canada*, so we knew Foster Hewitt and Danny Gallivan, but arriving here I didn't expect the Blues' play-by-play man to know hockey so well. Dan had been around the game a long time and they hired him to teach the game to the fans who were new to the sport in St. Louis.

When he would walk around with Mr. Francis it was like he was the assistant general manager, but it was more of a front. No one loved what they were doing more than Dan and we always gave him the respect. He deserved it, but we didn't really have a choice because when he was on the radio, he could make you the greatest player in the league or the worst player in the league. The one night in Philly that I mentioned earlier, the game before Jacques Demers scratched me against Washington, Dan made sure that everybody knew I was playing like horseshit. Dan didn't sugar-coat anything and good for him. If you had a bad game, he glared at you, and that was okay with me because I had a great relationship with Dan. Anytime we saw him out after a game, we made sure that we went over and said hello and bought him a drink.

It seemed unfair because first we lost Barc at age 46 and now Dan, 52, was dying. Why was this happening? Remember, Sid Salomon III, one of the original owners, had cancer, too. We hoped it was all coincidental, but honestly, we were all concerned that maybe there was something going on at the Arena that was causing this.

Dan finally succumbed to cancer on February 10, 1989. I remember the funeral at Ascension Catholic Church, and there were over 600 people at the service, including Scotty Bowman. Brian and I were honorary pallbearers. It was another sad day for the Blues' organization and another tough one for me. I always looked at Dan as being so special for my family. My folks couldn't watch me on TV a lot, unless there was a rare game televised on *Hockey Night in Canada*, but they were able to watch me play through Dan's eyes. I don't think anybody called a goal better than Dan Kelly, and he was involved in all 1,000 of my points, which is pretty amazing. I don't know how many announcers and players in NHL history could say that.

15

THE END IS NEAR

I COULDN'T HAVE imagined this at the time, but I didn't have many more goals left to score in a Blues uniform.

I scored 12 in the last two months of the 1988–89 season, including my last hat trick, on February 27, and finished with 22. I had 67 points in 66 games, which was second on the team behind Hullie. That was his first full season with the Blues and he had a big year with 41 goals and 84 points. I enjoyed playing with Hullie. He started the season on my wing and it was a learning process, like anytime with a new winger. Brett was young and raw, but no one could shoot the puck like he could. I'll never forget Hullie on the point on the power play. He had a quick release, but he was wild with it that first year.

I remember in Philly, I went to the front of the net and Hullie just wired one. As I turned, I saw it coming right by my head and it hit the glass. We went back to the bench and I said, "Hullie, when I'm going to the front of the net, you can't shoot the fucking thing that high, somebody is going to get hurt for fuck's sake."

He goes, "Yeah, yeah, sorry." So we got out next power play and I go back to the front of the net and I turn and the puck was coming right at me. I put my hand up in front of my head and the puck hit me in the laces of my glove. By the time I got back to the bench, I had a golf ball on the side of my wrist. If it would have hit me on the inside of my wrist, it would have broken it. Hullie said,

"Sorry, Bern!" That was just him. But you could see that he had something special.

As much as I give Brian shit for being bullheaded with me—and Hullie would say the same thing because Brian drove him crazy, too—I give Brian credit for understanding what he had in Hullie. You could see that if you could corral his talent, he was going to be really special. Of all the players that I played with, Hullie's release was better than anybody. Joey Mullen had the best balance, Hunts was a hard-nosed guy that went to the front of the net, and Babs was an overpowering shooter. But Hullie could release the puck in stride from anywhere on the ice. I would have loved to have had the chance to play with him for a few more years. I don't know if I would have been able to keep up because he was so much younger, but it would have been fun.

We finished the season second in the Norris Division and beat Minnesota in the first round of the playoffs in five games, setting up a second-round series against Chicago. We split the first two games in St. Louis, then lost Game 3 in Chicago to fall behind 2–1 in the best-of-seven series. On the off day before Game 4, we had practice at the University of Illinois-Chicago. Ron Caron wanted to talk with the team before practice, so he kicked all the coaches out of the locker room and gave this motivational speech that was the worst fucking thing I've ever heard in my life. It was all negative, belittling every one of us. He was dancing around like a chicken with his head cut off and went through this spiel for 10 or 15 minutes, and when he walked out, I knew that we were done. I looked into the eyes of everyone in the room and I could see the disgust. Not surprisingly, we lost the next two games to lose the series in five games, and a roller-coaster season was over.

We were finished, but a lot of the guys in St. Louis were paying close attention to the last couple of rounds of the Stanley Cup playoffs. That's because Calgary, thanks to a big influx of former Blues, won the Presidents' Trophy for the most points in the league during the regular season and had a good shot to win the Stanley Cup. They did, beating Montreal in Game 6 at the Forum to win their first-ever Cup. The running joke in the hockey world was that Ron Caron should have received a ring for all his trades to the Flames. They would have never been there if not for future Hall of Famers Joe Mullen and Doug Gilmour, defensive stalwart Rob Ramage, solid right winger Mark Hunter, defenseman Ric Nattress, and backup goalie Rick Wamsley. Where would we have been if we had kept them? Wow!

I had the option year left on my contract and I always said that I would only play as long as I knew I could still play and contribute. I really felt that I could because after starting the previous year at left wing I had had a respectable second half after moving back to center, and I led the team in scoring in the playoffs with 12 points in the 10 games. So I felt that I had proved I could still play, and I felt like I had done my job as captain—being there for the guys. But as I had told everybody throughout my career, I only wanted to play for the Blues.

It was really important to me to play my entire career with the team that drafted me, and as I pointed out earlier, I'd taken less money to try and do that. I didn't even have an agent negotiate my last contract because there was no sense in having one when the team knew that I wanted to stay in St. Louis. But looking back, that was probably a bad idea. It's too volatile of a business and though I had been in the organization 13 years, I never once felt secure that I was going to be a Blue for the rest of my life because I'd seen too many of the guys I had become close with over the years forced to leave. But I had that option year left and I wanted to stay, and since no one ever played out their option, I went in and asked the team to give me one more guaranteed year and an option—two years total—and then I'd retire. I had just turned 33 and back then, you were old at 35.

I had my end-of-the-year evaluation meeting with Brian and basically we talked about nothing, and then I went upstairs to see Ron. I told him that I wanted to get my contract done before I went home for the summer, and since he knew that I didn't use an agent, he assured me that wouldn't be a problem. That was a Monday morning and he told me to come back on Friday morning and we'd get it done. I agreed that Friday morning was fine, but told him that I had a charity golf tournament Friday afternoon, so we'd have to finish it pretty quickly. He assured me that if I came in at 9:00 AM, we'd have plenty of time to get it done. So Friday morning I was at the Arena at 9:00 AM, sat down in Ron's office, and before I could even settle into my chair he told me that their hockey operations staff had conducted meetings during the past week and that as an organization they had decided that I no longer fit in the team's plans.

I looked at him in disbelief.

He told me they were going to trade me. Then he told me that he would like me to give them four or five teams that I would like to go to and come back here on Monday and we'd discuss what we were going to do.

It was like someone had shot me. I was like, "Really?"

He said, "Yeah."

I got up and he said, "Have a great weekend!"

I walked out of there saying, "Are you fucking kidding me? Have a great weekend?"

This meeting only took five minutes, so it was over by 9:05 AM, and the golf tournament didn't start until noon, so I couldn't go straight to the course like I'd planned. This was before cell phones, so I went home to tell Bernadette the news. I walked in the house and she was very surprised to see me and asked what I was doing back home. I said, "You're not going to believe this."

I told her the whole story and I'm sure that I was crying. I told her there was no way they didn't know where they were trading me. They knew. I didn't have a no-trade clause—they were saying that as a courtesy—but there was no way they wanted me to give them a list of five teams that I'd approve a trade to. How in the hell would I know anyway where I wanted to get traded to? I didn't want to get traded. In hindsight, I should have immediately called my old agent, Art Kaminsky. To this day when I think about it, I still can't believe I was such an idiot and did not call Art. But on the drive home, I knew there had to be more to this and I'd figured out that the Blues must've already had a deal in place. I told Bernadette that it had to be Detroit. I knew Jacques Demers too well and it had to be Detroit.

Believe it or not, I actually went to the golf tournament that day. I'll never forget because I got interviewed by one of the local TV stations and the first comment was, "Bernie, you're the true Blue. It's so nice that St. Louis is home and it's going to be your home for the rest of your career...." If the reporter had only known what I had just found out. I don't know why I played dumb. The only reason I can think of now is that if I didn't say anything about the trade, maybe the Blues might change their minds.

It was a miserable weekend. You might have thought that Brian would have come down the street to at least talk to me, but hell no. On Monday, I went back to the Arena, and sure enough, without ever asking for that list of four or five teams I'd accept a trade to, Ron informed me that indeed a deal was done. But he said that they couldn't tell me who it was until I agreed to and signed a new contract.

In hindsight, I should have stayed composed and dragged things out, but I was so pissed off that I couldn't wait to get this over with and get the hell out of that office. I called my longtime friend and money manager, Tom Wright, and asked him to help me get this contract done as soon as possible. Remember, I had a lot of weird things in my contract because my last deal had been with Harry Ornest. There were flights and cars and carpet, and all that stuff that had been bartered now had to be given a financial value so that we could come up with a salary for my new contract. I was not going to take less than I was making with all the "perks," so we had to translate those items into dollars. What was it all worth? We figured it as best we could, and whatever it came out to, we added that to my base salary and that's what my new team would have to pay me.

During those conversations, Jack Quinn was such an asshole. Actually, he always was. Ron was trying to be nice and professional about it, but Jack was Jack. He was bickering about everything and there was no pity about anything. In all my years of hockey, I have never encountered any one person with less class than Jack Quinn. The nickname we gave him was "Honest Jack" because he was so dishonest. Whenever you shook his hand, it was so clammy that you knew that whatever he was saying was not genuine. Everything he told you was a lie, especially anything to do with money.

Even if you did get a bonus check from him, it took forever to get it, and the reason was because it was in his drawer the whole time and he was waiting as long as he could before he had to give it to you. I have never met a man who was so chintzy. We always talked about how hard it was playing under the purse strings of Harry Ornest, but everything had to run through Jack, so maybe it was him after all. But this time it was even worse because he was sticking it to me and loving it, and what I couldn't understand was why Jack was even concerned about the contract—the Blues weren't even going to be paying it.

We finally figured out how much all the extra stuff was worth and put it on paper, and we agreed to a one-year guaranteed deal with a one-year option, just like I wanted from the Blues. Jack said those were the only terms that the team trading for me would agree to. In hindsight, I should have asked for more years, even if I didn't want more years, just to be hard-nosed in negotiations. But I was so bitter that I said, "Let's just get this done and get me the fuck out of here." We looked over the contract and signed it. To me, there was no surprise as to where I was going—I was smart enough to figure that out on my own—and when they confirmed that it was Detroit, I learned that I was being traded to the Red Wings along with Tony McKegney for Adam Oates and Paul MacLean.

I was seething mad when I left the Arena because I couldn't believe it was happening. Ron Caron told me to stop by and see Brian on my way out, but by that time I didn't see the point.

Brian always swore that the only thing he was not in control of when he took the coaching job was me, that he was in charge of everybody else on the team, and that when it came to me, he had no say in what management decided. He stood by that, but I had a hard time believing it. He can deny as much as he wants that he was a part in the trade, but in my mind he absolutely had a say. For Ron Caron to tell me on Monday to come back on Friday and we'll get my contract done, and then tell me four days later that I was no longer in the plans—who changed the plans? Ron was the general manager, so obviously there was collective input. If Brian would have said, "Hey, you're not trading him," but he was all business. I had been instrumental in him becoming coach, but I guess it wasn't reciprocated.

I've never found out the way the trade really went down, but my take on the matter is that Jacques Demers probably called and offered Adam Oates, and if that is true, I'm not going to lie to you, it was a hell of a deal for the Blues getting Oates. But was there any principle here? I had been a loyal soldier for 13 years and had almost every individual record in the Blues' books. If they had come to me, explained the situation, and offered me an opportunity to rejoin the team later in my life, maybe I could have forced myself to understand. But all I have is my own speculation, and if that were not the case—Jacques Demers offering up Adam Oates—then I certainly think Brian was involved. You can ask any of the other guys, anybody who played with Brian, he didn't want any of us on his team. I can understand that. It's hard coaching someone that you played with and now all of a sudden you're giving them orders. I admit that it was a strange deal, but Brian didn't give a shit about me, he only gave a shit about his job. And after 13 years with the Blues, after I was so loyal to them, I had never felt so betrayed in all my life.

By the time I got home, the trade had been announced, so all of the TV camera crews were already outside my house. I agreed to do the interviews but it was extremely difficult. It was emotional and I had so much trouble holding back the tears that at one point I had to tell the cameras to stop rolling. There was so much bitterness in my heart and I am not that kind of person. I probably said some things that I shouldn't have said. I was pretty foolish to say that Detroit was a team trying to win and the Blues were not. I said I hoped to beat the Blues every time we played them. I was very one-sided, but that was obviously just human nature. It was funny, while they were interviewing me, Bernadette said the kids were playing outside and one of them asked Jordy, "Who did your dad get traded for?" When he said, "Adam Oates," Jordy's best friend, Shaun Sutter, Brian and Judy's son, started yelling, "Adam Oates sucks!" Then all the kids starting chanting, "Adam Oates sucks! Adam Oates sucks!" You gotta love the kids!

It was really hard on all of us. Bernadette and I were both distraught, totally distraught. We both thought that I was going to finish my career with the Blues. The kids were all born in St Louis and now Jordy was eight, Dusty was five, and Drew was two, and we thought they were going to grow up in St. Louis. It's amazing how that all blew up in one moment.

I dearly wanted to get out of town and away from all the stress, and I remembered that I hadn't used the plane tickets that were in my Blues contract the past three seasons. I got two business-class tickets to go anywhere in North America at the end of every year, and since I hadn't used any of them, they owed me six. In talking to Susie Mathieu, I found out her brother had a place in Maui and she said we could rent it, so we decided to go to Hawaii.

That was the best part of it. I called Jack Quinn's secretary and said, "We want to go to Hawaii on Friday." She tried to tell me that they needed more time to arrange the flights. I felt bad telling his secretary this because she was a great lady, but I said, "You tell Jack that it's part of my contract. You owe me six tickets. Business class. We're leaving Friday for Maui whether you like it or not." I had never called Mr. Quinn "Jack" before and it felt good. I should have always called him Jack, or something worse. Jack got all pissed off about the tickets, which made it so much better, but they did get it done. All of this transpired on a Tuesday, and I was on my way to Hawaii with my family by Friday. When we got back, it was like starting all over again.

16

JOINING THE
RED WINGS

WE HAD SO much to do and only a short summer to get it done. We put the house in St. Louis up for sale, and thankfully it sold quickly—as a matter of fact the first people that looked at it bought it. Bernadette and I left the kids with our parents and flew to Detroit to go house hunting. I had a phone conversation with Jacques Demers and he told me that he thought he was going to be the Red Wings' GM in the next couple of years and he wanted me to be part of his management team when I was done playing.

Jacques was a big deal in Detroit at that time. After leaving the Blues in 1986, he had taken the Red Wings to the Conference Finals in back-to-back seasons. He won the Jack Adams Award as the league's best coach two years in a row, becoming the first coach to do that since they started awarding the trophy in 1974. This was all good news, that I had somebody in Detroit who I trusted and who had plans for me.

We bought a house in Jacque's subdivision in Farmington Hills, and having him and Debbie close by helped a lot because we were going to a city that we knew nothing about. We held off the closing on our house in St. Louis until August, so that we could head back to Saskatchewan after finding a place in Detroit. But it was a hectic summer because we made an early exit from the lake to go back to St. Louis and get the house packed up. The reality of leaving St. Louis and all of our friends was now more difficult than we could imagine. Saying goodbye and not really knowing what the future held put a big knot in the stomach of both Bernadette and myself. We sent my car with the moving truck, and then the whole family jumped into our motorhome. There was a lot of sobbing on the eight-hour drive to Detroit.

As sad as we were to be leaving, a new adventure was kind of exciting, but we had a lot to learn. Detroit was a much bigger city than St. Louis and everything was foreign. We were taking new roads and freeways, going to Joe Louis Arena downtown and to the practice rink. This was Detroit, so we were asking ourselves, *Is it safe or not?* We were in a great area in the suburbs, but even the gas station down the road got robbed a couple of times, so that scared us. It was all so new and this never happened around us in Chesterfield. We just didn't know.

I was lucky because my teammates in Detroit were so welcoming. I knew Joey Kocur—he came to my hockey school in Yorkton as a kid—and I got to know more of the guys as I started skating with them before camp opened. Mr. and Mrs. Ilitch, the owners of the Red Wings, were wonderful people and they made me feel more comfortable right off the bat. And Jacques, of course, was so good to the team. With all my success in St. Louis, I had never had any local endorsements, and now all of a sudden, he's got me doing commercials and getting me a clothing deal, and even getting me a dealer car from one of the local car dealers.

But I couldn't stop thinking about Bernadette and the boys. She went from being the "Queen B" with the Blues for the last seven or eight years to being the new girl in town. Jordy and Dusty were in a new school and Drew was still a baby. One night, Jordy told her,

"I want to go back to St. Louis. I miss my friends." All she could do was hug him, cry a little, and say, "I want to go back there too." It was hard. As a family, it was really, really hard. But Bernadette was unflappable. She found the grocery stores, made sure the boys were comfortable at school and even got them signed up to play hockey at the nearest hockey rink in Southfield. As always, she was amazing.

Training camp started and it was really strange being out of my element. I was used to being in Regina or Peoria or wherever the Blues had their camp, and now I'm somewhere else. I remember we played a preseason game in Houston and just putting on that Red Wings' jersey for the first time, it was something that I never could have expected. The opportunity to put on an Original Six uniform was pretty special—I was wearing the same one that Gordie Howe wore!—but it felt weird.

Two nights before our opening game, Mr. and Mrs. Ilitch had a team dinner with all of the wives at Jacques Demers' restaurant, and it got even more bizarre. We were all enjoying a cocktail and then just before dinner, Jacques came in and said, "Mr. Ilitch wants to talk to all the players," so we all paraded into one of the banquet rooms. He was standing in front of the room, and in just a matter of a few minutes, he started blasting the players for the way they had been conducting themselves the past year off the ice. You have to understand that Bob Probert was in jail on drug-related charges and Petr Klima was possibly heading the same direction on drunken-driving accusations. It was clear Mr. Ilitch was sick and tired of the drugs and the drunken-driving charges. He paid everybody very handsomely and would have been be glad to pay everybody a lot more. But you knew if you screwed up, you were done.

He was extremely candid and very intimidating, and you could look around the room and see the fear in the guys' eyes. It was stern, but after all the stories I had heard, I actually thought it was a good thing he was doing. After Mr. Ilitch finished, we walked back in for dinner, sat down next to our wives, looked around, and all the booze that was on the tables just a few minutes ago was now gone. There was no liquor, no wine, anywhere. They gave us grape juice. Borje Salming and me, two of the new guys on the block who had thought we'd seen it all, just looked at each other and said, "Oh fuck, this is going to be a long fucking year."

My first regular season game without the Blue Note on my chest was October 5, 1989, in Calgary. I had worn No. 18 in training camp, but I switched to No. 42, which was my Blues No. 24 reversed, when the season started. No. 24 was Probert's number and unfortunately he was in jail. Jacques had asked me when I got there if I wanted No. 24, but I turned it down. Bob was scheduled to get out of jail in the spring, and if he was coming back to the team, I was the last person who wanted to be wearing his number.

At the morning skate, I had a conversation with Jacques and he kept telling me that he wanted me to do really well. He was the one that pushed for the trade, so obviously he wanted me to do well. There was a lot of pressure, but I kept reminding myself before the game, *You have a job to do. Who knows where this is going to go, but be the best you can be and everything will work out, like it always has in your career.* But even with those positive thoughts, I remember standing in front of the mirror in the Red Wings sweater and saying, "What the hell am I doing here?"

We were playing Calgary that night and that made it even more surreal for me because the Flames were getting their Stanley Cup rings from the year before and raising the banner before the game. Remember all those trades the Blues had made with Calgary? I looked across the ice and saw five of my former teammates being honored: Gilmour, Mullen, Nattress, Hunter, and Wamsley. As I was saying before, I felt great that I had been a staple for the Blues all of those years, but I was envious of those guys. They were the lucky ones going to Calgary and winning a Cup. It made me think that maybe being in Detroit was my opportunity to win the Cup, with the Red Wings. Maybe this was my destiny, maybe something great was going to happen out of all of this.

My debut with Detroit couldn't have gone any better personally, a four-point night with one goal and three assists. I did have a good game, but it didn't matter because we lost 10–7 to the Flames. I remember Jimmy Devellano, the GM of the Red Wings, saying the next morning, "Great game, Bernie!" That was nice of him but when you don't win, personal stats don't matter. You get paid to win and we didn't.

The first three games of the season were on the road and Steve Yzerman, who was only 24 years old at the time, was my roommate. Jacques wanted me with Stevie, which was good. He was a very nice young man, but very quiet. He probably thought I was crazy because I liked to have my beers. Jordy, who was really the only one of my boys who was old enough to know what was going on, became Stevie's biggest fan.

Whenever Jordy was off of school, he hung out with me in the locker room, and since Stevie was a right-handed shot and Jordy was, too, he would always get some sticks from him. It was so neat for him to take a real Yzerman stick out of the locker room and use it for practice and games. Jordy became a huge Red Wings' fan, but I think it was also because he had a disdain toward the Blues since they traded me. The boys really felt our anguish because it was a very traumatic experience for all of us. They were around when there were a lot of tears shed and I'm sure they heard a lot of swearing.

I was dreading my first trip back with Detroit to St. Louis on October 19, which was just eight games into the season. Of course coming back to the Arena was really, really difficult. There were signs in the crowd and just being there brought back so many memories. Jacques had me start that game, so there was a nice ovation and that was really special. But I didn't play much that night and didn't really deserve to anyway. I was way too nervous and it just didn't feel right. I think our guys understood how important the game was for me, and really came through, beating the Blues, 4–3. But I had no effect on the game whatsoever, and more than anything, I was just glad to get it over with.

After getting a goal and four points in my first game with Detroit, I didn't have a goal in the next 11 games. I don't know if there was a correlation, but the Red Wings ended up making a trade with Edmonton for Jimmy Carson in early November. I had been playing with Petr Klima and Shawn Burr on the second line, but with the addition of Carson, I was relegated to the fourth line and, after a few games, I became a healthy scratch.

Here I was, an old pro with almost 1,100 points in the league, and now I'm doing extra skating after practice because there's no room for me in the lineup. When they made the trade for Jimmy, who was a young, Detroit-born-and-bred boy and a really good player, I knew the writing was on the wall. I still believed in myself and knew I could play, but what do you do? It was especially hard on me because the Blues were having a hell of a year and Hullie and Oatsie were hitting it off right off the bat, which wasn't surprising. Oatsie was a helluva a player, and it probably helped him getting out of Detroit because Stevie played so much. I always wondered if Oatsie would have ever gotten the same chance with the Red Wings, or would he have been buried? That's why I always say, "It's destiny."

There weren't many magical moments that year in Detroit, but one will always be dear to me. It was the last game of the season, April 1, 1990, in Philadelphia, and it was No. 1,000 of my career. It was pretty remarkable because I played in 73 games that year and it put me right at 1,000 and that was not planned out. I had been a healthy scratch and I was hurt and missed a few games, and it just worked out that I reached that milestone in the last game of the year. I became only the 69th player in NHL history to play 1,000 games, and even though I did it with Detroit, this was a very defining moment. The Red Wings made it out to be a big deal. The trainer had me tape up six sticks—two for me including a backup, one for him and one for each one of my boys. I didn't know at that time what my future held, or if I'd play another game in my career, but I was so proud to achieve that goal because consistency and longevity is what I had always strived for, and on that day I felt fulfilled.

It wasn't a good year for me, but considering all the changes in my life and the limited amount of ice time, I felt like 17 goals and 57 points, which was third on the team behind Stevie and Gerard Gallant, was okay. But looking back on that season, the main regret I had is that I wish I wouldn't have been so vocal early in the season. A lot of things should have been said in that locker room and nothing was said. Stevie was not a talker, he led by example. He was always the first guy in the room lifting weights. Gerard and Mike O'Connell said more than anybody else, but not much. So I was the only one talking and only because Jacques had asked me to. He wanted me to be a leader and kept saying, "Bernie, I want you to be just like you were in St. Louis." So I did, but since I was new to the situation, I should have just taken a backseat for a couple of months and not said a word. Words count so much more when they come at the right time. In hindsight, that's what I should have done, but you live and learn.

I don't know that it would have mattered, however, because it was clear to me that Detroit had quit on Jacques. We'd come back and beat a team, and even though we won, there wasn't any excitement in the locker room, and that's when I knew it was bad. We were challenging for a playoff spot at the end of the year and we were right there, but you could see that there was no willingness to take it to the next level. They all knew if we didn't make the playoffs, Jacques was probably going to get fired. I'm not blaming the players, because when I was with the Blues we certainly weren't disappointed when Jacques Martin got fired. I wasn't disappointed when Leo Boivin got fired, or when Red got fired. Every coach has a shelf life and I think Jacques reached his with the Red Wings. So I understood the situation, but still it was hard.

Detroit relieved Jacques of his coaching duties right at the end of the season. But I was really happy for him when he became the head coach of the Montreal Canadiens and later went on to win the Stanley Cup in 1993. As expected, I received a phone call to come see the Red Wings' GM Jim Devellano. He brought me into his office and he could not have been any more professional, showing me nothing but respect for what I had tried to do with the Red Wings. He told me that they had experimented bringing in Borje and me and with it not working out, they were going in a different direction. He told me that I was not going to be part of the new direction, and that if I wanted, they would try trading me to another team. He also told me that if I chose to retire, they would honor the "option" year of my contract by paying in full. When he asked me if I'd like to go elsewhere, I immediately said no.

Bernadette and I had discussed the potential results of the meeting and we both knew that I'd had enough. As much as I would have liked to keep playing, I couldn't go through another year like I had just gone through. It wasn't worth it to move my family somewhere else for just one year. Darryl Sittler, the long-time Toronto Maple Leaf, did that at end the of his career, going to Philadelphia and then Detroit before retiring, and I just couldn't see myself doing that. Sure it would have been wonderful going out in a blaze of glory with the Stanley Cup in hand, skating a victory lap around the ice, but that was now just a fantasy. The reality was I went home and confirmed with Bernadette that I was done.

Although most of my experience had been a downer in Detroit, it had been nice to see a different organization and how it was run. Mr. Ilitch, goodness gracious, how much more could an owner care? In my time in St. Louis I had seen four different ownership groups, and none of them treated the players as good as the Ilitches. The Wings had no idea how good they had it.

One night we played Los Angeles in Detroit and Gretzky had just gotten traded, so it was his first trip to Joe Louis Arena with the Kings and the place was packed. That was a game where I wish I had a stopwatch on the bench because Stevie must have played 45 minutes. I don't think he came off the ice the first seven or eight minutes of the game. We went from power play to penalty kill to power play and he just stayed out there. I'm positive that I didn't play more than five or six minutes the entire game. We were down early and mounted this crazy comeback, and Stevie scored a goal from a crazy-bad angle with about a minute left and we beat Gretzky and the Kings something like 6–5. The crowd at Joe Louis was going wild and the players were pumped when we got back to the locker room. In the middle of the room there was always a cart with sodas and waters, and all of a sudden, Mr. Ilitch comes down the hall, runs around the corner, kicks the cart, and the drinks go flying everywhere.

I'm like, *Holy shit, what is going on?* Mr. Ilitch was just elated, telling us that it was the best game he had ever seen and the best ever comeback since he owned the team. Then he proceeds to tell us that the next morning there would be a check for $5,000 in each one of our stalls. Can you believe that? He gave us $5,000 each! Counting the coaches that was over $100,000! I felt guilty because I might have played a half dozen shifts tops, but that was Mr. Ilitch. On Christmas morning, ding-dong, the doorbell rings, a big-screen TV from Mr. and Mrs. Ilitch. It was amazing!

I had no control or choice in my move to Detroit, but I took it in stride thinking it was a career move. Jacques was going to be the GM and I was going to be part of his staff. But that's how fragile a career move can be, because it didn't turn out to be a career move. It turned out to be a career-ender. How do you know at the time? I've often wondered why that happened to me, why I couldn't have finished my career in St. Louis? I don't know. Destiny again, I guess.

17

POST-PLAYING CAREER

I DON'T KNOW how news of me retiring leaked because I I hadn't officially announced it at the time, but Jacques Demers probably had something to do with it. On the same day that I met with Jimmy Devellano, I got a call from Allan Cohen, the general manager at KMOV Channel 4 in St. Louis, asking if I'd be interested in working with Zip Rzeppa and Doug Vaughn in their sports department. Bernadette and I had already made a decision to move back to St. Louis, knowing that it was my best chance at finding another career. At 34 years old, and even after 14 years in the NHL, I hadn't made enough money playing hockey to retire and live happily ever after like they do today. I was still young, so I had to find something to do to support my family.

We could have gone back to Canada, but after playing for the Blues for 13 years, St. Louis was the best place for us. We loved the city and the boys were all born there, so it made sense. I was going to be paid by Detroit for the whole year anyway, but this offer from Channel 4 would allow me to get my feet wet in television and get acclimated in the business community, so why not? Fortunately, the interview went well and in mid-May I agreed to take the job.

I had no doubts that my playing career was over, but as it turned out, the door wasn't totally shut yet. I loaded up Bernadette and the boys, who were now three, six, and nine, in the motorhome, and drove back to our lake house in Saskatchewan.

In early July, we were on a trip in the mountains in Western Canada when I got a message from our old assistant GM in St. Louis, Dennis Ball. Dennis had got a call from Boston GM Harry Sinden, and he relayed the message that Harry wanted to talk to me. I called Mr. Sinden and he asked if I had any interest in playing for the Bruins. This kind of threw me into a spin. Sure some part of me knew I could still play, but it had been such a difficult year in Detroit. I told him I was interested, but not if it was just for one season. If they would give me a chance to prove myself for a couple of years, I would consider it. Mr. Sinden said he was just putting out a feeler and that he first had to clear it with Mike Milbury, who was coaching the Bruins at the time, and then he'd get back to me. A few days went by and I never heard from him, so their decision was obvious. That was it, and I was very comfortable about it. In mid-August, my official notice of retirement went out.

Who would've ever thought that a boy from Foam Lake, Saskatchewan, who didn't even play hockey for a few years because the rink in town burned down, would spend 14 seasons in the NHL? I finished with 369 goals and 1,130 points in exactly 1,000 games. When I retired, I was 16th all-time in scoring in the history of the league and 13th in assists. When you're playing, you don't really think about any of those things, you never concentrate on any of that personal stuff. But after it's all said and done, yeah, those statistics make you proud. They're just numbers, but for me, it meant that I was doing my job.

One of the stats that I was most proud of, and I didn't even know about it until my last season in Detroit, was the fact that I was the first player in NHL history to have 50-plus assists in 10 straight seasons. You know how I found out about that? We were playing a real important game at the end of the year in Minnesota, and it was the trivia question on the Jumbotron. I was sitting on the bench during the period and the trainer poked me and said, "Did you know that?"

I said, "What?" I looked up and the question and answer were on the board. That's a remarkable stat, and I had no idea, but that's how I found out. It was actually quite flattering that I had done that before anybody else and I was certainly proud of that.

I have never felt that I was truly respected for what I accomplished in the NHL. I finished among the Top 10 scorers in the league eight times in my career and only went to two All-Star Games. Heck, I didn't even receive my NHL "milestone award" for playing 1,000 games until four or five years after the fact. I was at an alumni golf tournament in Banff one summer, talking about it with somebody from the league offices. After checking their records, they realized their mistake and they ended up sending the award to my house. They actually sent two awards, including one for 600 assists, which I didn't even know existed.

It's funny, too, in Detroit they did a great job of recognizing me the day I played in my 1,000th game, but because it was the last game of the regular season in a season we didn't make the playoffs, and because that ended up being my final season, there was never a chance to have a little ceremony or anything like that. Dave Lewis, who was an assistant coach with Detroit the year I was there, finished his playing career with the Red Wings, too, but there were still some games left in the season after he reached 1,000 games. They had a ceremony for him and Mr. Ilitch gave him a gold Rolex.

I thought maybe I was going to get one of those, but that wound up being wishful thinking.

I also never got the opportunity to play for Team Canada, which always hurt. I played against the same people that everyone else was playing against in the NHL and put up as good of numbers as anybody, but I never got the same opportunity. The World Championships were in May every year and the only way that you could play was if your NHL team didn't make the playoffs, and since the Blues were usually in the postseason, it wasn't always possible.

The one time Team Canada asked, I couldn't go, and then they never asked again. It was 1979, my third season in the NHL, and the Blues weren't going to make the playoffs. Brian and I got a call from Team Canada, and they wanted us to go play in Russia. But both Brian and I were in the last years of our contracts with the Blues, and we knew we'd be taking a risk if we got injured at the World Championships. We met with Mr. Francis and he told both of us that we would be getting new contracts, but he also said, "Hey, guys, if you get hurt, we don't insure that." So Brian and I both said no to Team Canada and I believe that Brian and I may have gotten a bad rap for that.

The contract reason was certainly legitimate, and as it turned out, it wouldn't have mattered if I'd said yes, because I broke my wrist a week later and couldn't have played anyway. But that's one of my biggest disappointments, that I never got a chance to wear a Team Canada sweater for the World Championships or anything. Of all the numbers that I put up and things I was able to accomplish, I felt very slighted to not have ever represented my country.

Obviously, there were a lot of great players playing center for Team Canada, but it would have been nice to at least get a chance to go to the tryout camp.

But now my career was over and I was adjusting to post-hockey life. The boys were all young. Jordy and Dusty were back in school, Drew was in preschool and Bernadette was back with all her friends, and thankfully I had a job that was going to keep me close to the NHL and the Blues. Financially, we were fine, but it was still a little scary going from a nice NHL salary, which was going to run out in a year, to the unknown. We were lucky to be able to rent Greg Paslawski's house because he was playing in Philadelphia, so this gave us time to shop around and see if we could find a new house or even a lot to build a new home.

It was great to be back in St. Louis and around the team again, even though I had left under stressful circumstances. I don't think there were ever any fences that needed to be mended with the organization. The only problem I had was Jack Quinn. Mike Shanahan was the new owner and he was a wonderful and genuine guy. I only played one year under his ownership, so I really didn't get to know him that well, but he was local and he truly cared about making the Blues into Stanley Cup champs. The players all loved him. I have no idea why Mr. Shanahan allowed Jack Quinn to remain in charge, but I didn't have to deal with him anymore, so I guess it didn't matter.

Well, except for one occasion.

In December that year, Jack Quinn called me and asked if they could have the honor of retiring my jersey. I wish it would have been someone else that would have asked. It just didn't seem sincere coming from him, but of course it's the honor of a lifetime, so I agreed and they set the date to hang my No. 24 from the rafters for March 16, 1991. The Blues flew my parents and Bernadette's parents in from Saskatoon for the ceremony. I asked Jack to fly my brothers in, too—what a stupid question that was!—but of course he declined, so I did it on my own expense. It almost felt like it was something they felt they had to do instead of something they wanted to do. They had a little pregame reception in the executive offices with our closest friends, but it seemed weird. Maybe it was just me, unable to get over the hurt.

But on the ice before the game, it was a wonderful event. Mr. and Mrs. Shanahan gave Bernadette a beautiful necklace and presented me with my jerseys, which had been encased in wooden frames. This was a full house at the Arena ready for a Blues-Blackhawks game, and when they raised the banner to the roof, it was so loud and crazy that it was very emotional for us as a family.

Afterward, we had a private reception that Bernadette and I planned at Sportsman's Park for family, friends, and, of course, the alumni. There were well over 100 people, but strangely enough, Brian Sutter was one of the no-shows. Yes, the team had an afternoon game in Chicago the next day, but there were tons of flights to Chicago in the morning. I had been a big part of his jersey retirement night back in December of 1988, and of course just all the hours that we'd spent together, and I just didn't understand why it was more important to travel with the team to Chicago after the game than come to our special party. Were we surprised? Hell no. But to me, when you think about it, it just shows you what type of person he really is. As much as everybody talks about how great a guy he is and what a competitor he was, for him to not come to the reception, that was bullshit.

At the time, though, I was trying to put that situation in the past and continue my transition into the real world working at KMOV. It wasn't a lot of money, but again I was getting paid by the Red Wings, so I could take my time seeing if I liked it. I did some interviews and the game recaps, so it was a great opportunity. But to be honest, the job was kind of difficult because I still felt some hurt inside from getting traded by the Blues. I couldn't take out my frustrations on the team I was now covering, though, so I got over it. There was some talk about me becoming a sports anchor, and I thought about it, but Bernadette and I decided that if the offer came, I would turn it down. The idea of working 5:00, 6:00, and 10:00 PM, after being away all of those nights during my career, I didn't want to do that.

We also decided that it was time to build the home of our dreams. Bernadette and I had always lived our lives pretty modestly. That's the way we had been raised and that was our nature. Sure we had nice things, but we were never lavish and now more than ever it was important not to overspend. But Bernadette had always wanted to buy a house in this one particular subdivision in Chesterfield and I never thought I'd be able to afford it. However, with lots of stickhandling and help from our financial manager, we were able to find a way to make it work. Bernadette couldn't have been happier, especially when she found out that there were lots of other boys the same ages as ours in the neighborhood. We moved out of Pazzer's place and into our new home on February 15, and the neighborhood was wonderful, everything that we could have asked for.

I use the word "destiny" again here because little did we know that moving into that subdivision was going to mold my post-playing life. We had been in the house just a few weeks when we went to Sportsman's Park after a game one night, and that's where I met Dale Turvey, who still today, 25 years later, remains my best friend. Dale and his wife, Susan, were season-ticket holders and they came over and introduced themselves, saying they lived just three houses up the street from us.

We casually got to know them and ran into them a number of times after games, and Dale and I really hit it off. Early that summer, he dropped by the house and asked me to play golf over at his club. His wife, Susan, and his daughters were out of town for a few days, so after golf, Bernadette and I asked him to stay for dinner and a cocktail. Susan was gone three or four days and I bet Dale had dinner with us every night. He was always in a great mood and it was so nice to have a friend who had his own business and wasn't involved in hockey. When the Blues were out of town, I had a lot of time to kill, so I would go to his office, which was a few minutes from our house, and bullshit with him. Soon, it became almost a daily thing and usually we'd stop for happy hour on the way home.

There wasn't much stress in my life. The boys were growing up. They were doing great in school and playing hockey, and with my extra time I was able to get involved coaching them. Jordy was a pretty good player. In 1994, he was part of the pee-wee team that went to the prestigious Quebec International Pee-Wee Tournament in Quebec City. Watching Jordy play in the Colisee in a Blues jersey with his name and No. 24 on the back made me so proud and brought back so many memories. I understood right then and there how exciting it must have been for my parents every time they watched me play. He was one of the better players on the team, but my folks had never put any pressure on me, so I never put pressure on him, or any of my boys, to follow in my footsteps. It was enough pressure for Jordy just having the last name "Federko" on the back of his jersey. I just wanted them to have fun and decide on their own what their futures would be.

The boys were playing at Creve Coeur when we met a guy named Carl Tisone, who had kids that played with Jordy and Dusty. Carl and I had some conversations about how hard it was for the kids to get a lot of ice time. For the amount of them who were now playing hockey in St. Louis, there just weren't enough ice rinks to fill the need. There were five rinks spread out all over the county, so we had to travel from rink to rink to get as much ice time as possible. Carl wanted to change that and financially he could. He felt that there should be a rink out west where we all lived.

It took some time, but in 1996, the double ice rink in Chesterfield opened and we had the great pleasure of helping start the Chesterfield Hockey Association. It was great having ice so close to home and made life so much easier for all the local hockey parents. There were a number of parents like us who wanted to get the kids some extra competition to grow their hockey skills.

We decided that we were going to join the AAA hockey league, but before we could be a charter member, we had to prove to them that we were committed. So we had no home games the first season, traveling every weekend to cities like Chicago, Detroit, Cleveland, and Indianapolis. It was great to travel and spend that time with Jordy, and I was lucky that my schedule allowed me to help out.

I never wanted to be the head coach, though. As a parent, I don't think you should be coaching your kid. I know a lot of guys did, but if I would have been the head coach, I would have found a way to play my son either more or less than he should have played, and I didn't want to be in that situation, so I was fine being an assistant. I did everything I could to help in practice, but I didn't change lines or anything like that. I basically just stood behind the bench, helped, and talked to the kids when they came off their shifts, and, not surprisingly, bitched at the referees.

Jordy was progressing more and more as a player as the competition got better. He had really good hands and he could shoot the puck. His skating was not great, but neither was mine, or at least that's what everybody told me. He had his good games and bad games, but he was good enough after AAA to play two years of Junior B with the Junior Blues.

When he graduated from Chaminade Prep, he didn't get a hockey scholarship, but he was able to get a tryout at Union College in New York and made the team. That was fantastic for a walk-on and for a kid from St. Louis. He didn't play much his freshman year, but his sophomore year he won the award for most improved player on the team. He seemed to like it, but when he came home for Christmas his junior year, he told me that he didn't want to play anymore. I told him that was totally up to him, but if he was going to quit, it was going to be at the end of the season, not the middle of the year. He had made a commitment to the team and you don't leave halfway through the season. He agreed with that, finished the season, and even won an award for the highest grade-point average on his team.

Dusty, our middle son, loved hockey, but he got tall too quickly and, when it came to skating, he was just a little awkward. We used to laugh at him because he was so double-jointed and his body and would bend in all directions when he fell down. It just wasn't his best sport. He played all the way through minor hockey at Chesterfield and then at Chaminade, but gave up on organized hockey when he was a freshman. We had joined Meadowbrook Country Club when he was about 12 years old and he really got into golf. That became his real sport and he went on to receive a scholarship to play Division I golf at St. Louis University.

Drew, our youngest, was always one of the smaller kids when he played at Chesterfield. So while Dusty got tall too quickly, Drew was the opposite. He was the little guy who didn't grow fast enough, but he loved it. He also went through all the minor hockey teams at Chesterfield, and then played on the junior varsity team at De Smet High School for the first three years of high school. He got to play on the varsity team his senior year, but unfortunately he didn't get his six-inch growth spurt until it was too late. But of the three boys, I think he had the most fun playing hockey. I think he'll be a great coach for his kids one day.

I was a lot like my parents, so the most important thing to me was that they got an education and were the best students they could be. They have made us extremely proud with their career choices. Jordy graduated from Union College with a degree in economics and a minor in Spanish, then went on to Washington

University, where he got his Juris Doctor degree and a Master of Business Administration (JDMBA). He is now a lawyer. Dusty got his degree in international business with a minor in Spanish at St. Louis University and then got his JDMBA at Wash. U as well, and he too is a lawyer. Drew went to Southeast Missouri University and got his degree in broadcasting and communications. He won awards at school for production, but having a television broadcasting career is just such a difficult road. You've got to start in some small town in the middle of nowhere to become a reporter and then an anchor, and the more we talked about it, the more he came to believe that was a hard life he didn't want. So Drew decided to pursue a career outside of the broadcasting world. He's working in business development, and he's very good at that. We are very proud that everything has worked out well for all three of them.

18

VIPERS ROLL
INTO TOWN

MEANWHILE, I KEPT working as a reporter with Channel 4, and in 1993 I got involved with Roller Hockey International. Keith Blase, a former employee with the Blues, wanted to bring professional roller hockey to St. Louis with a team called the Vipers. RHI was a brand-new league and Keith contacted me about being the GM and coach. This was something new and different and it gave me the opportunity to get involved with something that was grassroots. It was a short schedule and they played during the summer, when I wasn't busy covering the Blues. This intrigued me, so after looking at their proposal I decided to get onboard. We talked Perry Turnbull and Rik Wilson into playing, so having a couple of former Blues involved made it more appealing. They had asked me if I wanted to play as well, but there was no way. I was already two years removed from the NHL and I had never really rollerbladed before, and at age 36, I was way too old.

I had no aspirations to coach, but thought it could be a stepping stone to get back in the game in management. The job was difficult because I was dealing with a lot of young guys that had never played professional sports. It was great having Perry because he knew what it meant to compete, but the other guys had mostly just played pickup hockey and had really never been taught how to be a pro. Perry gave me that NHL type who could show the guys the ropes, but even with his help, some just couldn't figure it out. They weren't getting paid much, so I couldn't get too upset, but I was always frustrated because it was hard to have to tell people over and over and over, "Didn't you understand what I said the first time?"

You'd be talking about the power play and trying to get everybody on the same page and they wouldn't do it. I would just lose it and Perry would have to calm me down. But the biggest problem for me when I was coaching was the officiating, which was all local. Whenever we were on the road, we'd get several penalties in a row called against us and I'd lose it. I got so upset one night in Pittsburgh that I got thrown out of a game, so I knew right away that coaching was not my cup of tea.

That fall, Channel 4 decided not to use me to cover the Blues, but I was thankful for the television experience I had acquired because it helped me land a color-analyst role in the International Hockey League. It wasn't much, but it was a new way of building a resume. The deal was with Prime Network and we were to do a game of the week, the All-Star Game, and the last round of the playoffs. It was a great experience and I learned a lot about live-action television. It also replaced the income I had lost with Channel 4, so it happened at a perfect time.

The Vipers were catching on, though, and that became a full-time business. The first year was a success and the RHI was getting bigger and better. The league had gone from 12 to 24 teams and it filled the summer hockey void. We had a good relationship with the Blues and in fact played the last professional game at the old Arena before moving into the Kiel Center in 1995. I coached again in the second year, but it clearly was wearing on me. I didn't want to be on the ice, or I guess you'd call it the "floor" in roller hockey, everyday. I had enough of that when I was playing, and those first two years verified that I didn't want to be a coach. After the season, we hired Perry Turnbull as the coach and I took more of a front-office role. My aspiration was to be a GM in the NHL and even though this was roller hockey, I really hoped this experience might help.

When I took the original job from Keith Blase, I was given a small percentage of ownership in the team. My best friend, Dale, was having a blast hanging around with Perry and me, and he really wanted to become involved with the team. So Dale and I put together a group of our friends and took complete ownership of the Vipers. It was becoming more and more popular and we had a really good team, winning the RHI championship in 1999. The funny part about that was that after putting all the work into it, I couldn't even go to the clinching game in Anaheim because I had a memorabilia card show. I'd looked at my schedule months earlier and had no way of knowing when the championship final was going to be, nor that our team was even going to be in it, so I'd agreed to do the card show. As it turned out, the card show was the same night as the Murphy Cup championship game, and I couldn't get out of the card show because they'd already spent money on advertising. It was terribly disappointing not to be there when we won the championship.

The RHI folded after that year, so I guess you could say the Vipers are still the reigning champs 18 years later. We did a lot of good things, but the league just couldn't crack that nut. We had a group, which included Dale Turvey, that went to NHL commissioner Gary Bettman about taking over the league, but unfortunately, when it was all said and done, the owner of RHI wanted the NHL to buy out his ownership or he would just fold the league, and that's what happened. It was a shame that it ended that way.

In addition to running the Vipers with Dale, I was now entrenched working for his company, and in the fall of 1996, I started working as a radio analyst for the Blues. Jack Quinn's secretary called with a message that Jack wanted to talk to me. The Blues had decided that they were not going to simulcast TV and radio anymore, so they needed another broadcast team. The season was starting the very next day, and they needed a color analyst to work the games with Ron Jacober on KMOX Radio. My name had come up and Jack asked if I'd consider doing the job. I knew from the experience that I had got doing the IHL color-analyst work that this was something that I would really like. I was in L.A. for some RHI meetings, but accepted the job on the phone and flew home the next morning. I had to study the Blues' roster on the plane coming back from L.A., as we were going to be landing in St. Louis just a few hours before game time. The first few games were stressful but I transitioned into it pretty easily. I had a lot of good advice from Kenny Wilson, who was calling the team's games on TV, and I guess you could say I can talk.

I spent one year with Ron Jacober and then in 1997 the Blues hired Dan Kelly Jr. I thought it was really neat when they brought in Danny. Obviously, his dad, the late great Dan Kelly, was a big part of my career and I had known the Kellys so well. Danny reminded me a lot of his dad because he had a lot of the same mannerisms. He was just a kid—22 or 23—but that was great for me because I was 41 and now I was hanging around all these young kids, including Danny McLaughlin, who was just starting his television career. He is a great friend and I learned so much from watching his work. I'm not surprised he's the voice of the St. Louis Cardinals and one of the top announcers in Major League Baseball.

The team was flying charters now, not commercial flights like in my day, and all of a sudden there was a team in Phoenix, a couple in Florida, and we're making trips to warm-weather cities during the winter. I was like, *Are you kidding me?* It was a dream job because I was part of hockey, but I wasn't under the microscope. I loved it, but deep down I still wanted to be in the infrastructure of a club one day. It was always a dream of mine to be in the front office, and it looked like there might possibly be an opportunity shortly after I started doing the radio.

The Blues finally fired Jack Quinn and Mike Keenan in December 1996. They brought in Mark Sauer as the new president and he began an immediate search for a new GM. I didn't have a great resume but I knew hockey and I knew St. Louis, so I applied for the position. I sent in my resume just hoping to get an interview and I was excited when I got a call from Sauer's secretary. She informed me to meet him at a hotel restaurant downtown for lunch, but unfortunately it wasn't what I was expecting.

I walked in, sat down, and Mark was very straightforward. He said they were not interested in hiring a GM with no experience, but he still wanted to pick my brain. I was extremely disappointed. *You want to pick my brain, but you don't want to hire me?* It was strange, but I was one of those guys that never wanted to rock the boat, so I told him as much as I could to help him out. I know Joe Micheletti applied, and he did get an interview. Joe and I were great friends from when we played together. He had been an assistant coach under Jacques Martin and Brian Sutter, and I recommended Joe to Dan Kelly when he was looking for a radio partner. But like me, Joe didn't have any NHL management experience and Mark wanted experience, so he went with Larry Pleau.

I knew it was a long shot for me ever being a GM because I hadn't exactly gone down to the minors and honed my skills, but I had a lot of ideas about running a team. Many of my friends were working in hockey at the time, in the minors and junior hockey, so I felt like I would have been a good choice. I would have needed to hire a bona fide successful NHL coach, but certainly Perry would have been part of the staff somehow. I always thought that Perry and I would have made a great team in the NHL. You look at the Vipers, yeah, it wasn't the NHL or even ice hockey, but we still assembled the team. I was the GM and Perry was the coach and we scouted guys and drafted them, and eventually we won a championship. I did put the Vipers on my resume when I applied for the GM job because we were very proud of what we had done and felt like we could have done the same thing with the Blues.

But I was "just a former player" and when you look back to that era, really the only guy who went from player right into management was Bobby Clarke in Philadelphia. It was frustrating because more of us felt that we could have done that same job, but they didn't give us a chance in those days. I knew when I didn't get that job, it would be my only chance in the NHL. I was 41 years old and if you don't get into the business by then, good luck, because that's a little late in life to start a career in that capacity. It's a road that I would have loved to have gone down and, to this day, I feel like it's something that my career is lacking. But at the time, it wasn't the end of the world. I was still the radio voice of the Blues.

Joe Micheletti had left St. Louis in 1991 to take the television analyst job in Minnesota. A year later he returned to St. Louis in the same role, working with Kenny Wilson. But after five years he got an offer with the New York Islanders that he couldn't refuse and so he left again. Bruce Affleck had been doing some sideline stuff for the Blues' telecasts, so he took over Joe's spot. During the course of the season, Bruce got sick and I was asked to move from radio to TV for about 10–15 games. I was very nervous at first because I had a little fear of the camera, but the guys at Fox— our producer Tommy McLocklin, director Tom Mee, and Kenny Wilson—helped out so much.

Kenny was so good. Back then, a lot of the announcers taped everything, but Kenny never did that. To him, it was always better live. When it's on tape, you know you can screw up and you'll screw up. He would say, "Bernie, I'm going to tell you this, you're going to give me something about that, then I'm going to ask you about this, and you're going to give me something back. And before you know it, it's all done." You could tell him that you had 30 seconds and he would nail it to the second. You didn't need rehearsal because he was bang-on every time. He was the ultimate professional, one of those guys who knew his job so well. He could have announced anything, and is still one of the finest broadcasters that I've ever seen. He helped me overcome all my fears in terms of getting in front of the camera. I'm sure that I made lots of mistakes, but he always made it easy and I became very comfortable.

I loved filling in for Bruce on TV, but when he came back, I returned to the radio chair with Danny Kelly. There was a lot of stuff going on with the Blues at that time, but as an employee of the team, I had to be very careful to not upset the apple cart.

One of those times was in 1998, when the Blues allowed Hullie to leave via free agency and sign with the Dallas Stars. He was the reason that hockey was so popular in St. Louis; he brought it back. Kiel Center was the house that Brett built. I always looked at those things as a former player, and I know we have more of a tendency to second-guess decisions made by management, but I always thought about what I would do if I were running the business. I just thought in the case of Brett, a guy who scored 527 goals in a Blues jersey, to let him go for nothing was a travesty.

I'm sure that Larry Pleau wanted to trade him before the deadline, but because Brett was becoming an unrestricted free agent at the end of the season, they weren't going to get his full value. They probably thought, "Well, if we trade him, it looks like we're getting rid of him," so instead, they chose to force him to make the decision. But letting a guy of that stature walk without any compensation made no sense. I got traded for a really good player in Adam Oates, and when you look at it that way, the precedent was set that it was business.

But to me, I thought the way they handled Brett's situation was asinine. He was the cornerstone and they should have found a way to keep him. They said he went for more money someplace else, but I didn't buy that. He was valuable to every team in the league and was worth whatever he was going to get paid. Brett was Brett, he liked to talk, but that's what made him so real and likeable. I know he never, ever wanted to leave. I couldn't say anything at the time, but that was just bad business.

Another time was 1999–2000, when the Blues won the Presidents' Trophy with 114 points and unfortunately lost to San Jose in the first round of the playoffs. The Blues were one of four unbelievable teams that year, including Detroit, Colorado, and Dallas, which won the Stanley Cup the year before with Hullie. But the Blues were definitely the new favorite in that group, and to lose in the first round was criminal.

An awful lot of odd things happened in that series. After the Blues won Game 1, Marc Bergevin accidently threw the puck into his own net in Game 2 and the Sharks evened the series at a game apiece. Then in Game 7, Roman Turek gave up that goal to Owen Nolan from outside the blue line. (It reminded me so much of the long-shot goal back in 1984, when Willi Plett scored on Mike Liut in Game 7 of the second round.) Everybody blamed Roman Turek, but with the amazing talent and the incredibly large payroll on that team, they should have had a more experienced and higher-paid goalie. I blame management more than anybody else.

Bill and Nancy Laurie were the owners, but there was no salary cap in place and it seemed like they never said no to anything. If a piece was needed, buy it and let's bring the Cup to St. Louis. We all thought the goaltending piece was missing. Did management try to maybe get a Nikolai Khabibulin, who sat out the whole year with Phoenix because of a contract dispute, or did he just think that Turek was okay? I'm just asking. I don't have the answer, nor would I ever know what it would have taken to make the deal. But it was the only Presidents' Trophy in Blues history, and we all thought that that was the year. To get beat in the first round, I think that ranks as the franchise's biggest disappointment.

That was my last season on the radio before taking over full-time for Bruce on the television side. He had been in the Blues' front-office sales department while doing the TV, and I'm under the impression that they thought having a front-office guy in the booth was not a good look. So Bruce kept his front-office job—which he deserves so much more credit for than he gets—and they made me the permanent TV analyst alongside Kenny Wilson.

The job came with a larger paycheck, and also came with a few breaks during the season. Instead of doing all 82 games like we did on radio, we only did about 60, so it allowed me to spend more time working with Dale. I had been learning his business over the years, and back when we were running the Vipers, he had moved his offices so that we had hockey on one side of the building and his company on the other side. With the Vipers gone, I was basically a fixture in Dale's office like everyone else. He had become like my older brother. All my blood brothers were in Canada, so Dale was my closest confidant. Perry had become my best friend on the hockey side, and he and I are still best friends to this day, and Dale became my greatest friend outside of hockey. Bernadette and Susan became very close, and for the boys, Dale has been like their uncle. He has always been there for all of us.

19

CALL FROM THE HALL

I HAD EVERYTHING I wanted in my life: a great family, wonderful friends, and a great job broadcasting the Blues. Some might have said the only thing missing was a call from the Hockey Hall of Fame in Toronto, but I didn't look at it that way. If it happened, it happened, but I wasn't losing any sleep over it. It was funny, though, because when I retired, every article written about me read "Future Hall of Famer," like it was a given. Mr. Francis was on the Hockey Hall of Fame committee and I know he pushed for me every year. When he saw my dad, he always told him, "Your son deserves to be in the Hall of Fame and he will be there someday." Every year when someone would go in, my name would always come up: "What about Bernie?"

I always thought my numbers were comparable to a lot of the other great players that were already in the Hall of Fame and I thought I was even better than some of them. Yes, I didn't win any Stanley Cups, but there were other guys in the Hall of Fame that didn't win Cups either. The hard thing about the Hall is that it's so subjective, meaning everybody has a different opinion. Either way, I did what I did, and it was totally out of my control. It was like being slighted for the All-Star Games during my career; I couldn't be bitter about something that I had no control over. Quite frankly, I was used to it.

I knew that the Blues had put together a nice presentation to make a case for me going into the Hall of Fame and I was thankful for that. Jim Woodcock, the Blues' new senior vice president of marketing, was behind it, and Woody was unbelievable. Kenny Wilson voiced a fantastic video and I know Mr. Francis helped, too. They had made a good push, but after eight or nine years, I started thinking it probably wouldn't happen. By 2000, I was pretty sure it wasn't going to happen, but within my little sliver of hope, was one thought: *If it's going to happen, please have it happen while my folks are still alive.*

The only time that I ever thought about it was when they announced the inductions every year. They voted in September and the inductions were in November, so if I was ever going to get a call, it was going to come in September.

Well, after that first year of working on the TV side, Fox asked me if I'd do a golf show during the summer. The premise was that I'd go play a round with the pro at the course, and then we'd talk about the course and the design. It was only a half-hour show, but it took all day because we had to shoot a lot of different footage and interviews, and then we'd edit it down. I love golf so this was a fun gig.

We had done a number of shows in 2001, and it was such a success that we started up again right after the hockey season finished in 2002. We were taping in early June at Winghaven Country Club, a new club just across the river in St. Charles. It was almost noon and we had just hit our shots onto the No. 18 green. My phone was in my pocket and I had the ringer off, but it just kept vibrating over and over. I finally took it out of my pocket to look and it was the same number that had buzzed a half-dozen times in the last five minutes. I figured, *Oh shit, it must be important.* But we were taping, so I went to put it back in my pocket and then it buzzed again.

I answered and a lady said, "Hi Bernie, this is Kelly Masse from the Hockey Hall of Fame." She then asked if I had a minute because Jim Gregory wanted to talk to me. I explained that I was in the middle of a taping a golf show, but she insisted that I just give Jim a couple of minutes. I knew Jim, so I said okay.

Remember, it's June, this was not voting time for the Hockey Hall of Fame, so nothing was going through my mind. I thought Jim either had a question for me, or he wanted me to do something for him because I worked for the Blues. Then Jim got on the phone and said, "Hey Bernie, how are you?"

I said, "Great, I'm just finishing up a TV show."

He said, "I know that you're busy and I don't want to keep you long, but you know why I'm calling you, don't you?"

I calmly replied, "No, Jim, not really."

He said, "You really don't know why I'm calling you?"

I said, "No, I don't."

So he said, "The selection committee just had the vote for the Hockey Hall of Fame and I'm so happy to tell you that you are one of the guys that was selected to be inducted."

"Jim, are you kidding me?"

He said, "No, Bernie, congratulations! We're going to release this in a half-hour and we really need you to be on the conference call." He told me who was going in—Clark Gillies, Rod Langway, and Roger Neilson—and I was just shaking. Then he handed the phone back to Kelly Masse, who instructed me to please not tell anybody until the official announcement, which was just minutes away.

That, however, was going to be difficult. I hung up the phone and Steve Sebastian, the club pro at Winghaven who I was playing with that day, said: "Are you okay?" I'm sure I looked totally discombobulated. I told him that as visibly shaken as I looked, I was better than okay. I couldn't stand the suspense. I had to tell someone and because the Fox TV crew was far enough away, I decided to tell him. I think he was just as excited as I was because he hugged me right away. I told him he couldn't say anything for a few minutes until I did the conference call. So the first person to know about me going into the Hall of Fame wasn't my wife or my family. It was Steve Sebastian.

The TV crew was ready to continue taping, so I apologized to them and said I had to do an important conference call that couldn't wait. I told them it was only going to take 10–15 minutes and then we'd have lunch. They must have thought that I was off my rocker because I was so excited that I was shaking. I snuck around the corner and called Bernadette before the conference call. I was so choked up that she thought I'd been in a car accident or something. She asked if I was alright and I told her what had just happened, so now she's freaking out. It was a magical moment. I didn't have much time, but I quickly called Mom and Dad and they were obviously excited. My dad was always a little more laid back, but he was tickled pink. That's the thing I was so glad about, that they were still here to see that I'd gotten in.

The conference call was so surreal that I don't even remember what I said. When I finished, I came back downstairs where we were to have lunch and told the crew what had just transpired. They were all so excited! Steve, the pro, had kept his word and not said anything to anybody, but amazingly, he already had some bubbly waiting on ice when I got back. What a fantastic gesture and unexpected moment!

They cracked open a few bottles right there, and we had the first toast of the day at 2:00 PM. Immediately, word started trickling out everywhere, and the phone calls started coming in. The reaction that I kept getting from everyone was, "It's about time!" I drove home and a lot of our friends had already started showing up at our house to celebrate, and celebrate we did, until the wee hours of the morning.

The way I found out about the Hall of Fame was probably the best surprise that I could have ever gotten. There are guys who are first-ballot Hall of Famers like Wayne Gretzky and Brett Hull and they know they're going in, but for the rest of us, it's a judgement call. You have to get at least 75 percent of the committee members to vote for you and that's a lot. For me, it was probably the most unexpected pleasure of all time, and it will always go down as one of the best moments of my life.

The boys were overjoyed because they had been too young to see me play when I was in my prime. We didn't have all the video tapes or anything that they have now, so they'd just heard stories about my career. But now all of these exciting things were happening and they were able to attend the events. They remembered my Blues jersey retirement in 1991, but they were only three, seven, and 10.

Then in 1996, when the boys were a little bit older, we went back to Saskatoon when the Blades retired my No. 15.

I was the first player in the organization's history to have that honor, so it was a big deal. The Mayor of Foam Lake, the Premier of Saskatchewan, the Mayor of Saskatoon, the President of the Western Hockey League, and even Mr. Francis were at the ceremony. I never envisioned anything like that, and the Blades really did a magnificent job. The boys were so proud to be able to wear Blades jerseys with my No. 15. It was special, too, because Saskatoon was such a big part of our lives. Bernadette was from there and we went back every summer after the hockey season. It was basically our hometown, so for them to do that with Bernadette's family and my family in attendance was unbelievable.

Then in February 2002, I was inducted into the Missouri Sports Hall of Fame in Springfield. That was my first induction into any Hall of Fame, so it will always be very special in my heart. I had grown up in Canada, but now I was clearly a Missourian.

Later that summer, Foam Lake held a banquet to honor me, along with three other local residents that had made their mark in hockey: Dennis Polonich, who played for the Detroit Red Wings; Pat Elynuik, who was drafted by the Winnipeg Jets and had played for Winnipeg, Washington, Tampa Bay, and Ottawa; and Ted Hargraves, who had played years earlier on Canada's national team. It was such a nice gesture by Foam Lake and we were honored to go back. Seeing the Foam Lake Recreation Center brought back so many memories and it was extremely satisfying knowing that the money the town received from the NHL for my development had been used to put in an artificial ice plant. It was a fantastic day that included a parade, and to top it all off, they unveiled a large action hockey card photos of the three of us in a roadside display just off the side of the Yellowhead Highway.

But now it was November and time for the Hockey Hall of Fame induction weekend, which was one for the ages. The ceremony wasn't until Monday evening, but we arrived in Toronto on Thursday afternoon. We had a plane full from St. Louis: Dale and Susan, Perry and Nancy, and dozens of our friends. Jordy was on a term abroad in Spain and I will never forget the smile on his face when he got off the plane in Toronto. My parents, my brothers and their wives, Bernadette's parents, they all came in from Saskatoon. Our greatest friends and family from all over Canada and the U.S. were with us, and there were so many moments to savor.

On Saturday, the inductees were introduced at the Toronto Maple Leafs' game with other Hall of Famers in attendance. Jean Beliveau of the Montreal Canadiens was my hero, and I had met Mr. Beliveau over the years, but now I was standing next to him on the ice and joining him in the Hall of Fame. That is mind-boggling to me and it was one of the big thrills of my life.

On Sunday, putting on the Hall of Fame sweater and skating onto the ice in front of a packed Air Canada Center was overwhelming. That night, we had a private reception at Wayne Gretzky's restaurant and rented out half the place for a group of about 100 people. We'd partied like rock stars a couple of nights in a row, so even though the rest of them kept it going late, that was a quiet night for me. The most important speech of my life was the next day and I wanted to make sure I had a clear head. Writing my Hall of Fame speech was one of the hardest, yet most pleasurable things I have ever done in my life. I only had five minutes to spill my heart and soul to the world and thank everyone who helped me along the way. Even thinking about it now brings back so many emotions.

On Monday morning, we received our rings and blazers. I had never imagined how amazing it could be until I looked at that HHOF logo that was now on the ring finger of my right hand. I had never even been to the Hall of Fame before and now, my very first time there, I'm being inducted. I had to pinch myself a few times.

On Monday evening, it was showtime. We were seated in the small, quaint trophy room at the Hockey Hall of Fame and it was packed. I don't know if I had ever been that nervous in my life. I had rehearsed my speech over and over, but with the cameras rolling, the pressure of the situation seemed greater than ever. I was fortunate that the inductions went in alphabetical order and my name was up first. So after a short video presentation, I was introduced as the newest member of the Hockey Hall of Fame. I walked the few steps to the podium and you could probably hear a pin drop, along with the sound of my beating heart, but it seemed like there was a calming that came over me.

My parents, my brothers, Mr. Francis, Bernadette, Jordy, Dusty, Drew, seeing them filled me up with so many emotions. There was no teleprompter to read off like there is these days, it was just the notes I had in my hand and in my head. I still think that this was the only genuine way to do it. As difficult as delivering the speech seemed, I was through it in the blink of an eye. It was everything I wanted and needed to say. It was five minutes of my life that I will always cherish and I walked away from the podium with the most amazing feeling that I'd ever had.

The etched glass portrait of me was now on the wall in the Hockey Hall of Fame and my signature was officially in the register. I've always said that when you're a little kid in a small town, you're not trying for greatness. You're just trying to have fun and then eventually you're trying to make a living and win a Stanley Cup. If anything, every kid's dream is to score the game-winning goal in overtime in the Stanley Cup Final. The Hall of Fame is the pinnacle of personal accomplishment, but it's not something you dream about it, or at least I didn't. I can't say that being inducted changed my life, but I think the respect that comes with it immediately changed the way I was looked at. I felt that I was now recognized as one of the great players of the game. I always had great respect in the St. Louis community, which meant the most in my mind, but now it had gone to the next level.

When I got back to St. Louis, the Blues had a special pregame ceremony to commemorate my induction into the Hockey Hall of Fame. Bernadette told me they were doing something for me that was unbelievable, but she wouldn't give me any clues. Bill and Nancy Laurie and Jim Woodcock joined Bernadette, the boys, and me at center ice, and they presented me with a miniature bronze statue. During the presentation, the crowd was so loud, that I couldn't understand anything they were saying. So when they handed me the miniature statue and I said, "Thank you," I really didn't know what they said. I'll never forget that because when we headed up to the suite in the freight elevator for the game, Bernadette said, "Bernie, you don't understand what's going on, do you?"

I said, "What do you mean?"

She said, "Do you understand that they're making a life-size bronze statue of you like the miniature one?"

I hadn't understood, because I couldn't hear. She said she thought it was a little weird the way I'd reacted. She quickly explained that the little replica wasn't what they were giving me. That was the big secret they were keeping. I was now taken aback. I was embarrassed because initially I didn't react very graciously, but I would have if I had heard the announcement. The little trophy was nice, but what she had just explained—a life-size bronze statue—I had never ever expected myself to ever be in that spot. How can anyone ever believe that there could be a life-size statue sculpted in your honor? That's iconic, that's forever, that's crazy.

Harry Weber, the sculptor, had been coming to Dale's house and Bernadette and the boys had been helping with the design. Now it was my turn to put my final stamp on the almost-finished product. Bernadette and I drove out to Harry's studio where he asked me to make any changes that I saw fit. Harry is an unbelievable sculptor, so with his attention to detail, there was very little we wanted to do differently. It was then sent off to be bronzed.

Early the next hockey season, the statue was ready, and in November 2003 it was officially commemorated. We had a good-sized crowd of friends and dignitaries in the lobby of Scottrade for the commemoration. I pulled the veil off and had a very bewildering feeling, standing next to a life-size bronze statue of myself. To my sons, this was the greatest. They were able to add an inscription in the gloves:

We love you, Dad.

—Bernadette, Jordy, Dusty, and Drew

Ironically, that night the Blues played the Chicago Blackhawks, whose coach was Brian Sutter. We invited him up for the dedication, but once again, he didn't show.

The statue remained inside Scottrade Center for six years, but they moved it outside in 2009 when they unveiled Al MacInnis' statue. A year later, they unveiled Brett Hull's statue, so now the three beautiful bronze pieces stand guard in the plaza before you walk in the rink. I don't look at mine every time that I go by it, but I know it's there. It's the first thing people that Bernadette and I know say when they see us, "Hey, we drove by Bernie's statue." I've had a lot of honors bestowed upon me, including the jersey that hangs in the rafters and being a member of five different Hall of Fames, but the statue is surreal.

20

FOREVER
GRATEFUL

IT'S AN AMAZING feeling to be personally recognized in the manner I was, and I feel extremely fortunate for every moment this franchise has afforded me. I've been able to witness the growth of the Blues in St. Louis and experience all of the highs and lows that we as a city have shared together.

The Salomons created something so special here, and yet there were days at the end of their ownership when we didn't know if the team would stay here. With the help of Mr. Francis, Ralston Purina came in and infused some fresh blood into the organization, and yet a few years later, we almost ended up in Saskatoon.

Harry Ornest came in, and he might have been the cheapest owner in the history of the NHL, but he saved hockey in St. Louis for the fans and the players who never wanted to leave. Mr. Shanahan then came in and made the Blues exciting again with his passion for the franchise, and of course, everything changed when Ron Caron made the trade for Hullie. It's funny, before Brett, when the public-relations department used to set up appearances for the players at local Target stores, we'd spend two hours there and maybe five people would show up. But Hullie brought intrigue; he changed the whole city. When he scored those 86 goals, hockey wasn't just a sport anymore in St. Louis, it was a cult. Kids were playing hockey like never before and new rinks were popping up all over the Metro area.

We then saw Kiel Partners come in, and we were graced with Wayne Gretzky for a short time, but as good as that seemed, we saw Mike Keenan blow it all apart. The Kiel Partners didn't really want to run the team, and that was apparent when they let Brett leave as a free agent, but thankfully they put the club in safe hands.

Bill and Nancy Laurie came in, and I don't think the Lauries get enough credit for what they did for the St. Louis Blues. No one spent more money trying to bring a cast of players in here and win a Cup like they did. The NHL lockout in 2004–05 was a travesty, but no one can ever accuse the Lauries of not trying their best to win it all.

When Dave Checketts' group, including John Davidson, came in, the Blues were back at square one. Al MacInnis retired and Chris Pronger had been shipped off to Edmonton in what looked like a selloff. For the first time in club history, the Blues finished in last place in the league standings and fans had to remain very patient.

In 2012, Tom Stillman and his local group of investors re-took guardianship of the franchise and restored faith in the fanbase. We have a group of owners now who care so much about the Blues and the pride in the city that no one ever has to worry about their intentions. Yes, they're running a business, but they want to win for everybody associated with the game of hockey in St. Louis, and after everything we've been through over the years, that's all you can ask.

Forty-one years after I stepped off a plane in St. Louis, I remain thrilled to still be part of the Blues' organization and thankful for the memories and friendships that will last a lifetime.

After starting as a reporter at Channel 4, I'm really happy to still be a part of the Blues television broadcasts. Fox Sports and Jack Donovan gave me the opportunity 17 years ago, and they've provided me with one of the best jobs that I could've ever asked for. Like my playing days, I'm still on a team with great guys, like John Kelly and Darren Pang. To have worked with all three of these great Kelly voices means I must have scored another big hattrick. John continues to do a marvelous job carrying the torch his dad lit. Panger and his humor keeps the whole crew loose. And what more can I say about our great Fox crew, led by Tim Pabst and Phil Mollica. No one does a better game than they do.

I'm also still part of one of the NHL's best alumni groups. No other city in the league has had as large of a contingent that stuck around after their careers. We have ice available to us twice a week and many of the guys still show up to play on a regular basis. I hung up my skates after the Hall of Fame induction, but I have made a couple of worthy exceptions.

In 2005, Peter Stastny asked me to attend a charity fundraiser in Bratislava, Slovakia, honoring his local team that won the Czechoslovakian championship 25 years earlier. It was like a World Championship to me because I got the opportunity to play a game with some great international players, like Slava Fetisov, Alexander Yakushev, Borje Salming, and many more.

In 2015, after the terrible tragedy that took the lives of Pavol Demitra and the entire Locomotiv hockey club in 2011, our alumni was able to participate in a fundraising effort for Pavol's foundation. We played three games in three different cities in Slovakia in front of packed houses, and the tribute to Pavol was unbelievable, and just being there and visiting his gravesite made you realize how fragile life can be.

In 2017, we had the unbelievable honor of skating in the Winter Classic alumni game in front of a sold-out Busch Stadium. I can honestly say that with all the hype that it got, it was much more than we could have ever anticipated. To be on the ice with Wayne Gretzky, Brett Hull, Pierre Turgeon, Keith Tkachuk, Al MacInnis, Chris Pronger, Martin Brodeur, and Mike Liut, what a moment! For a fleeting moment, we still felt like we were real hockey players, and to beat the Chicago Blackhawks, it was like a blast from the past. The game brought back the memories of all the blood, sweat, and tears.

The beautiful thing about our game is that we all come from different parts of the world, and when you end up on a team together, that becomes your family. You develop many relationships over the years, and few are closer than the roommates you have. I really only had three in the 13 years that I played for the Blues. The key to deciding who was a good roommate or not was whether I had control of the TV remote—that was imperative—and I did with all three of them.

One of them was Joey Mullen, who became like a little brother to me. Joey was quiet, but he had a great sense of humor, and he was such a great player that I wish I could have played my entire career with him. No one was more talented for a guy his size, and I was so proud when he went into the Hall of Fame because to score over 500 goals from where he came from was simply amazing. I was so glad to be a part of his career and he'll always be a dear friend.

Another was Greg Millen. Very rarely do goalies have room-mates because they are a different breed, so they usually had their own room on the road. But not Millsie, who was the most easy going, happy-go-lucky goalie I ever met. We could spend hours talking hockey or talking nothing at all, but no matter what, we always had a good time. I remember we used to have enough Chinese food delivered to our room in Toronto that after the bars closed, we could have fed the whole team. I think we both kept each other's sanity through the latter years of our careers.

I've talked a lot about Brian Sutter, who was my first roommate and who I spent the first 13 years of my career with. We had our great times and we had our differences, but no matter what, our accomplishments both on and off the ice will always be special. We've grown apart over the years, and the rare times that we do see each other, it's different; the bond that we had is gone. He's the one who made the decision to pull away from the closeness that we had, not me. But we're cordial and Brian will always be that person who helped mold my career.

As important as my hockey friends are, I also have friends outside of the sport, and I was lucky that I had an everlasting one in Randy Pangborn, whom I met in Saskatoon. No matter how far Randy and I were away from each other and if we didn't see each other for months at a time, we were always at each other's side. When you're dealing with the stuff that I was dealing with every-day, it's great to have an objective outside voice that you really trust, and he was always that person.

I am so lucky that there are so many other great friends that we met along the way. Whether they were there with us in St. Louis or away in Canada or beyond, whether they were in our hockey world or outside of it, they are the reason our lives have been so fulfilled. I wish I could mention every one of their names, but of course that would add way too many pages to the book, and I am afraid that I would probably miss someone too important to miss. I just want all of them to know—and I know they all know who they are—that I cherish each and every one of those friendships. I want to express my sincere gratitude and want you all to know that you are family, not just friends. There are no successes in life without someone to share it with.

For Bernadette and myself, family has always been the most important thing. Our parents instilled that in us at a young age, and I will always thank them for blessing us with great family values. They made us God-loving and God-fearing people. Religion was always a big part of our lives, not to the point where it was pushed on us, but we knew how much it meant to say your prayers and go to church, and we've taught the same to our kids. It was perfect coming to a Catholic city like St. Louis, because our boys have grown up in that same environment that we did. I guess I have always believed in the powers above, and the good Lord was looking out for us.

I have been blessed with an awful lot of things in my life, but none greater than Bernadette. We were just kids when we started dating: I was 18, she was 16. Two years later, I left for St. Louis to start my NHL career and we had no idea how a long-distance arrangement would affect our relationship. Thankfully, when I called her for the first time in two months to spend that first Christmas with me, she still cared enough about me to come. I know that was the most important phone call of my life, because 18 months later we were married. I'm sure there were a lot of doubters, saying, "Oh, this isn't going to last because he's a professional hockey player, blah, blah, blah." I guess for some people it might not have been ideal, but for us it truly worked. Communication was always an important part of our marriage, and we made sure we didn't lose that. We tried to share what was always in our hearts.

I know it wasn't easy living with a professional hockey player. The game's ups and downs are very hard on one's psyche, and that was grueling at times. I had a lot of crazy mood swings and needed to vent a lot of times after games. You need a strong person by your side, and Bernadette was always that person listening and consoling me, thank goodness. What I love about her was that even though we didn't agree on every issue (as most normal couples don't), she had a mind of her own and said what she felt. She would reel me in, in a good way—she still does!—and was always the one that I could count on.

Bernadette is that one person that, when she walks into a room, it lights up. She's beautiful, bold, and brawny, and she's always been that way. I thank the Lord every day for giving me such a great person, who is also the best mother in the world to our three wonderful children. I will always thank her for being my best friend and confidant. I'm the luckiest guy in the world to have her as my wife. Words can't describe how much she means to me.

I'm so proud of Jordy, Dusty, and Drew. It seems like just yesterday that I was racing from the house to the hospital to the rink so that I could watch them come into the world, and it's crazy how fast time goes. Watching them grow up before our very eyes has been the greatest gift of all. They are my best friends, but when I look at all three of them, I will always just see them as my little boys. They will always be the first thing that I think of each morning, and the last thing I think of each night before I go to bed. They have already accomplished so much in their lives, but most importantly they have become wonderful gentlemen. They are such polite and respectful young men, and that's something we always hoped for. Thankfully, they still want to be around us, and we couldn't be happier, because that keeps Bernadette and me acting a lot younger than we are. We're still waiting for grandchildren—heck, we're still waiting for them to get married. We'd never be pushy, but Mom has the pink and blue paint ready to go.

I still pinch myself every day, and for the last time, I'll go back to that word: destiny. I worked very hard to be a good hockey player, but it's still all about timing. What if Father Fenrich didn't get me the tryout with the Blades? What if Shaky was looking another direction when I scored that goal at the Blue-Gold game and he didn't see it? What if Ron and Don weren't going to college in Saskatoon, would Mom and Dad have let me go try out there? What if I hadn't made the Blades that year, what would have happened to me? What did the Blues scout, Gerry Ehman, see in me? What did Mr. Francis see in me? What did Barc see in me? Like they say, beauty is in the eye of the beholder, and luckily I've had a lot of great beholders. There were so many instances where things could have gone sideways and, if they did, I would not be where I am today.

The Blues' organization has meant so much to me and my family. The fact that I still hold the franchise record for games played (927), assists (721), and points (1,073) is something that I'm very proud of. If I would have stayed in St. Louis my entire career, I'm sure my numbers would have been better, although Hullie may have broken my records if he wouldn't have gone to Dallas. My biggest disappointment is that I didn't start and finish my career as a Blue, and, most importantly, that I didn't win a Stanley Cup in St. Louis.

But even without a Cup, I know my parents, Nick and Natalie, were proud of me before they passed away in 2012 and 2017, respectively. Beginning with the early years with the Blades and all the way through the Hockey Hall of Fame, they were extremely happy for all of my achievements. Dad never bragged once about any of my accomplishments, but he lit up whenever anybody wanted to talk about my career. Mom was the same way. Even after Dad passed away, she and her girlfriends would watch Blues games on TV. There was no bigger fan than Mom, and I know if there are TVs in heaven, she's tuned in to Fox Sports Midwest.

This great game of hockey has brought me everything. It's made me laugh and cry, it's brought me pain and jubilation. But when I look back at it all, it's not really the hockey. It's life that brings you all of this. It's destiny and a greater being. You can't change the past and you can only live in the present and look toward the future. My past has been fantastic, my present is so fulfilling, and I can only hope that my future will be as good as I dream it to be. But that dream won't be complete without me in the parade, riding through the shadow of the Arch, overlooking a euphoric sea of Blues fans and being blinded by the glare of the Cup.

> "Of all those memories we share when we're old,
> None are more clear than that hard bitter cold.
> You'll not find among us a soul who can say:
> 'I've conquered the wind and a cold winter's day.'"
>
> —David Bouchard
> *If You're Not from the Prairie*

NICKNAME KEY

Babs = Wayne Babych

Bourby = Rick Bourbonnais

Bubba = Barry Melrose

Chappy = Blair Chapman

Crommer = Mike Crombeen

Dougie = Doug Gilmour

Dunner = Blake Dunlop

Durby = Steve Durbano

Fats = Fred Williams

Flocky = Ron Flockhart

Gasser = Bob Gassoff

Hullie = Brett Hull

Hunts = Mark Hunter

Legs = Glen Leggott

Lutey = Mike Liut

Maxy = Bryan Maxwell

Millsy = Greg Millen

Oatsie = Adam Oates

Pazzer = Greg Paslawski

Ralphy = Ralph Klassen

Rammer = Rob Ramage

Rosy = Claude Larose

Reedsie = Mark Reeds

Shaky = Jack McLeod

Smrkie = John Smrk

Ungie = Garry Unger

Wammer = Rick Wamsley

Wick = Doug Wickenheiser

Zuky = Mike Zuke